Ronan O'Gara was born in 1977 in Sacramento, California, and educated at Presentation Brothers College and University College Cork, captaining Pres to the Munster Junior and Senior Schools Cup and winning an All-Ireland Under-20 winners' medal with UCC in 1996. In 1998 he helped the Ireland Under-21 team to the Triple Crown and the following year guided Cork Constitution to the AIB League title, before making his international debut against Scotland in 2000. That same year, he scored a Six Nations record 30 points against Italy.

O'Gara was the inspirational force behind Munster's Heineken Cup victory in 2006, scoring 13 points in the final, and is the leading points scorer in the history of that competition, with another 11 points in Munster's 2008 victory against Toulouse. He was also the leading points scorer in the Six Nations Championship in 2005, 2006 and 2007, won the Triple Crown with Ireland in 2004, 2006 and 2007 and was a member of the British & Irish Lions touring teams in both 2001 and 2005.

Denis Walsh, who helped Ronan O'Gara in the writing of this book, is the chief sportswriter with the Irish edition of the *Sunday Times*. He is a former sportswriter of the year in Ireland and winner of the McNamee Award for Gaelic Games Writing. His first book, *Hurling: The Revolution Years*, won the Boylesports Irish Sports Book of the Year in 2005.

RONAN O'GARA

My Autobiography

with Denis Walsh

TRANSWORLD IRELAND

TRANSWORLD IRELAND
an imprint of The Random House Group Limited
20 Vauxhall Bridge Road, London SW1V 2SA
www.rbooks.co.uk

First published in 2008 by Transworld Ireland

A CIP catalogue record for this book
is available from the British Library.

ISBNs 9781848270084 (cased)
9781848270091 (tpb)

Extract from Brendan Fanning's *From There to Here*, reproduced courtesy of Gill & Macmillan.

With thanks also to the following journalists for the use of quotes from their reports: Gerry Thornley of the *Irish Times*, Neil Francis of the *Sunday Tribune*, Brendan Fanning of the *Sunday Independent*, George Hook of the *Sunday Independent*, Barry Coughlan of the *Irish Examiner* and Tony Ward of the *Irish Independent*.

Addresses for Random House Group Ltd companies outside the UK
can be found at: www.randomhouse.co.uk
The Random House Group Ltd Reg. No. 954009

The Random House Group Limited supports The Forest Stewardship Council (FSC), the leading international forest-certification organization. All our titles that are printed on Greenpeace-approved FSC-certified paper carry the FSC logo. Our paper procurement policy can be found at
www.rbooks.co.uk/environment

Typeset in 11/16pt Berling by
Falcon Oast Graphic Art Ltd.
Printed in the UK by CPI Mackays, Chatham, ME5 8TD

2 4 6 8 10 9 7 5 3 1

To Jessica, whose love, personal sacrifice, understanding and fun far exceeds my highest expectations, and to our future family life together.

To Colin, Fergal and Morgan, for being brothers of the highest quality.

To my parents, Fergal and Joan, for their unconditional love and support.

ACKNOWLEDGEMENTS

I would like to thank all the many coaches I have worked with through the years. Without them I wouldn't have had anything like the career I have. From Con under-8s to the many senior coaches I have worked with – each played a part and I thank them all.

I would also like to thank all the players I have played with. I was lucky to be on teams with some of the greats, and some of the greatest characters of the game.

It would be remiss of me not to mention the role of Cork Constitution and the great team spirit that exists at that club.

For all my years in Munster, we had something special. I never take for granted the special bond among us. I would like to thank all my supporters around the country who fill me with pride as we stand singing 'amhrán na bhfiann'.

Thanks also to all the people who made this book possible, especially Denis Walsh for his great skill in putting my thoughts and actions into words, and Brendan Lenihan and Jonathan Harris for putting Denis and the publishing team together. Finally, thanks to the whole Transworld team in Ireland and the UK, including Doug Young, Eoin McHugh, copy editor Mark Handsley, and editor Giles Elliott.

PROLOGUE

16 February 2007

I was upstairs when the buzzer sounded from the intercom at our front gate. It must have been after three o'clock because Jess was home from school. We had moved into our new home before Christmas and I was going through bits and pieces with the quantity surveyor. It was five days after Ireland lost to France in Croke Park and we'd been released from camp for the weekend. My ankle was sore and swollen. Nothing serious. Apart from that it was a normal Friday. Then the buzzer sounded.

Jess answered. On the other end of the line was a guy with a Dublin accent.

'Hi, Jess, I want to ask you about the break-up of your marriage?'

Jess thought it was her brother Philip, messing. She started to laugh and give out to him at the same time. Then he repeated the question.

'No, Jess, I'm a reporter. Have you any comment on the break-up of your marriage to Ronan?'

I came down the stairs. I knew there was something up. I asked Jess who was there and as soon as she told me I charged through the front door and down the driveway, as fast as I could move with my limp and my slippers. If it wasn't so serious it might have been comical. I was freaking.

The reporter was from a Sunday tabloid and he had a photographer with him. Their car was parked across the road and the photographer was behind the wheel. The reporter was just getting in and they were ready to take off. I wrenched the door open. I was pumped. He was a big enough fella. He probably could have knocked the head off me if he wanted. In my state I didn't care.

'What the fuck are you doing here?'

'I just wanted to ask your wife a few questions.'

'About what?'

'About your new home.'

I got him out of the car and over towards the footpath. I tried to take a picture of him on my mobile phone just to have some kind of proof of what was going on. I asked who sent him and demanded that he get his boss on the phone. I challenged the editor and he came up with what to me was a cock and bull story.

'We were told by a reliable source in the IRFU.'

At that point I lost it. I let fly.

'You're a disgrace, harassing people like this. People like you are what's wrong with modern Ireland. You're a low-life.'

He got all defensive and I hung up the phone. Jess was standing at the top of the drive with our quantity surveyor. I asked her to come down and I brought yer man over to the gate. I told him to apologize to my wife. He made a pathetic effort so I made him apologize again.

When we got back inside I rang Ger Carmody, the Irish team manager. I wanted to put this whole episode on the record with the IRFU in case we took it any further. We were going to make a statement to the local Gardaí in Douglas but instead we rang Jess's brother-in-law, Gary McPolin, who's a Garda inspector in the city. He said write down every detail of what happened while it was fresh in our minds and store it away. That's what we did.

Jess is a strong person and she was remarkably calm. I was bulling. I couldn't believe it. I knew that a couple of the Dublin-based Irish lads had been followed around by photographers on nights out but this kind of intrusion was in a different league.

I don't believe for a moment they had any IRFU source for their story. They were just acting on the same malicious, groundless rumour that had been doing the rounds for months. When they came to our gate they didn't expect I would be in the house. That's how much they knew. Nothing. They knew nothing about us, our marriage, our lives. They were acting on a black, spiteful rumour that had sprung up from God knows where. We were living with that but in a way we weren't. It was out there – somewhere, everywhere – out of our control. Our family and friends knew the truth. That was enough. You can't live your life wondering what strangers think.

How do you make these rumours go away? We ignored them.

They didn't go away.

A few weeks before the World Cup Eddie O'Sullivan and his assistant Niall O'Donovan raised it with me in camp. They knew there was no truth to the rumours but they were concerned that it might be weighing on my mind. Niall O' had suffered something similar as a Shannon player in the 1980s and he'd been faced with the same dilemma. How do you kill it? Squashing a rumour is like trying to shoot a ghost.

We discussed the options. If you call a press conference and address the rumours you're giving them legitimacy. People will say that you're hiding something. Elements of the tabloid press will say that we had brought it into the public arena so it was fair game for them to go prying and snooping. As far as I was concerned that wasn't an option.

And if you don't address the issue are you running from the problem? It was a no-win situation.

We decided that it was best to say nothing. It wasn't affecting our marriage and it wasn't hurting my rugby. I wanted to focus completely on the World Cup. No distractions.

Did I think it would go away? I didn't know. It was out of our control.

CHAPTER 1

Summer 2007

It was the morning of Friday, 13 July when my knee collapsed. The last day of our training camp in Spala. We had a seven-on-seven game. I twisted. My right knee went. The same knee that nearly kept me out of the Lions tour in 2005. My bad knee. The World Cup was eight weeks away and I lay on a bed in Poland. Tormented.

We had done four weeks of pre-season already. It was savage and brilliant. Everybody had been really pushing themselves. Pushing each other. I was in the best shape of my life. All of us were. Everything we did was tested and compared. The results confirmed what I was feeling. I was flying. Power was up. Speed was up. Then this.

My brother Fergal was getting married a day later. I was joint best man and before the injury they had already allowed me to fly home a little early. I couldn't get my knee scanned until Monday but I knew there was damage. They gave me crutches in Poland and that's how I arrived at the wedding: hobbling, drawing attention to myself, inviting questions I couldn't answer.

I was in a world of my own that day. It's one of the things about the life of a professional sports person: it makes you selfish.

Everything is about us: our fitness, our diet, our mood, our needs, our schedule, our next match. People make allowances and make adjustments and you carry on being selfish. My brother's wedding should have been the best day of the year but I couldn't stop thinking about my knee. My speech was all right but it wasn't as good as it should have been because I was worried – distracted. You're asked to stand for photos and you're thinking, 'Should my knee be elevated?' Four or five times during the day I disappeared to the bedroom to ice it. Nobody gave out. It's what they expect.

On Monday the scan was a massive relief. As good as I could have hoped. No ligament damage. The problem was at the back of my knee. I hardly even heard what the specialist, Ray Moran, said once I knew the ligaments were all right. He said I'd be back in four weeks. That was a huge chunk out of my build-up but it was manageable.

The first warm-up match was against Scotland on 11 August. They were pushing me to play but I knew I wasn't ready. The scan was clear but I couldn't run 20 metres. I have a high pain threshold but this was killing me. It wasn't right. I knew they weren't convinced. They were telling me that I had to push through it but this pain wasn't like that. I couldn't run properly. It came down to heated arguments between me, the Irish doctor and the Irish physio before they believed me. In the end they relented and suggested a few more days' rest. That worked.

I sat on the bench against Scotland and came on for the last fifteen minutes. We didn't play well and lost by 10 points but nobody was that worried. The final squad was being announced the following morning so we had fielded a second-string team with the exception of about three or four players. The biggest worry was Shaggy – Shane Horgan. He did his knee in the warm-up. A grade two medial tear. Everyone knew it was bad straight away. He wasn't out of the World Cup but he was under pressure. Murder.

Our next game was on the following Thursday against Bayonne, a club side in the south of France. We set up camp near Biarritz for five days. A beautiful hotel on the beach. It was an important week. We knew we had to step it up. Scotland had looked more match-ready than us. France, our opponents in the pool, had already played a hugely physical warm-up match against England and were facing another one the following weekend. Because of injuries Brian O'Driscoll and Paul O'Connell had played their first match in over five months in Murrayfield. The 15 that started against England in Croke Park had been left out of the summer tour to Argentina. Nobody questioned the wisdom of that decision but we needed serious game time now.

The selection against Bayonne was basically full-strength. We knew they'd hit us hard and that was the point of the exercise: a hostile crowd, pumped-up opponents, a tough work-out. What nobody expected was their attitude. They were completely over the top. From the beginning they were dirty and nasty. The verbals were flying. Richard Dourthe in the centre was mouthing obscenities for most of the night. Base stuff.

We expected them to mill into us but they weren't satisfied with that; they wanted to knock our heads off with cheap shots. Off the ball. Drico and Paulie spoke to the referee because they thought it was going to get out of hand. Then it did. One of their guys punched Drico in the side of the face. A sly dig. Straight after the game he was taken to hospital with a suspected broken cheek-bone; what the X-ray showed was a fractured sinus, which meant he was extremely doubtful for the first game of the World Cup against Namibia.

Afterwards Eddie O'Sullivan took a lot of stick in the media for arranging the match. The gist of it was that other countries were gearing up for the World Cup with proper Test matches while we were being knocked about by a club team in the south of France. In hindsight there was some merit in that argument. Before the

2003 World Cup we had played Wales, Italy and Scotland in the build-up. This time we were short at least one Test match. But it was wrong to hammer Eddie for the Bayonne game. In Spala he'd discussed the fixture in a meeting with senior players: Drico, Paulie, Shaggy, Simon Easterby and myself. We thrashed out the pros and cons and if we had a serious objection we were at liberty to raise it. We didn't. We saw the potential benefits of that game the same as the management did.

Things didn't get any better against Italy in Belfast eight days later. In fact they got worse. We won by 3 points. I got a drop-goal and a massively dubious try in the last few minutes but the performance was a shambles. We were flat. No spark. Dead. The pack was delivering slow ball and backs are screwed by slow ball. We carved them open three times in the first half but each time we blew a try with poor execution or poor decision-making. The off-loading and micro plays between forwards and backs that we'd worked on in training weren't happening on the pitch. There was no flow to our game.

Eddie was furious in the dressing room afterwards. He didn't say anything that we didn't already know. The faults were plain for all of us to see. We looked nothing like the team that had beaten England by 30 points in Croke Park and run eight tries past Italy in Rome six months earlier. That team had fallen off the face of the earth.

No Irish team had ever gone beyond the quarter-final of the World Cup but we had huge ambitions. Our intention was to win it. We stated that to each other. We agreed that it was achievable. Our form over the previous twelve months justified it. Four years earlier the big thing was just to get out of the pool and take it from there. Our pool this time was just as tough – the hosts plus Argentina. But we weren't judging ourselves by the standards of 2003 or 1999. We'd progressed miles since then. At one meeting in Spala we were given a day-by-day itinerary for the World Cup.

The itinerary, though, only took us as far as the quarter-final. Shaggy was the first to notice it and he raised it immediately. He wanted to know why the itinerary didn't account for the semi-final and final. That was our mentality.

Naturally you're not going to get everybody on exactly the same track. In every squad players have different goals according to their circumstances. Some fellas were just delighted to be in the 30, other fellas were aiming to be in the 22, a few guys were hoping to break into the first 15. I understood that. I'd been in that position myself before previous World Cups. But for the core of experienced players in the group this World Cup was only about one thing: winning it. And now we couldn't put one foot in front of the other without falling over. We were trying not to panic. There was no panic. We had two weeks of training left before the World Cup. There was still time.

After the Italy match we had the weekend off and were back into camp on Tuesday. I went to the gym and trained like a dog. Other fellas did the same. Looking back it was a mistake. Pre-season had started on 11 June. This was the last week of August and we should have been tapering off. We found ourselves in a situation, though, that nobody had expected. The only response we could think of was more hard work. Stronger, faster, fitter. Push it.

The Italy game was analysed in detail, like every game we play, and when we returned to camp we were fed the information like medicine. Hold your nose and swallow it. In the Ireland set-up the feedback is blunt and delivered in front of your peers. If you've cocked up everybody knows chapter and verse. That's good. You have to be strong to take it and if you can't take it you've no business in an Irish jersey.

And in the back of our minds we thought it would come right. We thought we'd get to France and it would click. That our hard work would get the reward it deserved. That we would be the team we were before. In spite of everything we still thought we could do it.

Then our worst nightmare came true.

Namibia had six professional players in their squad. In their final warm-up match they had lost to South Africa by 105–13. We were expected to beat them by 50 or 60 points at our ease. Instead we got a dodgy late try to win by 15. We were brutal. The worst performance any of us could remember.

What happened? Mistakes. Simple mistakes. Too many of them. We were trying to play high-tempo rugby but the execution wasn't there. We should have been more patient. Gone through the phases. Instead we tried to play the kind of rugby we produced against Italy in March at a time when our confidence was sky-high. After half an hour we were 20–0 in front and for the next fifty minutes they outscored us. Their pack fronted up in the second half and we didn't do anything about it. Incredible.

Fellas were saying all the right things afterwards. Disgrace. Unacceptable. Take a look at yourselves. All the things you'd expect. Eddie hammered us. Brian hammered us. We hammered ourselves. But where was it getting us? Nowhere. Attitude wasn't the problem. We couldn't try any harder. We couldn't have been more desperate to make it right. We analysed ourselves to death. We knew what was going wrong, we just didn't know why. Everyone was making two or three errors that they hadn't been making in the Six Nations. Multiply that by fifteen players and you're looking at thirty or forty mistakes. Namibia made twelve unforced errors; we made eighteen. We're the professionals. How do you explain that? We couldn't.

Brian stopped me in the corridor at the hotel one night. It was a couple of days after we played Namibia, a few days before the Georgia match. He was tearing his hair out. Totally bewildered. He asked me what the hell was going wrong and I honestly didn't have an answer. Brian is a great friend of mine and as our captain I wanted to say something that was supportive. I don't even remember what I said but I know it was pretty useless.

With things going so badly on the field a whole load of other things seemed worse. Like the hotel. The original plan was to stay in the Radisson in Bordeaux but it wasn't finished in time. Instead, we stayed in a dismal, two-star hotel in the middle of an industrial estate, miles from anywhere. Totally isolated. No buzz. The only amenities nearby were a man-made lake and a go-karting circuit. Useless. It was like you were devoid of reality in that hotel. You were living in a surreal world.

On top of that the food was brutal. When we're in camp at Killiney Castle in Dublin the chef is brilliant and mealtimes are a social occasion. You sit down, enjoy your meal and have the craic. We didn't bring a chef to the World Cup. In Bordeaux you were shovelling in as much grub as you could stomach and heading back up to your room. There was a greasy spoon type place across the road, serving all the wrong kind of food, but we used go there one night a week just to give ourselves a break. If the rugby had been right, though, you could have coped with the hotel and the grub. In our state of mind, everything was worse.

I'm not sure exactly when the rumours started back home about disharmony in the camp. About fights between Munster and Leinster players, about Geordan Murphy walking out and players going on the booze and God knows what else. How do these things start? Who makes them up? We're a nation of gossipers, that's at the heart of it. When we hear bad news, we can't wait to pass it on. We don't question it. If it's bad news we assume it must be true.

The rumours were flying around on emails at home and some of the lads got them. They printed them off and read them out on the bus going to training. At least it gave us a laugh. We didn't have much light relief.

To this day there are people going around saying they *know* what happened at the World Cup. These people invariably have it from a 'good source'. Who? Name the source. Bullshit. They refuse to accept that we under-performed for a whole load of mundane reasons. Over-trained. Tired. Not match-ready. Crucially important stuff that we got wrong. For these people, though, there had to be a Big Reason. A Bust-up. A Meltdown.

I suppose we created the vacuum for all these rumours to exist. We couldn't explain our performances at the time. Six months earlier we were minutes away from winning the Six Nations. We had turned from that into a crowd of plodders. Expectations had been enormous and now it was all collapsing around our ears.

Plans to rotate the starting team for the Georgia match were shelved. This was a great source of slagging for people like Alan Quinlan and Frankie Sheahan – thanking the first 15 for cocking up their World Cup. Of course fellas were disappointed but I didn't see anybody sulking. Somebody like Brian Carney never got a look in but he was a fierce positive influence around the place. At one stage in the Georgia match the television cameras must have picked up Quinny and Frankie in the stand. Next thing they get a text from Mick O'Driscoll, sitting on a bar stool back in Cork. 'Stop smiling and put down that Georgia flag.' The only thing left to laugh at was ourselves.

Georgia was a disaster. Humiliating. They killed us up front. We lost too many collisions. The ruck area was a shambles. Every time we took the ball into contact it was slow coming back. At that stage it was about knocking their heads off. Half of that is technique, half of it is mental. Having the edge to go and do it. There's a phrase in rugby: Hammer the hammer. When their big men are carrying the ball you drive them back. One guy hits him and then another guy hits him. We weren't doing it.

When we let Georgia into the game they grew another few inches. The crowd got behind the underdogs and they came lashing into us. They had a very limited game plan but it was hugely effective. As a top team, should we have been able to counter that? Absolutely.

Things got heated in the second half. Drico ate the head off Peter Stringer for their intercept try. I had a go at Isaac Boss near the end. People were shouting at the pack to sort themselves out. It was a bad scene. In that situation you don't have time to think about the big picture. All you're thinking about is the next restart, the next possession, the next tackle. My head was fit to explode.

A couple of months after the World Cup I watched the last few minutes on DVD. Sitting down, a long way from the battlefield, and watching it on screen it looked even worse. They were within inches of beating us. Losing that match would have been the lowest point in the history of Irish rugby.

Winning that match seemed the lowest point in the history of Irish rugby.

After breakfast on Tuesday morning I was approached by Karl Richardson, the IRFU's media manager. He said there was an article in the French sports paper *L'Équipe* that I should read. Monday had been our media day and I was interviewed by a group of French reporters. One of them was Benjamin Massot from *L'Équipe*. He had been covering the Irish team for a while and I had been interviewed by him before in Limerick. Massot was there for the group interview with the other French reporters and then he had a prior arrangement to speak to me, one-on-one. We went downstairs to find a quiet spot but I didn't have much time because we had a backs meeting. I offered to do the interview afterwards if he wanted to wait. He preferred to carry on. As it happened it didn't take long.

The Irish team had been announced for the match against France four days later. Peter Stringer and Denis Hickie had been dropped. Massot wanted to talk about Eoin Reddan and how he was different to Peter. I wasn't prepared to go there. I'd known Peter for twenty years, we'd played together for club, province and country, we'd been through a lot as a partnership and now he had been kicked in the teeth. For me to go talking up Eoin in a French newspaper would have been incredibly disloyal and I wasn't prepared to do it.

Word for word, this is my recollection of the exchange we had.

'Ronan, does the fact that you'll be associated with Reddan and not Stringer, will that change the Irish game?'

'What it's going to change I'm not going to say.' Silence.

'Do you not want to answer the question?'

'If you want you can ask me the question after the match on Saturday, OK?'

At that point the interview ended. Did we part on bad terms? Yeah. We didn't have a row but it was clear that neither of us was happy with the interview for completely different reasons. In his article the following day he said that I was 'as usual, very unpleasant'. Was I in bad form? Absolutely. I was cranky. We were playing brutal, I was playing badly, our World Cup campaign was falling down around us. Everything we'd worked for, everything we'd dreamed about, was falling apart. I couldn't divorce myself from that. It meant too much to me. I wasn't going to fake being happy when I wasn't.

Was I unpleasant to him? Yeah, probably. Am I usually unpleasant with the media? No. But these weren't normal circumstances. I wasn't in a normal frame of mind.

In the article, though, the Reddan–Stringer question wasn't the big issue. In the twelfth paragraph, in a sentence which I felt was intended to hurt me and my family, it read: 'Among these rumours [about me] is an enormous debt he would have built up playing the races (the sum of €300,000) as well as others concerning his private sphere.'

Massot knew the Irish scene. He knew some of the Irish rugby journalists. He would have known that these rumours had been flying around for ages. He didn't have one shred of evidence to substantiate any of the rumours and still he went to print with his story. The libel laws in France are different to here, looser and more liberal, but I feel that what he did was despicable and beneath contempt. It was a piece of gutter journalism, nothing else.

Not all of the Irish papers picked it up the following day but it was on the Pat Kenny radio show and by the end of the week all of the Irish media had got stuck into it. That was very difficult for Jess and my family. When people see something in the paper their first reaction is that it must be true. They don't question it.

In a bizarre way I saw some good in it. Crazy rumours about my gambling had been going around for years. The whole world seemed to have heard them. It was in the papers now. What difference will that make? After a few days the story will have blown over and it'll be somebody else's turn.

I'm not saying that thought made things easier. Nothing could have made that week easier.

I've had a passion for horse racing for as long as I can remember. Some days after school myself and Anthony Horgan used go to Cashman's Bookmakers. Instead of getting the 3.20 bus home we'd get the four o'clock and catch the last couple of races. I guess we were about sixteen at the time.

There was no history of horses or racing in my family but I loved it. When Presentation Brothers College got to the final of the Munster Senior Cup there were pen pictures of all of us in the match programme. We were asked for our interests outside rugby. Mine were tennis, football, horse racing and greyhound racing. Hoggy ducked it. He said soccer, golf, snooker and 'sport in general'. I didn't care who knew.

The first racing animal I got involved with was a greyhound called All Steel. A group of us in Cork Constitution formed a syndicate: myself, Frankie Sheahan, John O'Driscoll, Ian Murray, Dave O'Brien. She broke our hearts. I don't know how many times we backed her at short prices and we did our dough every time. Then she won in Cork one night at 8/1 when we thought she'd no chance. We didn't have a bob on her.

After that it was horses. About seven years ago I bought one in partnership with a friend of mine, John Dineen. We wanted to call him Claw in honour of Peter Clohessy because he was small and fat. We were also under the impression that he was fast. That name, though, had already been taken so we translated Claw into French: La Griffe. The French always had a soft spot for Claw. As it turned out the horse was nothing like Claw because he was a serial loser. He was sold to England and he hasn't won over there either.

Pat Hughes trained that one and since then I've had a share in horses with a string of trainers from Gerry Cully to Mouse Morris, Michael Grassick, James Nash and John Gosden. Everything from low-grade jumps horses to Group horses on the Flat. I had a point-to-pointer as well. John Dineen trained him for me and Jason Holland. We called him Munster's Best even though it was clear after a while that we should have called him Munster's Worst.

Jess's dad, Dom Daly, is a big point-to-point man and we used to love heading off on a Sunday during the winter. Cork racecourse outside Mallow was another favourite haunt. The O'Driscolls, Mick and John, love their racing too and their father Michael is on the board at the track so we'd go up there, settle into a quiet corner and have a right good day.

Since I was a teenager I've loved a bet. It's part of the game. There was never a time when I regarded it as a problem but there was a time when I did too much of it. It was too easy and I liked it too much. I had money in my pocket, I had plenty of friends in racing so there was no shortage of tips. All I had to do was pick up the phone. If I had a couple of hours off in the middle of the day between training sessions I'd kick back on the couch, stick on the racing channel and have a bet. It became a lazy habit. Part of my routine.

Did I lose money? Of course. To have any chance of making money from gambling you must be very selective, highly disciplined, a brilliant student of the form or massively well informed. I was none of those things. I was a recreational punter. Recreational punters back their share of winners and end up losing money. The good professional punters know when to play and when to walk away. If you switch on Channel Four on a Saturday afternoon and have a tenner on every race they show you'll lose most Saturdays. Probably eight Saturdays out of ten. Those are the odds.

It probably took me two years to cop on to myself. My losses weren't the issue because I was always betting within my means. I wasn't going out drinking like other fellas my age. Having a bet was what I did instead. But you can get too much of a good thing. I came to that realization and I cut back. There was a time in my life when I had a bet most days but that time is long gone.

Where the stories came from I haven't a clue. I was never in debt because of gambling. Nowhere near it. I have nothing to hide and nothing to be ashamed of. Any money I lost was money I was prepared to lose. But the stories kept coming. The list of people who are supposed to have bailed me out is a who's who of the rich and famous in Ireland. The one that keeps on coming up is J.P. McManus. I've never met J.P. or spoken to him and if we ever meet I'll be as embarrassed as hell shaking his hand.

Probably the most comical story of them all was the one where I was supposed to have thrown a Heineken Cup quarter-final against Llanelli in 2007 when Munster were the defending champions. The story goes that J.P. and I backed Llanelli to cover my gambling debts and I deliberately missed shots at goal to make sure Munster lost. There's no point getting annoyed about a story like that. The people who spread it and believed it deserve to be pitied for their stupidity.

Other stories were just as outlandish. That the IRFU warned every bookie in the country not to accept a bet from me. That I flew to the UK just to get a bet on. Do these people not realize that it was never easier to have a bet? Twenty-four hours a day, seven days a week, on the phone, on the internet. There was no intervention from the IRFU because there was no problem. It was nobody's business except my own.

With the rumours, though, came the slagging – in the Munster dressing room and with Ireland. The Munster lads are merciless but they also know where to draw the line. If they thought I had a problem with gambling it would be off the agenda. As it is, they kill me about it. During the World Cup Quinny picked up on the story of the Tongan guy, Epi Taioni, who was given €10,000 to change his name by deed poll to Paddy Power for the duration of the tournament. So Quinny started calling me William Hill while also telling everyone that ten grand was a drop in the ocean with my debts.

Horse racing remains a great passion in my life. I still watch it when I can but I only have a bet now when the mood takes me. Owning shares in horses has been a huge thrill in recent years and watching them run is the greatest kick I've had from the game. I would love to do what Michael Owen has done: set up my own stables with a private trainer and a string of good horses. But I don't earn Michael Owen's wages and I don't expect that dream will ever come true. The biggest drain on my pocket from racing has been from owning horses. The bracing reality of the game is that most racehorses never pay their way. I have yet to own one that did but I haven't given up the search.

Of course none of that appeared in the *L'Équipe* article.

* * *

The other killer phrase in the article referred to rumours 'concerning his private sphere'. To elements of the Irish media, that brought Jess into the picture. I was photographed one day in the week of the France match having a walk with my parents in Bordeaux. The implication of the picture was 'Where's Jess?' and readers were invited to draw their own conclusions. The simple answer was that she was at home teaching primary school kids in Douglas. The new term had just started so she wasn't in a position to drop everything and spend a month in France. She flew in every weekend for the matches and when she arrived in Paris that Friday it was deemed worthy of a front page photograph by one newspaper. Jess didn't ask for that kind of attention and she didn't deserve it.

I managed to keep my head together. People assumed I was in bits but I wasn't. I was all right. I'd been living with all these rumours for ages. The media fuss was new and unwelcome and a distraction but it didn't blow my mind. I was all right.

Drico brought it up at the team meeting on the night before the game. The feeling in the room was that this story had been calculated to undermine us. The attitude was that we were going to ram it down their throats. The mood was good. We knew that France were under savage pressure. They had lost their first match to Argentina and if they lost to us they were basically out. We'd already been written off. In most people's eyes all we could do now was come back from the dead.

Before the match we stood for the national anthems. The camera panned along the line for the usual close-ups. When I got home people told me that I looked haunted. That's not how I felt. I was buzzing. The Stade de France is my favourite venue in the world. This was one of the biggest games I was ever going to play for Ireland. The atmosphere was amazing. I was emotional for the anthems but my focus was where I wanted it to be.

I was living the game in my head. Picturing a dream scenario. Last-minute drop-goal. Running over to the crowd. I thought about the Leicester match a year earlier in the Heineken Cup. My neck was on the block that week for comments I'd made in the press. I overcame that pressure. Kicked a penalty from half-way to win it. I said to myself, 'This could be fantastic. This could be the best day of your rugby life.' Maybe when you looked into my eyes on television you couldn't see any of that but that's how I felt.

It didn't happen. We couldn't make it happen. They were as nervous as we were but they made us pay for our mistakes. Our mistakes were killing us. Even when we were 12–3 down in the first half we were well in the game. We were close to getting a try and if we had scored then we'd have rattled them because they were bricking it. On the field you can always sense it when a team is vulnerable. If we'd got a try I'm certain we'd have got another. But we couldn't execute when we really needed to.

We shot ourselves in the foot too. Their second try was a move we'd covered in training. We practised defending it over and over again. But on the night there was a massive breakdown in communication on Andrew Trimble's wing and when Michalak put in the kick there was nobody within 20 metres of Clerc for the touchdown. Madness.

I didn't play well. My first kick at goal was a shocker. It flew like a dead duck off to the right. Couldn't believe it. I'd been kicking well all week. Me and Shaggy cocked up a high ball later on. My fault. I was in the full-back position and I was coming on to the ball but I left it for him. If things were going well that wouldn't have happened.

We couldn't snap out of it. We were probably better than we had been in the first two matches but nowhere near the level that was required. They beat us handy.

After all these matches there's a mixed zone where reporters stand behind barriers and try to grab a word with players as they walk to the bus. You can ignore the dictaphones and keep walking. After the France match I chose not to. I was about three-quarters of the way down before anybody mentioned the story in *L'Équipe*. I had nothing prepared. People might say that's naïve but I've always felt capable of handling myself with the media. In the absence of any rehearsed answers I spoke from the heart.

'That I have a troubled marriage is quite disappointing to hear. It's not for me to say I have a perfect marriage. Like everyone else little things happen behind closed doors. I love my wife and I think she loves me. That's all I can say on the matter. There's been rumours about me going around for a year now. The only good thing is that it's all come out and has now been put to bed.'

Maybe if I'd thought about it I would have expressed myself better. Maybe I should have kept my mouth shut. The papers got another two days out of those quotes. Speculating about what I really meant when I said, 'I *think* she loves me.' Why didn't I just say, 'I *know* she loves me' – because that was the simple, wonderful, uncomplicated truth? Our marriage is the best thing in my life. Jess is the best thing in my life.

Wives and partners were allowed stay with the players that night. There was a reception on the twenty-first floor of our hotel but I didn't stay long. No mind for it. The match had been late, my head was wrecked. I went to bed and at 2 a.m. I had to call the team doctor, Gary O'Driscoll. My leg was out like a balloon. Beautiful.

The squad returned to Bordeaux by train the following day. Wives and partners were permitted to stay in the team hotel until nine that night but Jess had an early flight back from Paris to Cork on the following morning. Doing a six-hour round journey to Bordeaux would have been ridiculous. Some of the other women were in a similar situation so they stayed behind in Paris and had a night on the town. It didn't hit us at the time but it struck us later: what if Jess was photographed in the early hours of the morning, dancing in a club or whatever? Would that have made the papers? Would it have fuelled the story for another day or two? We'd never had to think like that before. We were private people living private lives.

For one terrible week all of that was violated.

To qualify from our pool we needed a bonus point win against Argentina. Four tries. The cold, objective, outside view was that we had no chance. Their World Cup had already been a success; ours had already been a flop. As a player you try to live without that kind of objectivity. It was no use to us. We had a week to make ourselves believe we could beat Argentina with four tries. Nobody else believed we could. Did we believe it? In our hearts? I don't know. All I know is that we didn't give up.

The captain's meeting on the night before the match was brilliant. Honest and positive. I don't usually speak in these meetings but I thought we needed to put it on the line in the starkest terms: we have one last chance. If we go home after this match we're an embarrassment, a disgrace to ourselves and the country. The buzz leaving the room that night was as good as anything I'd ever experienced before an international.

The performance against Argentina was our best of the tournament. What did it count for? Nothing. How good were we? Better than brutal. Not good. Nowhere near it. Our two tries were well worked but we never looked like getting four. The collision area was a disaster again. If you don't win the collisions you can't make offloads and that leads to turnovers. We must have coughed up a dozen turnovers. A couple of weeks later I had a chat with Denis Leamy and he said it straight out: the pack was beaten up in three of the four matches. Without that platform we had no chance. Not that the backs were firing either. We weren't.

For the second game in a row we conceded a try that we had specifically practised a defence for. An ordinary 8–9–14 move down the shortside. We spent twenty minutes in one session working on it. We'd stopped the session, we'd argued about it and we kept going until we got it right. Then the first 5-metre scrum they got Lucas Borges got in. The first score of the match. That kicked everyone in the guts. How do you explain that? We'd practised it. We knew what we had to do. And they still scored.

My kicking out of the hand was bad, just as it had been in the other matches. One of my missed touches went straight to Juan Hernández who took one look and banged a brilliant drop-goal. The exact same thing had happened against Argentina in the World Cup four years earlier. Unbelievable.

On the pitch there was all the usual bad blood between us and them. Felipe Contepomi complained afterwards in the Argentinian press that he was sledged by Irish players. So what? That goes on in every match. You give it and you take it. Contepomi is a talented guy and he had a good World Cup but he can be fragile too. In the 2006 Heineken Cup semi-final against Munster he cracked. When a player has that reputation other teams are going to twist his tail and see if he copes. That day, he coped.

After the final whistle one of the Argentinian props gave me a sarcastic pat on the cheek and a feed of abuse. That was the final insult. Our World Cup was over.

I skipped the mixed zone afterwards. Took a different exit. One of the security guys tried to stop me but I brushed past him. Just wanted to get away. Didn't want to talk about it, didn't want to put on a brave face, didn't want to share what I was feeling with strangers.

Jess and my three brothers were at the reception in the team room at the hotel. My parents were staying in a different part of town but I spoke to them on the phone. We're a close family and that has been a precious thing in our lives. That night I needed them.

CHAPTER 2

Frankie Sheahan never shuts up about my dad's final trial for Ireland. He says that was the line I always used when we were kids and I wanted to impress people. 'Hi, I'm Rog, my dad played in a final trial.' He's exaggerating but I probably did go on about it. I can't remember a time when I wasn't impressed by my dad. He has shaped me and my career in rugby more than any other person. The biggest thing in our relationship is that he always seemed to know what I needed, whether that was a kick in the ass or an arm around my shoulder. As a young fella there were times when I thought I knew everything. He knew better.

My brothers tell me how much stress I've caused in his life, because he lives every moment of every game. Fergal is in his late fifties now and it's not good for him but I don't think he can get out of it at this stage. My mum, Joan, is a bit like that during matches too but I think mothers are different – they want you to do well and they don't want you to get hurt, but my mum isn't playing every ball of the match like my dad. She is always incredibly caring and I suppose like all Irish mothers she adores her sons. We didn't have to lift a finger. She washed our mucky gear and put our meals on the table. Spoiled us.

Dad was never pushy. He has a great way of being balanced and reasonable about things. I never felt under any pressure from him to do well. Faith plays a big part in his life and he believes that we all have God-given talents that we should make the most of – that was it. Fathers can be blinkered about their sons but that isn't his way. I know I occupy a lot of his thoughts but he never took the soft option of telling me what I wanted to hear when there was something that needed to be said. In life and in rugby he's been my go-to guy. If I needed an opinion on something I would ask him, knowing that he'd be honest and smart.

In his playing days he was a winger with UCG Connacht and Sunday's Well and when I was a kid he did some coaching with underage teams in Cork Constitution. I've worked with a lot of good coaches but he's sharper than most of them. Before big matches over the years he'd write me a note with his thoughts on the game, the things I should be concentrating on, the things the opposition might try to do to me and brilliant stuff on the mental side of the game. He'd leave it in an envelope and he'd say something like, 'If you have time, take a look at that.' I'd be dying to read it. The second he was gone out the door I'd open the envelope. He doesn't do it as much now as he used to but he typed out some thoughts for me before the World Cup and gave them to me with a miraculous medal from my mum.

They met in the early 1970s when they were students in University College, Galway: Fergal O'Gara from Ballisadare in county Sligo and Joan Langan from Ballina in Mayo. Mum qualified as a teacher and Dad as a microbiologist and shortly after college they spent a few years in California. My older brother, Colin, was born there and so was I, on 7 March 1977. I was only about six months old when we moved to Central Avenue in Bishopstown, a new middle-class suburb on the southside of Cork city. My two younger brothers, Fergal and Morgan, were born there.

My parents gave us every chance in life, which is something you never appreciate when you're a kid. We were sent for elocution lessons when that wasn't the done thing and we were sent for piano lessons to open up that horizon to us. I didn't want to know. Tuesdays and Thursdays were the days for lessons and I dreaded them. All I wanted was to be out on the street, playing ball. One day I took my protests too far. I got an old rugby boot and scrawled on the piano: 'I hate music.' I tried to blame one of my brothers but my parents knew it was me. There was murder.

My parents really wanted us to have a good education; our homework was checked every night and they were strong on discipline, but they indulged us too. When BMX bikes were the cool thing for kids to have we had the Mongoose model with the small saddles that you had to import from abroad. That was unheard of around Bishopstown. We had great summer holidays in France and we didn't want for anything.

My brothers were big into sport too. Colin is a brilliant windsurfer and represented Ireland when he got older. Morgan and Fergal played rugby in Presentation Brothers College, University College Cork, Cork Con and Highfield and they were both good players. As it happened, they were out-halves as well, but were happy to play anywhere. In Pres, Morgan played with Peter Stringer's younger brother, David, which was a weird coincidence. It also invited comparisons and that wrecked Morgan's head a bit.

From where we lived, Highfield and Bishopstown GAA were only up the road but as kids we played everything. There was a bunch of young fellas around the place who just loved sport: the O'Reillys next door, the O'Loughlins on the other side, down the road to the Burkes and across to the Nestors. There was so little traffic in our estate that we could chalk out a tennis court on the street during Wimbledon and use a rope for a net. We played pitch and putt in Murphy's Farm, where the pins were nearly always missing, and I played soccer for Summerstown. My position was the right side of midfield. I was so small I could hardly kick the ball but I remember having my own Summerstown jersey with matching shorts, which seemed like a big deal.

At the same time I was playing in the Bishopstown GAA Street Leagues. I was better at Gaelic football and stuck at it longer. I loved hurling too but I gave it up when I was about twelve. I wasn't one of the best on the team and I didn't see a future in it. Even back then that would have been my attitude. Wanting to be the best.

I went to Scoil Spioraid Naomh primary school, where the GAA was strong. It was a great school and they gave you a good education but it was cold and bleak too and we had some hard teachers. I remember being very scared of one in particular. If you were being disruptive he'd hang you by the jumper on one of the coat hangers in the corridor for a few minutes. It didn't hurt – it was just the public humiliation. I wasn't a trouble-maker but I suppose I was cheeky. The school reports were usually: has ability, loses attention, could do better. The fact was that I didn't want to be in class. All I wanted was sport.

Rugby started at home. My friends still talk about the birthday parties where my dad would launch a garryowen from the patio in our back garden and thirty kids would try to catch it. A great friend of the family called Fred Casey got me involved with Cork Con. It was odd for somebody from our side of the city go over there, passing Highfield, Dolphin and Sunday's Well on the way, but Fred was in charge of the U-12s and that was the reason.

Even though we were young it was quite competitive. One summer they brought us to a kind of European championship over in France and we won it. For kids that whole experience was unbelievable. We travelled in cars, across on the ferry, and we slept in dorms, a squad of U-12s on tour. We ate in restaurants, glasses of Coke with our meals – all of that must have been a massive kick at the time because twenty years later I can still remember it. Con wear white but for some reason we wore black for that tournament, which made us feel like New Zealand. That U-12 team in Con was my first time playing with Peter Stringer. People seem to think that I've been playing alongside him all our lives but that's a myth. He's nine months younger than me which meant that he was a year behind me in school and after Con U-12s we didn't play together again until he broke through with Munster ten years later.

Rugby got serious for me in Presentation Brothers College but going there wasn't the original plan. My mum was teaching in Bishopstown Community School and when I finished in Spioraid Naomh that's where I went too for a year. The problem, then, was me. I saw myself as a bit of a hard man and a little gang of us were of the same opinion.

We were only in sixth class in primary school when we started smoking. We'd have a packet of John Player Blues and at lunch-time we'd sneak off into the palm trees between Highfield and Bishopstown GAA. We'd get six cans of Club Shandy that had 0.001 per cent alcohol and convince ourselves that we were getting a buzz off it. Somebody would get the fags for us and we'd puff away. It was a ridiculous carry-on. I had asthma for one thing and the other thing was that I hated the taste of the cigarettes. It was torture but you'd have to put on a brave face for the sake of appearances. If the boys were watching I'd have to inhale, but if they weren't looking I'd puff-blow the smoke away. To get rid of the smell before we went back into class we'd chew on a bit of a palm tree. I remember getting sick a few times but that didn't stop me. Not if you wanted to be a hard man.

The other thing we used to do was walk into Dunnes Stores with one of their plastic bags and rob fun-size chocolate bars. Eventually, we were caught and held until our parents were called. Our worlds fell apart that day. All the other lads were like myself, from respectable families. There was hell to pay. I was grounded for a good stretch. A proper grounding. One of my friends still remembers calling up for me one day during my sentence and I was shouting out of the top window, bawling, crying: 'Please come back.'

By then we had moved about two miles away from Bishopstown, out the Model Farm Road to an estate called Hilton. At the end of first year it was decided that I needed a different environment, away from my little gang. I was afraid to tell my buddies that I was going to Pres. It was even beyond slagging. This was deadly serious and it was bad the way it worked out. When I was in Bishopstown Community School I used to cycle to school and pick up a friend of mine, Alan Forde, on the bike. Alan was ringing before second year started and I said, 'Yeah, I'll see you in the morning.' I couldn't face telling him. Pres is a fee-paying school and it would have been seen as posh and elitist, so it was a big move for a Bishopstown young fella to go there.

Nobody cut anybody off but communication just fell away. It was just the way it happened. I went one way and they continued doing their own thing. They were all living around Bishopstown anyway and you wouldn't have been going in there after school. You did your homework, had dinner and you weren't really allowed out when it was dark.

I was very nervous going into Pres. I knew a couple of lads from Con but there were 120 kids in second year and they all knew each other. Rugby was my way of gaining acceptance. I was made captain of the U-14 team and that was the start of it.

Pres was where I first came into contact with Declan Kidney. He was in charge of rugby in the school and he was a big influence on me in those years. Deccie was really good, very organized, and the fitness programmes were savage. We'd train on Christmas Eve, Stephen's Day, crackers stuff. In fairness, he gave me a good understanding of the game and he invested a fair bit of time in me. I used to meet him a lot at lunchtime and break time. He'd draw out a pitch on a sheet of A4 and then fire the questions at me: 'What would you do here? What would you do there? What would you do off this scrum? Off this lineout?' Being the captain meant that you needed a grasp of strategy and that's what he was instilling in me. He wanted to know what I was going to do most times with the ball, what I was thinking. It was a simple game plan but I enjoyed the tactical side of it. I had my head fairly well screwed on about what we wanted to achieve.

I don't know if I was the best player on the team. I probably wasn't but I would have been pissed off if I wasn't captain. People probably would have said I was a bit cocky but that can be a front too. Over the years you'd see plenty of cocky fellas who were crumbling underneath. Whatever doubts I had, though, I always had good belief in my ability and that counts for a lot when you're a young fella. I was fierce competitive but that also made me a terrible loser and my parents didn't let me away with that.

We won the U-14 cup and I was kept on as captain for the junior cup team a year later. Schools rugby in Munster doesn't have the same profile as it does in Leinster but it was a big deal in our school and you felt that. We had a decent team and when you were playing for Pres you always had a chance. Frankie Sheahan was hooker, Anthony Horgan was on the wing and we got to the final against St Munchin's from Limerick.

Ollie Campbell had come to Con years earlier to do some coaching and I still have a letter that he sent me before that final. 'May you kick like a mule and run like the wind,' he wrote at the end. I'm not sure I did any of that in the first match, which ended in a scoreless draw in Musgrave Park. The replay in Thomond Park was heading the same way – no score with the clock ticking down and extra-time looming. We had one last attack and off a lineout I went for a drop-goal. It was a fair bit out and we were playing with a small, size four ball on a windy day. It was ninety seconds into injury time and I knew it was our last chance but I had the confidence to try it. Bang. Over it went.

That was the first big event in my rugby career: write-ups in the paper, a victory dinner in Jurys Hotel, getting selected for the Munster schools team, my first representative honour. You feel like you're the business.

Out-half was always my position but I was a different player back then. For one thing, I wasn't the front-line kicker. Eddie Hogan-O'Connell was the kicker on our school team, right up until senior cup. He was a big young fella and he had a great boot on him. The other thing was that I was very small. In one of the match reports from the junior cup final I was described as 'diminutive' and that's exactly how I looked on the field.

We would have heard about the weight training that the schools players were doing in Dublin but the belief in Pres was that we were too young and that eighteen was time enough to start in the gym. I was skinny and I wasn't tall but Deccie's training was tough and that stood to all of us. When I got up to sixteen or seventeen I did an awful lot of tackling practice. I used to hate it but it was beaten into us for our own good. The tackle bags weighed a ton and they used to hold water when it rained, making them even heavier. I was creamed plenty of times but it wouldn't have mattered if I was two stone bigger, I still would have been creamed. You have to be brave to a certain extent but I wasn't extra brave. I didn't look on it like that. You had to make your tackles and that was it.

When rugby got serious in school I basically had to give up soccer and Gaelic football. During the summer months, though, I took up tennis and I got mad into it. My dad shelled out for lessons that didn't come cheap and I kept playing until I was about eighteen. Rugby was my number one game but I wasn't obsessed about it. I was sorry to give up the other sports but it just came to a stage where I had to choose.

I used go to Con matches in the All-Ireland League and I'd watch Munster if they were playing in Musgrave Park. When I was a young fella there were only a handful of Munster games every season. One of them was a famous victory against Australia when they were the reigning World Champions. Musgrave Park wasn't full that afternoon, not even close. Anybody that tells you there was always great support for Munster teams hasn't a clue. I managed to go home with one of the match balls that day. It landed in a crowd of us and I wrestled it off another young fella. Into my school bag and away. Class.

Dad used to bring us to the Ireland matches in Lansdowne Road. He had a guaranteed supply of tickets for the same spot in the front row of the West Stand but there weren't enough for all of us so my brothers and I were taken in turn. That was a big day out and there was a set routine: the 7.30 a.m. train out of Cork, a late breakfast in Bewley's on Grafton Street and maybe a burger in McDonald's a bit later. Then we'd go into the bar in the Shelbourne Hotel on St Stephen's Green, where Dad would have a pint with old friends from university.

We always only had two tickets but that was enough to get three of us in. Dad would stand me by a lamppost next to the turnstile, go in with my brother, deposit him in his seat and come back down with the two tickets, minus the stubs. He'd give some yarn to the fella on the gate so that he could get out and then he'd come back in with me, giving the same yarn again. It always worked a treat. Our seats were in the front row of the West Stand, right in the corner at the Havelock Square end, and for some reason there was a tiny space at the end of our row that was too small to be a ticketed seat but was the perfect size for a little young fella like me. That was my perch.

One of my earliest memories is the 1985 Triple Crown match against England. Dad brought myself and Colin that day. I was only eight and Colin was nine so you can imagine the excitement.

Ciaran Fitzgerald was the Ireland captain and Dad had played with him in UCG which, as kids, made us feel that little bit closer to the heart of it. The game went down to the wire and that was a disaster for us. Our routine also included getting the 4.50 p.m. train back to Cork which meant being on the platform at Lansdowne Road station before 4 p.m. to make the connection. The upshot was that we had to leave our seats with about ten minutes to go at a time when the teams were level, 10–10, and the tension in the ground was unbelievable. Me and Colin didn't want to budge. We kept leaning forward, trying to ignore Dad's urgings to move. In stressful situations my cheeks give me away and at that moment I could feel them turn red with frustration.

We got to the platform at Lansdowne Road Station and word went round that Rob Andrew had missed a penalty. Our carriage was packed, mostly with Cork people heading for the same train as us, but one of them had a radio and there was such a hush that the only voice you could hear in the carriage was Jim Sherwin doing the commentary on RTE radio. I've seen Michael Kiernan's winning drop-goal many times on television since but I remember the commentary as if I never saw it: 'Drop-goal on. Drop-goal taken. Drop-goal good!' When the kick went over people were roaring and jumping around and my dad half-thought we were going to be derailed.

I dreamed of playing for Ireland and in my senior cup year I got the chance. With dozens of other schoolboys from around the country I was picked for an Irish schools trial. We assembled in Blackrock College and Deccie was the coach. I can still see it, all of us gathered in a room on the morning of the trial with Deccie addressing the group.

'Hands up here who wants to play for Ireland?' he said.

Everyone put up their hand.

'Now,' he said, 'get out of my sight. I don't want to have

anything to do with ye! Hands up here who wants to play for a winning Ireland?'

Deccie has changed a bit over the years but in those days he was still a school teacher in every way.

I was picked on the Probables team and I had the game of my life: two tries and kicked all around me. I remember going home on the train with Dave O'Brien, a friend and team-mate from Pres, and he was disappointed because he had lined out for the Possibles and felt he hadn't played well.

I'll never forget the shock when I was told I hadn't been picked. Australia Schools were touring here that winter and Ireland were fielding two teams against them in the week before Christmas 1994 – Ireland Schools and an Ireland B XV. I was named on the bench for the B team. I had gone from having a blinder for the Probables in the final trial to being third choice. Emmet Farrell was now first choice and Richard Ormonde was ahead of me.

I was rattled and it took me a long time to get over it. I remember Deccie trying to make jokes about it years later but I couldn't laugh. I was still sore. That might sound crazy now given the career that I've had, but it's something I'll never forget. That was the first time rugby had given me a savage kick in the teeth. I can see some good in it now. I have had plenty of down times in rugby since then but that was the first major setback and it definitely prepared me for what was coming down the tracks. Ultimately, setbacks either make you or break you and I think they've made me.

I played in a couple of minor matches for the Ireland Schools that season – I remember one against the Leinster U-19s – but for the important fixtures I was off the radar. Dave O'Brien made the team at full-back afterwards and I went to see him play against Australia. It killed me to stand there and watch.

My dad was important around that time. 'There's politics in

that decision,' he said. 'You couldn't have done any more.' I guess that's what I needed to hear but I know he believed it too.

Munster Schools played Australia on that tour as well and we did really well to get a 12–12 draw but it wasn't enough to change the mind of the Irish selectors. After that it was back to the senior cup campaign in Pres. I was captain again and the commitment expected from everybody was huge. Between training and matches we were doing something probably five days a week, including weekends.

On the odd days that we weren't training a few of us would go down to the Victoria Sporting Club straight after school. We played pool or computer games and the girls from Scoil Mhuire school at the top of Patrick's Hill would be hanging around. You'd meet lads from Christians as well, our arch rivals on the rugby pitch. We played them in the semi-final of the senior cup that year and murdered them, 24–0. That was a big event in our little world. In those days I always regarded myself as an out-half that got a back line moving, but there's a paragraph in the *Examiner* report of that match by Barry Coughlan which will be more familiar to people who've watched me in the Munster jersey for the last ten years or more: 'Pres kept it tight after their brilliant start. Out-half Ronan O'Gara recognised the immense threat posed out wide by Christians' speedy three-quarters and opted for a safety first approach, keeping his pack moving forward with clever use of the boot.'

I suppose it's easy to get notions about yourself too. Schools rugby is all about winning and very little about style. We used do a lot of back-line moves in training that didn't work in the real world. You had the famous move of dummy switching the first centre, dummy switching the second centre and then giving it to the full-back. We'd score forty training tries and then catch one or two bad teams with that move.

In the final against Crescent Comprehensive, though, we got a great try and that was basically the difference between the teams. I played a long pass to Paul Barry in the centre and he played another long pass to Anthony Horgan who got over in the corner. David Wallace was the Crescent captain – another fella who didn't make the Irish Schools team that year – and we've shared many great days since for Munster and Ireland but that day it was me or him.

Their kicker had a nightmare and missed nine shots at goal. With the wind in the second half Eddie Hogan-O'Connell nailed three kicks for us and that was it, 14–7. I climbed the steps of the stand in Musgrave Park to accept the cup from my mum and the two of us lifted it together. There was a victory dinner a few weeks later and I had to make a speech. I was absolutely dreading it. Whatever confidence I had on a rugby field didn't spread to public speaking.

There's no doubt that rugby interfered with my studies in Pres. I can't blame anybody but myself for that. Plenty of fellas combine the two and succeed at both. My parents were always anxious for us to do well academically and there was good discipline in our house when it came to homework and studying. My Junior Certificate results were not too bad but I know my parents were expecting a bit better.

I'll never forget the day I got my Leaving Cert results. My dad drove me into Pres and he waited in the car. I wanted to do Commerce in University College Cork but you needed about 420 points for that and I ended up with 400. I messed up my English paper. I was in the honours class but I only got a D2 and that cost me about 30 points. My dad was gutted. He didn't give out to me but the silence as we sat in the car expressed all of his disappointment. I hated that. I hated letting my parents down. Without putting pressure on me I knew their expectations were high. Colin was already studying medicine in UCC and they would have expected me to reach my goal.

The game turned professional that year, 1995, but the prospect of having a career in rugby was only a dream. My first thought was that I was going to have to repeat my Leaving Cert, but I had enough points to do Arts and that's what I did. One step closer to the big bad world.

CHAPTER 3

In December of 1995 the UCC rugby team was tested by the Human Performance Laboratory in the college. I had never been tested like that before and I had barely started to address all of the physical requirements for top-class rugby. I was slight and I spent most of my teens being small as well. It never bothered me. I never regarded it as a barrier to playing rugby or being good at it. But rugby was changing fast and for the next few years the condition of my body was going to be an ongoing issue.

In the test I scored well in flexibility and aerobic fitness, but my body fat level was very high and I only weighed around 11 stone. Years later John Hayes described me as a 'skinny, fat bastard' and that's what the test results were saying too. I played in the centre for UCC that season in Division Three of the All-Ireland League and I must have been concussed four or five times. I was always complaining to the forwards about the beasts that were running at me, looking to them for better protection. They got a great kick out of my distress.

I was only eighteen and I looked it: slight with a boyish face. In the match programme for the first inter-varsity game of the season, against Queen's University Belfast, everybody had the piss taken out of them in the pen pics. 'On a reinforced diet of Cow & Gate and Milupa baby food,' was how my one started. After that it gets a bit coarse in the tradition of undergraduate write-ups.

I had started on weights and I was going to the gym a lot but you couldn't say that I was leading the life of an athlete. The craic was too good. After matches on Saturday there was always a drinking session and it was all the better if you were playing away from home. You'd start with a few bottles on the train, thinking you were cool in your college blazer. When we got back to Cork we'd have a couple upstairs in the Mardyke pavilion, then across to the Western Star, the most famous of all UCC sporting pubs. The Star was next door to the greyhound track and a few of us would climb over the wall at the back, stick on a few bets and have a few more jars before heading into town to finish the night off. When I started in college I was also eligible to play for the juniors until I had made a certain number of senior appearances. Those games were on Sundays but that didn't keep me in on Saturday nights.

The other big college night was Tuesday. You'd rush home from training, grab four or five cans of beer and drink them on the street with the lads before going into the nightclub. 'Bushing' I suppose you'd call it – the kind of thing we thought we were doing as ten-year-olds in the palm trees with our packet of John Player Blues and cans of shandy. I wasn't stuck for money in college but I wasn't loaded either. I had a normal student's pocket and having a few cans first gave the night a longer tail. My dad was a professor lecturing in UCC – as he still is today – and through his work he had an account with Cork Taxi Co-Op. For a while I chanced my arm and ordered my taxi home on his account but I was rumbled soon enough and that was stopped.

We had a serious team that year. John O'Mahony – who went on to be the leading scorer in the history of the All-Ireland League – was playing at out-half. John Kelly was captain and playing at outside centre, Frankie Sheahan was at hooker and Dominic Crotty was at full-back, only a year away from winning his first Irish cap in the autumn of 1996. At that level Crotty was unbelievable. In one match against University College Galway in the inter-varsity Dudley Cup that season he scored seven tries, and on the day we won promotion to Division Two of the AIL he scored a brilliant try against University College Dublin. I'd say he beat half a dozen players to score. He got a hat-trick of tries that day, for the second week in a row.

He was a complete freak, so far ahead of everyone else, and I really looked up to him. I'd say he was training three times a day and watching his diet at a time when that kind of thing wasn't the norm at all. I did a lot of kicking practice with him during the summer of 1996, after my first year in college. Two or three nights a week I'd cycle in to the Mardyke on my shitty mountain bike and meet him at the rugby pitch. He'd arrive on his moped with seven or eight balls and I'd bomb him with garryowens for catching practice. He stood behind the posts for my kicking drills and I'd listen to anything he had to say.

Because the League was being restructured six teams were promoted that year and we went up on the last day, despite only winning six of our eleven matches and losing all of the first three. I didn't go to UCC as a recognized front-line kicker but I was given that responsibility for the college and I thrived on it. In all competitions, with the seniors, juniors and U-20s, I scored 462 points that year.

At the end of that season I reached the first major crossroads in my career. Paul Burke was leaving Cork Con to take up a contract with Bristol and the club approached me to be his replacement. It was normal practice to play for UCC as long as you were in college but I was ambitious and this was a huge opportunity. Con were one of the top teams in the country and in those days the First Division of the AIL was the place to be if you wanted to be noticed. My dreams were to play for Munster and Ireland and I saw this as a big stepping stone. Michael Bradley and Ralph Keyes, two former Irish internationals and huge figures in the club, approached me in May of 1996 and I jumped at it. Obviously, I wasn't given any guarantees about my place and in the back of my mind I thought they'd go off and sign a current international like Eric Elwood but they assured me that they wouldn't. The way I looked at it, if I turned them down they were going to get somebody else and how could I be sure that an opportunity like this would ever come round again?

Word got out about my decision and it went down very badly in college. I was doing a bit of part-time bar work in the Western Star and one Sunday afternoon a crowd from the rugby club came in after a junior match. I didn't realize the resentment my move had caused until one of the alickadoos started abusing me, telling me I wouldn't make it and stuff like that. I'll never forget it. At the AGM later one of the lecturers associated with the club made a speech about players 'selling their soul' to join other clubs. He didn't mention me by name but it was clear who he was talking about.

Before the approach from Con I had already applied to UCC for a sports bursary in second year. From my application form it would have been clear to them how ambitious I was. Under the heading short-term goals I wrote: Munster U-20 96/97, Combined Universities 96/97 and Irish U-21 team 96/97. Below that I set out my long-term goals, in black and white: Munster senior team, Ireland A, Ireland senior team. In my mind, moving to Con fitted in with all of that.

Obviously I withdrew my application for a bursary and cancelled the scheduled interview that was part of the process. A few days later I received a letter from Kieran Dowd, Director of Physical Education and Sport in UCC. He wasn't happy either:

'It is particularly disappointing as Head of Sport in UCC that as the College is making strenuous efforts to make college sport more attractive and successful with the provision of improved facilities and additional funding for sport that the erosion of young talented players should nevertheless be continuing.

'It's a choice you have made and I hope that for your sake it will benefit your game. Yours is still a very raw talent and I know from my years of experience that it would be better developed within the current set up at UCC Rugby Club which during the last year, your first year in College, helped in no small way to develop your skills and help make you the player whose services another club now consider desirable to acquire. Regrettably I had no input if indeed it would have made any significance in your decision.

'I wish you well in your career ahead both sporting and academic.'

While all that was going on I'll never forget the support I got from Cillian Twomey, who was the UCC rugby club president and a gentleman. He rang me a few times and gave me his support. 'Do what's best for your career,' he said, 'and back yourself.' That was the conclusion I had come to but it was reassuring to hear it from someone else.

I didn't know whether I was going to make it or not. I knew that I badly wanted to succeed and I knew I had ability but I wasn't a superstar whiz-kid. I made the Munster U-20 team that year and was named in a 45-man squad for an Irish U-21 training camp during the summer. I was also considered by the IRFU to be part of their National Foundation Programme but I didn't make the grade. The scheme was designed to 'assist young players of international potential in the development of their skills.' Basically, they were looking to groom future internationals. Each branch nominated players to go to an initial training camp in Blackrock College and I was sent from Munster. About fifteen players were picked for the scheme and I didn't make the cut. In their eyes that's where I stood: good, but not that good. When your dream is to play for Ireland that's a kick in the teeth. I still have the letter from Ray Southam, the IRFU's Director of Rugby Development, informing me of the bad news: 'I would suggest that when you finish your season you take a break with some recreational activities involvement,' he wrote. 'Then set off-season goals that will see you establish yourself in your Provincial U-20 team and pushing for National U-21 selection at the end of next season.'

I already had plans for 'recreational activities'. With a gang of my buddies from Pres we headed to Martha's Vineyard in the States: Paul O'Mahoney, Aiden Fitzgerald, Eoin Walsh, John Powell, Steve O'Brien, John O'Sullivan, John O'Connell. Some of these lads had nothing to do with rugby and couldn't care less about it and I've always valued those friendships.

I got a job stacking fruit and vegetable shelves in a local A&P supermarket for $6 an hour. The manager was a good guy who, for some reason, nicknamed me Ace. It wasn't great money but it was enough. The plan was to work for a month and take a two-week holiday at the end. We had brilliant craic even though we couldn't get into bars over there. None of us was twenty-one and fake IDs didn't work. I definitely had no chance of fooling a door-man. To be honest we got a bit fed up of drinking at home every night.

Having been born in Sacramento I had a US passport so I could have stayed as long as I liked that summer. I had no plans though and it was just as well. In my first-year college exams I failed French, which was a massive pain in the ass. It meant studying again when I got home. I took grinds to make sure I didn't cock up in my repeats and then it turned out later on that I hadn't failed at all. They had forgotten to add my oral results to my written paper and that would have been enough for a pass mark. In first-year Arts you must do four subjects and I was dropping French anyway. For the remainder of my degree I took Economics as my major subject and Psychology as my minor. I stuck at it, got my degree and did a Masters in Business Economics a year later. I'd have been happy to finish up with my degree but my dad felt strongly that I should continue and he was right. Again.

The funny thing was that I had another opportunity to leave UCC after first year. Somebody at the University of Surrey who knew my dad sounded him out about the possibility of me enrolling there on a rugby scholarship. They had a link-up with Harlequins and the suggestion was that I could continue my studies while training as a professional rugby player. Professionalism was still new in rugby and nobody was sure how it was going to turn out, but the English clubs had really embraced it and there was a lot of money sloshing around over there.

Harlequins was a big club and that kind of offer would turn your head. My dad, though, spoke to Donal Lenihan and Ralph Keyes about it and they both thought it was risky. Harlequins were losing players at the time, it was a tough league and my opportunities would probably have been very limited. We made the decision to stay and I was happy with that. Making it with Con was going to stretch me enough. Other players though were made offers they couldn't refuse and there was an exodus of top players from All-Ireland League clubs that summer. As well as Paul Burke, Con also lost David Corkery to Bristol and Gabriel Fulcher to London Irish – three players of international class. Len Dineen and David O'Mahony were two other big players who left for other Irish clubs and the general view was that Con would be in for a tough season.

In those days the pool stages of the Heineken Cup were played off very quickly in the early part of the season and the All-Ireland League didn't get going until after that. Munster weren't a force in the competition and nobody expected them to reach the knock-out stages. I needed to prove myself with Con before Munster were going to take me seriously but I was invited to train with them early that season, and when they had a couple of injuries I sat on the bench for an inter-provincial against Connacht at Temple Hill, Con's home ground. After that I was back to the Munster U-20s.

I had put on the guts of a stone over the previous year and I was going to need it in the All-Ireland League. In the *Sunday Independent*'s preview of the season I was highlighted as one of the young players to watch but everybody was picking up on my lack of power. 'Big on skill if light in physique,' wrote Brendan Fanning. 'O'Gara has tremendous balance and footballing nous. He will need it to survive his first season at this level; soft ground and hard flankers will ask questions.'

My first taste of a hard prop came in the second game of the season at Tom Clifford Park, the home of Young Munster. It was a comical scene when I look back on it now but at the time there was nothing funny about it. A melee broke out mid-way through the second half and Des Clohessy came after me. He said I was after kicking one of their front rows in the face. I could have fallen over a ruck or something but of all the stupid things I've done in my life kicking a Young Munster player in the head at Tom Clifford Park isn't one of them. Anyway, Des wasn't waiting for video evidence or an independent inquiry. I was scared, simple as that. He charged at me and I back-pedalled for all I was worth. Somebody said it was like hare-coursing with Des as the greyhound. What was I supposed to do? Stand there and have the head bashed off me? He was raging and I was running.

Coming off the pitch I got an earful of abuse. 'Open the gate, O'Gara is coming', 'Where's your mammy' and all this. On the way home that night the Con lads didn't spare me either, which is what you'd expect. I became friendly with Des over the years and I often call to him in Limerick. We still have a good laugh about it. 'You have to play to your strengths, Des,' I say to him, 'you were never going to catch me.'

As a young fella in that league I was conscious of being targeted but I was tough enough too and I was able to look after myself in my own way. I had great battles over the years with another Young Munster wing-forward, Ger Earls, father of Keith, a rising star with Munster now. One day I caught him a beauty. I was clearing to touch and he was running through, trying to charge down my kick. I held my finish, like a golfer, and jabbed my studs into his ribs. That's the law of the jungle. When I'm kicking the ball I'm in a vulnerable position and wing-forwards will bury you every chance they get.

I was the kicker and I was comfortable with that. Con finished only in mid-table but 146 points made me the second-highest scorer in the league behind Andrew Thompson, who was playing for the champions, Shannon. Given all that I've learned about kicking in the last ten years my technique was primitive, but I had a way of doing it that I trusted and I didn't mind sharing it with the world when I was asked. I had my initials etched into my kicking tee and that's what I aimed for. 'Kick my initials and that ensures the perfect strike,' I told Tom English in the *Sunday Times*.

That's all wrong but that was me, thinking I knew it all. When you kick it like I was back then the ball rotates quickly, end over end, and it's less likely to hold a true line. Now, I'm looking at a spot two-thirds of the way up the ball. You can see from old action shots of my place-kicking that I'm leaning off too which means I'm not getting through the strike in the way that I do now. I had no drive through the ball. My routine was probably three steps back, three to the left and another one. Why? Probably because Neil Jenkins or Rob Andrew did it that way. There were no kicking coaches in Ireland at the time. You found a way that worked for you and stuck with it.

There was some money floating around the All-Ireland League but not much of it came my way that season. Other lads would have had different deals but all I remember is getting a £100 win bonus and no basic match fee. The season went well and there was a lot of positive feedback for my performances but I wasn't the brightest young star on the Con team – my scrum-half, Brian O'Meara, was way ahead of me on that score.

Brian was a year older than me but I knew him as a kid growing up in Bishopstown and we would have played together on the green. He went to Pres but we didn't really play much together in school because of the age difference. At the beginning of my first season with Con he was being linked with a move to Bath and the IRFU put him on a special contract for young players, as long as they committed to staying in the All-Ireland League. The deal was £9,600 a year, which was serious money for a nineteen-year-old student in UCC.

He broke into the senior Irish squad for the autumn internationals of 1996, before I had even made my All-Ireland League debut for Con, and at the time he seemed to have everything that I wanted: a full-time contract, a place on the Munster team, an international career and ownership of a Ford Mondeo car while I was sharing my mum's Mini Metro. I was friendly with him in college and he was a bit of a celebrity around campus. I was dying to make the breakthrough that he had made but it was much too soon for me and I wasn't nearly good enough. In the long run, waiting was no harm.

Brian made his first senior start for Ireland on the first Saturday of March 1997, a day after I made my debut for the Ireland U-21s against Scotland. Richard Governey was promoted to the 'A' squad and that opened the way for me. The match was played at Watsonians ground and I'll never forget the bitter cold. Barry Coughlan in the *Examiner* described it as an 'accomplished debut' but it was a handy game for an out-half because we murdered them up front. We had some pack that day: Frankie Sheahan was captain and our back row was Leo Cullen, David Wallace and

Simon Easterby. We won 31–0 and walked off to a standing ovation. Eddie O'Sullivan was in charge and it was my first serious contact with him. He tells a story of noticing me at an U-14 training camp in Clongowes years earlier, but this time he was my coach and the level of technical detail in our preparation was something I'd never experienced before.

I felt like I had made good progress but the challenges kept coming and for the following season the bar was raised. The IRFU came up with a new contract system for the provinces where ten players would be full-time and twenty others would be on a part-time deal worth £7,500. I was given one of those contracts and became a recognized member of the Munster squad.

For a young fella that dressing room was an amazing place. One quality about Munster in all the years I've been involved is that new people are always welcomed and accepted. It's hard to think of a prize wanker who's been in that dressing room. Once or twice with Ireland you'd be saying, 'Fuck it, I need to stay away from this fella – I don't have any time for him.' That's never been the case in Munster. That squad was full of internationals and players that I had admired as a kid but they didn't make me feel like a stranger or an impostor. The other side of that, though, was the pressure to deliver on what you said you'd do or what your team mates expected you to do. There has always been huge honesty in the Munster dressing room and that honesty could be uncomfortable if you had failed or fucked up. There's an old saying about fellas who don't produce it on the day: train like Tarzan, play like Jane. How you train doesn't count for much unless you're backing it up on match day, and if you don't you'll be shown the door at Munster. Nobody can argue with that.

Mick Galwey and Peter Clohessy ran the show. Mick – Gaillimh – was captain but more than that he had presence that you can't get from a title. He had a fierce capacity to affect people. His speeches before big matches would have fellas in tears and he'd be crying himself. There are a fair few spoofers in the world but Gaillimh isn't one of them. There was no ego or bullshit with him. You knew that it was sincere, that he felt genuine pride in us and the jersey. It got to the stage where I'd go into team meetings thinking, 'You've got to keep a check on your emotions here.' He had a gift for unifying a group of players. It's hard to define but you responded to him without ever questioning it.

As a young player he was generous to me. If you had a bad day or you had doubts he would pick up on that and have a quiet word. When I landed a kick he would always say, 'Good boy, Rog.' It might seem like a small thing but I valued those simple words in a way that I would never have noticed coming from somebody else. I really missed that when he retired. At the same time, if I was getting above myself Gaillimh and Claw would tell me that too. I might have said something in an interview that was out of line and one of them would pull me aside. Whenever they needed to speak to me I deserved it.

Every team was afraid of Peter Clohessy, the Claw. You could see that other teams never messed with our front row or any of the forwards when he was playing and that's changed since he left. In many ways he was the perfect rugby player. He was an animal, he was hardy, he was able to mix it and he was cheating as much as he possibly could. He was a great scrummager but his ball skills were unbelievable for a prop forward. A freak. His fitness was good but he wouldn't do much for you in the gym and he wouldn't post great scores in a fitness test, but he'd do it for you on the pitch. Give him a cause and give him a ball and he had an aura about him that generated huge respect.

Gaillimh would be more polished in terms of addressing people whereas Claw would just say it as he saw it: bang, bang, bang. Everyone knows about Gaillimh's emotion but Claw wasn't far behind him. I think the older he got the more it meant to him. For the first part of his career he was going with the flow a little bit but he turned into a serious rugby professional. They both came from the amateur culture of boozing after matches and you could see it in their body shape and conditioning, but they both changed and they inspired everyone that's played for Munster over the last fifteen years.

Leadership off the field was more of an issue at the beginning of the 1997 season. John Bevan from Wales agreed to take the job and then did a U-turn. If that wasn't bad enough the IRFU announced that Andy Leslie from New Zealand would be Munster's new Director of Rugby, until it turned out that he hadn't agreed at all. When those two appointments fell through Munster turned to my old school coach Declan Kidney and Niall O'Donovan, with Jerry Holland as the manager.

I didn't have any strong feelings about it one way or another. I certainly didn't think that Deccie's appointment would fast-track me onto the team. Killian Keane had taken over from Paul Burke at out-half for the previous season and he was an excellent kicker. He would have seen me as a threat but it didn't stop him from being helpful and generous with his time and thoughts. But he had a knee problem at the end of the summer and I got my chance against Edinburgh in a short pre-season tour of Scotland at the beginning of August. I kicked five penalties, a couple of conversions and felt good. Killian was named as one of four out-halves in a preliminary Irish squad at the start of that season but he could also play centre and I knew the Munster number 10 jersey was a realistic short-term goal for me.

Harlequins at the Stoop was our first pool game in the Heineken Cup on the first Sunday of September, but our form had dropped badly after a good start to the season and the team selection was really shaken up for that match. David Wallace and Anthony Foley were among the players dropped from the team and not even brought in the travelling party. Until the end of his final season in 2008 I think it was the only Heineken Cup match in Anthony's Munster career in which he played no part. To this day Alan Quinlan will use it as ammunition if he's stuck for a jibe in a slagging match against Axel Foley.

Our target that season was to win our home matches. Simple as that. We didn't travel to the Stoop the way we would now, confident we could win. You wouldn't say it but deep down none of us believed we had a chance. They were a full-time professional outfit and a star-studded team: Keith Wood, Thierry Lacroix, Will Carling, Jason Leonard, Laurent Cabannes. We had a handful of guys on full-time contracts. Going over there we were stepping into a different world. We had manky O'Neill's tracksuits, they had names on the backs of their jerseys. You'd love to have swapped jerseys with them after the match but we were barred from doing that – even now Munster jerseys must be handed back in the dressing room.

For me it was nerve-wracking. The biggest game of my life. Everybody copes differently with anxiety on big match days; some fellas puke, I get a dose of the runs. I was on the bowl half a dozen times on the morning of the Harlequins game. But when it started I was all right. I held my own. It was an amazing match. We were 20–3 behind after only eighteen minutes and staring down the barrel of a hiding but we got back into it and were level at 30–30 early in the second half. Eventually we went down 48–40 but in a match of eleven tries we scored five of them and there was a feel-good vibe about the whole thing. People were half expecting us to get thrashed and we weren't.

Brian Ashton, the new Irish coach, was there and he was kind about my performance. He said that my kicking was excellent, especially my drop-outs. He pointed to a few defensive failings but he thought I was promising.

A week later, though, against Cardiff at the Arms Park, I got a bracing dose of reality. They beat us by 20 points and I felt blown away. Their winger Nigel Walker scored a try that I'll never forget. He picked the ball up 30 metres out and about two seconds later he was under our posts. I couldn't get over the speed of him. I remember thinking, 'Fuck it, I shouldn't be playing here at all.'

The next game was against Bourgoin at home the following weekend and I wasn't even in the 22. Killian Keane was moved from centre to out-half, Conor Burke came into the team at centre and took over the kicking, Sean McCahill was the utility backs replacement on the bench and I was out in the cold. The Munster manager, Jerry Holland, explained the press that Killian could give us more control. When you're a young fella and you see something like that in the paper you take it to heart. I'd have been annoyed, I'd have been thinking, 'I can do as good a job as him.' But of course they were right. I wasn't able to control a game at that level yet.

In Munster's four remaining pool matches I got five minutes of game time, as a late replacement for Killian over in Bourgoin. We ended up beating Harlequins and Bourgoin at home but we hadn't even reached our base target of winning all our home games. By the middle of October, Munster's year was over. Our last game was on a Sunday against Harlequins and on the following day we went on the piss. There was a big party in Schooners, a pub-restaurant in Limerick, and we went out to Killaloe where Claw had his boat and messed around on the water. It was the first time that I felt I was leading the life of a professional rugby player, ducking lectures to hang out with the boys.

I went back to Con and tried to get my season back together. I was picked on the bench for an Ireland Development XV against an Exiles XV at Thomond Park on a Wednesday night late in November but that turned into another hairy experience. I felt it was a big deal to get into that squad and I'd built it up so much that when I came on early in the second half my mind was scrambled. A few minutes later I was lining up a conversion attempt to bring the teams level and I made a complete mess of it. The kick was on the right-hand side and I found touch by the left corner flag. I was so nervous I took my eye off the ball and the thing squirted away a couple of feet off the ground. Frankie Sheahan and Dave O'Brien were at the match and they thought it was hilarious. The slagging started straight after the game and here I was, climbing the walls about it. No mercy.

After Christmas I nailed my place on the Ireland U-21 team and we clinched the Triple Crown with a 9–7 win over England at Richmond in early April 1998. We had a classy team that contained nine future senior internationals but it was still a serious challenge and I would have seen it as a test of my nerve. In those days goal-kicking always dominated my thoughts. On the day of a game those were my blues: that fear of not kicking well, that fear of failure. I always hated when people didn't distinguish between my goal-kicking performance and my overall performance but at the same time I knew that kicking goals was what was expected of me and that was a pressure I had to deal with.

That was one of the good days. I landed three penalties in the first half and we hung on after the break. There were bottles of champagne in the dressing room afterwards, something that I'd never seen before. We all changed into our number ones – our IRFU suits – and there was a party for us in a London hotel. The reality is that very few people really care about the U-21s but when you're playing at the time you think, 'This is some life.'

I went to America again that summer with Jess and a group of friends but before I went I got a call from Eddie O'Sullivan out of the blue. He had taken up a job coaching the US Eagles and he knew that I was qualified to play for the States. We arranged to meet at a restaurant outside San Francisco owned by Frank McCourt's brother Malachy: just me, Eddie and the team manager, Jack Clarke.

In typical student fashion I hoovered up all the grub that was on offer – starter, main course, dessert – and I listened to their pitch. The upside was that this was a chance to play international rugby straight away and they were building up for the 1999 World Cup. The money was good over there and they only played a few games a year. The plan was that I could continue playing for Con and Munster. But clearly it was a serious decision and Eddie didn't try to hide that. If I joined them I was turning my back on Ireland. He knew he was chancing his arm and he didn't push it too hard in fairness.

I didn't give them an answer on the spot. Eddie rang me a couple of times after our meeting and I didn't say no in the first phone call either. I was desperate to play international rugby so I didn't dismiss it as a non-starter. I went away and thought about it and discussed it with my dad. To be honest, though, my heart was never in it. It must have been two months later, after I'd returned home, when I finally gave them my answer. No deal.

I came home to an enhanced IRFU contract of £15,000 a year and a sponsored Rover car from Con. Gone were the days of driving to Limerick for Munster sessions in my mum's Mini Metro with the choke out all the way or in Frankie's Micra, where it felt like we were going to be airborne whenever he pressed down on the accelerator. I also came home to the most difficult season of my career.

I started Munster's opening pool match at home to Padova in the Heineken Cup but we struggled to win 20–13 in front of less than 1,000 people at Musgrave Park. I was poor. 'O'Gara lacked presence,' wrote Gerry Thornley in the *Irish Times*, 'missed tackles, and though he place-kicked well and occasionally connected sweetly out of the hand his kicking game was mixed. The up-and-under, until the try, was badly executed.' Killian Keane was obviously still on the scene but Barry Everitt was bursting through as well and there were high hopes for him as my rival for the number 10 shirt. The Neath match was only a week later but I ripped my hamstring in training that week. I was desperate to make it and keep Barry out of the team but I was only fooling myself and I couldn't fool Deccie.

Declan Kidney is known for his savage fitness tests and on the day before the game he put me through my paces in Musgrave Park. I tried to bluff it and knowing him he sensed there was something wrong. He kept asking me, 'Are you sure it's OK?' giving me a chance to speak up. He loves a mind game too and I wasn't giving in. He ended up flogging me and I made shit of my hamstring. It was a valuable lesson to learn. I thought I could hide it and all I did was hurt myself.

Munster qualified from the pool for the first time and in the middle of December played Colomiers away in the quarter-final. That game wasn't on telly and I listened to commentary on the radio, a million miles away from where I wanted to be. After the Padova game I played no further part in the Heineken Cup that season. My hamstring took a long time to heal and in my absence Barry made a big impression. Before the Colomiers match he played really well against Leinster at Donnybrook in what was a final game decider for the inter-provincial title. Brendan Fanning of the *Sunday Independent* spotted me in the crowd that night. 'O'Gara was an uncomfortable onlooker,' he wrote. 'The torn hamstring was the least of his pain.' I was down in the dumps. I had lost my place on the Munster team, Con had lost three of their first four games in the All-Ireland League and for the first time in my career it seemed like I was going nowhere.

It got worse before it got better. Every player on an IRFU contract was subjected to regular fitness tests and I scored really badly in tests done in April of 1999. There were twenty-four backs on IRFU contracts and our tests results were compared against each other. My results were shockingly bad. For the bench pull I was last. Jonny Bell at the top of the list was able to shift 110 kg – I was able to do 80, which put me 10 kg behind the guys who were second-last. For some reason that I can't remember I didn't do the bench press test but in the counter-movement jump I was joint last with Simon Mason.

Away from the power tests my results should have been much more positive but they weren't. I was last in the 15-metre sprint, last in the 30-metre sprint and my bleep test score was only in the middle of the pack. A good few Munster players came out badly from those tests and there were serious questions asked at Union level about the set-up down here. But we all had personal responsibilities too and I was failing in mine. Simple as that. I didn't score any better in the next test in mid-summer and I received a letter from the IRFU reminding me of my contractual obligations. Who was I codding? Nobody.

I remember, though, resenting the emphasis that was being put on power. Ever since I was a kid I was usually one of the weakest guys on the field but it hadn't stopped me. I saw rugby as a game of brain over brawn and I knew that I had the brain to prosper on a rugby field. Looking back now it's easier to see the big picture. These were still early days for the full-time professional game in Ireland and a lot of the other top test nations had stolen a march on us in terms of physical conditioning. I couldn't bench press 100 kg and I remember thinking that this was being held against me and that it was an absolutely ridiculous yardstick for picking a rugby player.

At the same time I knew I needed to be bigger. It wasn't in my make-up to be muscular so I had to force it. Even when I got my act together with my diet and gym work I was still a slow-gainer. At times it got on top of me. You'd be wondering if other fellas were taking illegal substances to bulk themselves up and, Jesus, there were days when it crossed my mind. 'Will I chance something?' I never did and I never gave it serious thought.

I was taking courses of Creatine to try to beef up but I wasn't doing it properly. There's a loading phase where you must take 5 grams, five times a day for five days, and then one helping a day for thirty days but I wasn't disciplined enough to follow that programme. I was still going on the piss after every Con match and I wouldn't be able to eat anything the following day, not to mind get some Creatine down my neck. The stuff was costing about thirty quid a pot and I was basically pissing it away. If you look at action photographs of me from the late nineties I'm wearing a T-shirt under my jersey and the jersey is still blowing in the breeze. Everything was weak. There was no muscle definition in my legs, I had no core strength.

My form, though, returned in the second half of the season. Michael Bradley was the Con coach and he met me for lunch around the turn of the year. He gave me a kick in the ass that really got me going. He asked me where my ambition had gone. And that was the key to it. Everything I had achieved in rugby up to that point had been driven by ambition and without noticing it I had slipped into cruise mode: here I was with a nice car, a pocketful of money, leading the handy life of a student. I had made a breakthrough with Munster the season before and I had fallen in love with myself. He said I needed to start taking responsibility for the team as well as my own performance and I took that to heart. Whatever Brads said was gospel to me.

Con set off on a roll that took us to the final of the All-Ireland League at Lansdowne Road. There was a great atmosphere around the club and I was really buzzing. Shannon were going for five in a row and we knocked them out of the play-offs in the last round of regulation matches. Con usually played in front of small crowds at home, even in the heyday of the All-Ireland League, but there were 7,000 people in Temple Hill that afternoon and I got 16 of our 26 points, including a try. The photographs of Con players celebrating that appeared in the following day's papers would bring you back to a time when the All-Ireland League was a really big deal. It was massive for us. Con had won the very first title in 1991 but the competition had been dominated by Limerick teams for the next eight years and we would have felt the pain of that more than any other club outside Limerick.

In the semi-final we played Buccaneers, who were coached by Eddie O'Sullivan, splitting his time between Galway and the States. We won by 12 points, 32–20, and Eddie described me as 'magnificent' afterwards. In an interview that week I was after blowing some smoke up Eddie's ass too. 'Eddie is a great coach, I have nothing but the utmost respect for his ability. He brought me up a few levels [with the Ireland U-21s], encouraged me to make decisions for myself on the pitch.' All very cosy.

My form with Con pushed me into contention for a place on Ireland's summer tour to Australia, but while I was getting my act together in the first few months of the season a couple of other players had joined the queue ahead of me. Barry Everitt's form with Munster earned him Ireland A caps, and when he was injured for the final game of the campaign Jeremy Staunton was picked to start against Italy with me on the bench. I got on for the last two minutes to win my first Ireland A cap but the reality was that Staunton was on a fast-track and I was being left behind. He didn't turn nineteen until the end of that season, which made him three years younger than me, and he still hadn't played for the Munster senior team but he was being talked up as the new sensation of Irish rugby. Was I envious? Of course I was.

He was the Garryowen out-half and they were our opponents in the final of the All-Ireland League. There was a lot of media attention on our duel that week and neither of us was pushing it away. Gerry Thornley interviewed both of us for a big feature in the *Irish Times* on the morning of the match and while he was positive about me he was gushing about Jeremy: 'Although he's error-prone, he's young, gifted, deeply self-analytical about his game, fiercely competitive, eager to learn and destined to be a pin-up boy of Irish rugby. It's almost scary to think how good he could become.' There was a panel alongside the interview where we were analysed in different categories. Under the heading of 'Potential', Thornley wrote a long paragraph describing how I might eventually play for Ireland. For Staunton he wrote just three words: 'Sky's the limit.'

They asked us both to comment on each other and, amazingly, we did. We were full of compliments, of course, but one of Jeremy's comments was interesting. 'He's very good at what he does,' he said. Here he was, being portrayed as a flair player, a free spirit, and I thought in that remark he was hinting at my limitations. 'He'll obviously be out to get me,' he said too, 'because I've sort of jumped ahead in the ranks.'

On both counts he was dead right. I was dying for a crack off him. In my own mind this was the day I was going to settle the argument. Jeremy was stronger than me but in every other way I believed I had the measure of him. I felt I had an edge over him mentally. Even then I felt I had the right mindset for performing at the highest level. A lot of that was built into my personality but I worked on it too because you will always have doubts. Either you control them or they will control you. My dad put a lot of emphasis on mental preparation and around that time I was reading a book he gave me called *In Pursuit of Excellence* by Tom Peters. I'd make my own notes before matches and keep referring to them to get my head where it needed to be.

We won that match in extra-time and I scored the winning penalty. It was a brutal match and a crowd of just 6,000 made for a strange atmosphere in Lansdowne Road. I felt I had done well and the consensus in the media was that I had out-played Staunton. George Hook did a piece analysing the game for the *Sunday Independent* and came down in my favour:

'The pre-match hype on the respective out-halves never lived up to its billing,' he wrote. 'Jeremy Staunton looked to be carrying an injury but his positioning was in marked contrast to his opponent. Staunton stood deep and made the kick the first option. O'Gara attacked the advantage line unlike any out-half since Ollie Campbell. The result was that the Cork backline always threatened.'

The big mistake I made was reading too much into that game. Staunton was picked for the tour to Australia and I heard later that the decision was made before the final. He was going, regardless. Given the way things had gone in the first few months of the season I should have been delighted to be so close to a place in the Irish squad but that wasn't how I looked at it. I was gutted and I saw it as another painful setback.

Garryowen got their revenge on us in the Munster Cup Final afterwards and one of their props, Niall Hartigan, caught me lovely. I bumped into him and he gave me a look so I told him where to go with himself.

'What's your problem?' he says, so I told him where to go again.

'Who is it you are now? Jeremy is it? No, you couldn't be. Sure Jeremy's in Australia, isn't he?'

Fair play to him. The Garryowen fellas were bursting themselves laughing and some of the Con lads too. I was just stunned. At the end of that season I probably didn't deserve the last word.

CHAPTER 4

After the summer the road ahead was clear and I was driving on again. I wasn't getting in my own way and other obstacles no longer existed. Jeremy Staunton made just one appearance for Ireland against a provincial side on the summer tour to Australia and when he came home Munster decided to try him at full-back. Barry Everitt moved to Leinster in the close-season, which meant that the red number 10 jersey returned to my back. I was working harder in the gym and I had put on some extra bulk. The confidence I'd gained with Con over the last months of the previous season was still in my tank, ready to fuel a new campaign.

Ireland were gearing up for the 1999 World Cup a couple of months away and I had Eric Elwood in my sights. At the start of the year I was a long shot for a place in the squad but as the tournament got closer my prospects improved dramatically. David Humphreys was nailed on as the first choice out-half and realistically my best chance of being in the 30 depended on Ireland bringing three out-halves, but I started the season playing out of my skin and hoping to put pressure on Elwood.

With an eye to the World Cup the inter-provincials started in August and Munster hit the ground running. We beat Leinster and Connacht and I was named Man of the Match in both games. A couple of weeks later we beat Ulster in Belfast for the first time in twenty years and by then I'd been named in a preliminary squad of 34 for the World Cup.

Among the rugby writers there was a big push for my inclusion but I knew the reality of my situation. The Irish manager was Donal Lenihan who I knew from Con. He was happy with my form and gave me plenty of encouragement but he's a very straight guy and he didn't give me any false hope. In one interview he laid out the heart of my problem – inexperience. He put it as a question: if David Humphreys broke his leg could they play me against France in a World Cup quarter-final? The answer didn't need to be spelled out. In another interview Warren Gatland, the Ireland coach, raised my fitness tests. I felt like I was still paying a price for the sins of the previous season. I was up to about twelve and a half stone, or maybe more, and when we were tested again in the autumn my performance was better than the disastrous results of the spring. I still wasn't where I needed to be on the strength tests but my speed had improved and aerobically I was good. Gatland, though, made it plain that I wasn't up to scratch yet.

'Munster have got themselves sorted out now but last year things weren't happening and I think it was a bit of a cruise mode [down there]. Now it's sorted but he [O'Gara] realizes he's missed a year.'

I came on as a sub in a warm-up match against Connacht in Galway. I thought I did well but the overall performance was poor and Ireland struggled to win. The World Cup squad was announced in the team hotel afterwards and Donal tipped me off in advance that I wasn't included. They had picked an extra prop forward and gone with two out-halves: Humphreys and Elwood. I had made my run too late. I travelled back to Cork with Donal's wife and even though I'd known the odds were against me I was still disappointed. It wasn't in my nature to take it any other way.

Three weeks after the Connacht game Ireland continued their

World Cup preparation with a match against Munster and we beat them 26–19. Ireland were having a shocking build-up and this put the tin hat on it. They didn't field a full team but that didn't matter to us. There were about 4,000 people in Musgrave Park and the atmosphere was electric. It was like the old days when touring sides would come to Limerick or Cork and get a belly-full. Apart from me there were a few other Munster lads who had been left out of the squad and we were really fired up. Dominic Crotty put us in front with a great try midway through the second half and I got a drop-goal and a penalty in the last few minutes to seal it. Elwood started for Ireland and I thought I out-played him again. I couldn't argue with their reasoning for not picking me and, at the same time, I couldn't have made my point with any greater force. I was playing the best rugby of my career.

Ireland bombed at the World Cup and as the Heineken Cup got going there was no great hope for the provinces. Ulster were the defending champions but the English clubs were back in the competition now and nobody was predicting an Irish winner. Things, though, were changing for the better in Munster. Keith Wood had come home from Harlequins for a year and we made some other great signings during the summer: John Langford, a former international second row from Australia, Mike Mullins, a Kiwi centre who could also play at full-back, and Jason Holland, another New Zealander, who was playing for Midleton in Division Two of the All-Ireland League. Dutchy came out of nowhere but he was a brilliant signing too.

We already had a savage pack of forwards and for the first time we had real depth in our squad. On the bench that season we had guys like Frankie Sheahan, Marcus Horan, Eddie Halvey, Brian O'Meara, Tom Tierney and Donncha O'Callaghan. To have any chance you needed subs like that.

Did we think we could win it? Not me. Not most of us. To

think that way simply wasn't in the culture of Irish rugby at the time. At the start of every season we spend a day in the University of Limerick planning our campaign and setting our goals. It was Wood's first time at one of those meetings and he said, straight out, our goal should be to win the Heineken Cup. Fellas couldn't believe what they were hearing and a couple of lads started giggling. The first thing we needed to do was to think like him.

Wood made a huge impression. He raised the whole thing up a level. I know our set-up wasn't as professional as the one he had just left in Harlequins but he liked the spirit in our dressing room, the real sense of friendship. On the training field, though, he thought we were a bit easy on ourselves and he confronted that. One day he had an altercation with John Kelly. Rags was on the wrong side of a ruck in a training exercise and Woody gave him a shoeing, just as you would to one of the opposition in a match situation. Rags didn't like it and had a go at Woody but Woody wasn't having any of John's complaints. He was on the wrong side, he had to get a taste of what he was going to get on Saturday. They were both hugely respected players in our dressing room and you could see it from both points of view. That debate would never even have occurred before Woody joined us. Woody's way, though, was the way forward.

He was captain of Ireland at the time and around the Irish scene he was the loudest voice – on the pitch, on the training field, in the dressing room. With Munster, though, he respected the fact that Gaillimh was captain and he didn't step over that line. There was a forum for everybody to make a contribution and we got a lot from him through those channels. Langford was another guy who brought new ideas about lineout variation and stuff like that. Australian rugby was ahead of us in terms of professionalism and he brought that to the party.

There was a good buzz around the place and we were trying new things. One weekend we went on a bonding session to

Kilkee. On the Friday night we had a great drinking session and on the following morning they ran the shit out of us. We were sent on a killing run, up a track that overlooked the lake. Murder. Frankie Sheahan and Tom Tierney ducked out. I don't know how they managed it but they were sitting by the water while we spilled our guts on the run. They were eventually caught and fined £20. Best twenty quid they ever spent.

We beat Pontypridd at home in the first pool match, 32–10, and then we were away to Saracens. Munster had pulled off a couple of good results in the Heineken Cup in previous seasons but that was the day it really kicked off for us. Everything about that weekend was a step up. We travelled on Friday for a Sunday match and the preparation was good. Deccie had us up to speed with all the razzamatazz that accompanied Saracens' home games: the cheerleaders, the loud music after every try, the little remote control cars bringing out the kicking tee. All those things could be distractions if you didn't block them out.

Saracens were the glamour club in England at the time. There was massive money behind them and they had put together a team of stars on the pitch. They had a pack of internationals led by François Pienaar, South Africa's World Cup-winning captain. Thierry Lacroix, a legend, was their out-half and they didn't expect to lose to us.

Saracens were ground-sharing at Vicarage Road, Watford FC's home. Watford had a game against Sunderland that Saturday and a few of us went along, to get a look at the ground as much as anything else. Niall Quinn was playing and Alan Quinlan had met him once at the races. Quinny wouldn't be shy by nature and during the warm-up he went down to the bottom of the stand to try to get Niall's attention. You could tell that Niall didn't know who the hell he was but he was very nice about it. We gave Quinny a terrible slagging. Niall Quinn knows exactly who Alan Quinlan is now but you'd forget about the time when being a

Munster player wasn't the same thing as being famous. Quinny, though, always believed he belonged in that section of society. A celebrity. He collects the mobile numbers of famous people, as if this confirms his status. He got Aidan O'Brien's a couple of years ago and he taunts me about that. No fear he'd give it to me.

It was an amazing match. We were 15 points down midway through the first half and we were still 11 points down midway through the second half but we never cracked. Gaillimh was in tears in the dressing room at half-time, trying to get us to believe that we could do it. Could we? We never have to think about the answer to that question now. Back then? We had to prove it to ourselves first. Axel got over for a try to bring us back into it with less than ten minutes left and then Jeremy Staunton got another one to put us a point behind with my conversion to come.

Pressure is always relative. I had kicked plenty of penalties and conversions that were important at the time but doing it away from home in the Heineken Cup in a cliffhanger against one of the biggest clubs in England was a level of pressure I had never experienced before. I missed the conversion for Axel's try and the word I got from the line was that I lifted my head. That's the kind of novicey mistake bad golfers make when they're worried about a shot and it shows where I was in my development as a kicker.

The conversion to win the match was from out on the right. Got my head together. Kept my head down. The posts were quite low and, Jesus, it looked for a second as if the ball had gone over one of the uprights. The referee gave it but that didn't stop Sky News playing it on every bulletin the following morning. Got away with it.

They still had time to come back at us but we held on to win by a point, 35–34. The scenes afterwards were unbelievable. We only had a couple of hundred supporters, many of them living in London, but they invaded the pitch and we were going around as if we'd won the World Cup. In the papers the following day there were photographs of Munster players with the tricolour, roaring like bulls. With the standards we've set for ourselves over the years we wouldn't allow that kind of celebration for an ordinary pool match now but all of this was new to us. Irish rugby was in the pits at the time and we were the only good news story in town.

That was our ninth win in a row and the momentum was sweeping us along. Two weeks later we beat Colomiers 31–15 to win in France for the first time in the Heineken Cup. They had hammered us in the quarter-final a year earlier, almost to the day, but we were a different proposition now. Claw had to pull out with a back injury on the night before the game but Marcus Horan stepped up and we carried on. In other years losing a player like Claw would have been a handy excuse for us to believe that we were never going to win anyway. It was my first time playing in France and having to deal with the abuse that kickers get over there. I think I coped. All of it was experience in the bank.

In the space of a few months we had pulled off big away wins in France, England and Belfast and, more than anything we did in Thomond Park, that reflected where we were going as a team. To achieve anything in this competition we had to prove that we were more than a team of home-birds.

And still the pool came down to the second-last match against Saracens in Thomond Park. Every year we seem to have a monster match at home in January to decide our fate in the Heineken Cup but that was the first of them. We had an away game against Pontypridd to come so it wasn't a tightrope act, but if we won we were guaranteed a home quarter-final and Saracens would be out. It was the biggest crowd I ever saw in Thomond Park. After that match the fire and safety people put the capacity at 13,500 but that evening there must have been at least 18,000 in the ground.

For all the noise they made there was nothing but stunned silence when the Saracens full-back Mark Mapletoft touched down to put Saracens 30–24 ahead with three minutes left. Mapletoft was dodgy under the high ball and I had bombed him with garryowens from the start. He couldn't deal with them and the crowd went wild. Now it looked like he was going to have the last laugh.

Gaillimh gathered us behind the posts and told us we were going to march down the field and score a try. Simple as that. No panic. And that's what we did. We worked ourselves into position, Langford won the lineout, the pack drove it up to the line and Woody got over. He handed me the ball. It was down to me. A kick to win the match.

In those situations the two most important things are to trust your technique and to control your mind. My technique wasn't nearly as good as it later became but I had faith in it and I believed that it worked for me. When I kick now I'm able to blank everything out of my mind but I didn't have that capacity back then. Negative thoughts are always trying to barge in and for some reason David Humphreys crossed my mind. A year earlier he had a last-minute kick to beat France at Lansdowne Road and he missed.

I lined it up again. I had to get a positive thought into my head. Then I thought, 'Relax, this is going over.' I was nervous but I was confident. Edgy but good. The Saracens players charged too soon, trying to mess with my head and the referee pinged them. It meant they couldn't charge a second time. A Limerick fella gave me a present of a great black-and-white photograph later. François Pienaar, Richard Hill, Paul Wallace and all these guys are standing there, hands on hips, staring at the posts from the goal line, not allowed to move. Helpless.

I caught it well. From the left-hand side I was trying to draw it in from the right-hand post. There were people in the stand behind me who thought I'd missed and you can see from the action photographs that I had an anxious look on my face under my bandaged head. The ball moved just enough to glance the upright and drop over.

The place went bonkers. We were on the road.

Deccie said afterwards that he had done the maths and he knew that we didn't need the conversion. A one-point defeat would have been enough to guarantee us top spot in the pool whatever Saracens did in the last match. But Deccie decided that it was better for me not to know that. Cheers, Deccie.

After a disastrous World Cup the Irish squad was shaken up for the first-ever Six Nations and a rake of Munster guys were brought in to the mix. The way we were going they couldn't ignore us. The first game was away to England. I was picked. My big chance. The chance I'd been waiting for all my life.

What happened? I got myself crocked. I couldn't fucking believe it. I was doing a tackling drill with Elwood and I was holding the tackle bag. I had my knee in the wrong place and after the impact I knew I was in trouble. Damaged knee ligaments. There was some talk of taking a jab to get me on to the field but even in my state of desperation I knew that was ludicrous. In those situations the first thing that goes is perspective. I was in despair. I thought, 'This is it, my chance is gone.' Crazy stuff. In the end it probably turned out to be a blessing. England slaughtered us in Twickenham and if I was there that day I'd have been cut to pieces too. Nobody came out of it well.

Scotland were next, at home, but I had to get myself right and prove my fitness. Con played Ballymena, up there, on the Saturday before that game and some of the selectors came to watch me. My knee was strapped and I hate playing with strapping but that's no excuse. I played badly and I thought I'd blown my chance. When I got to training on Monday, though, the vibes were good. The team was announced to the players on Tuesday morning but as I walked into the meeting room David Humphreys came over and shook my hand. The guys that are dropped are always the first to know. I was in.

Over the next few years that handshake became a regular feature of our relationship. The number 10 jersey was passed between us over and over again and, somehow, our friendship survived the rivalry. I can think of, maybe, two occasions when things became heated between us on the training pitch but that was it. I have huge respect for him as a rugby player and as a person and during the years when we fought for the same jersey those feelings were enhanced.

It was my first experience of an Irish team announcement and the mood of that day never changes from year to year. The bus journey to training is always quiet. Plenty of guys are dealing with stuff: being left out of the team, being left out of the 22. That morning the wind-up merchants at breakfast have a field day: 'Did Eddie get you there, he was looking for you?' You knew it only meant one thing if Eddie O'Sullivan was looking for you on a selection morning – or Warren Gatland or Declan Kidney. The wind-up merchants knew I was an easy target too because for years I could never be sure of that jersey.

Everything about the week was new to me. On Thursday we shifted base to the Berkeley Court Hotel. Nearer to the ground, nearer to the centre of the action, closer to kick-off. My parents called in for tickets and a cup of tea and I was getting more and more wound up. People kept telling me that it'd pass so quickly and that it'd be over before I knew it. I hated being told that. I remember thinking, 'I'll decide that – I'll have my own say on that.' Wrong. Again.

There was a tradition in those days of going into Rala's room for pizza on the night before matches. Paddy O'Reilly is the name on Rala's birth cert but nobody ever calls him Paddy. He's the bag-man with the Irish team though his presence is far, far, bigger than that. There's always a good atmosphere around him and on the night before matches his room is buzzing with people coming and going. You go down there to pick up your socks and shorts and a training top for the following day and he has everything laid out to get your boots ready: polish, wet cloths, studs. There will be jerseys to sign for a charity or whatever.

There was a pizza place around the corner from the hotel and the grub was ordered on an IRFU credit card – pizza and cans of Coke, fuel for elite athletes. That practice was stopped later on – they were afraid of food poisoning I think – but Rala's room was still the place to be. The night before an international is a lonely time and being down there always breaks the loneliness for a while.

Eating breakfast was torture the next morning. I forced down a small bit of cereal and a banana. When the time came to go to the ground we were clapped onto the bus by Irish supporters who were milling around outside. I couldn't even look up. I'd spent half the morning on the toilet. The usual.

There were five new caps: myself, John Hayes, Shane Horgan, Peter Stringer and Simon Easterby. Eight changes in all from the England game. The Irish management were taking a big gamble and we were their chips on the table.

Hayes doesn't go in for any bullshit but I remember we shook hands in the dressing room that day and it's something we've done before every match since. We lined up for the national anthems and I stood next to Gaillimh with Stringer on the other side. The photographers loved it. The picture made Gaillimh look like a mother wolf with a pair of little cubs under each arm. I know Stringer stood next to Gaillimh deliberately because he wanted to tap into Gaillimh's emotion during the anthem. I hadn't planned it. I was thinking of the match and my goal-kicking. Always the goal-kicking.

In those days under Gatty our game plan was simple: set a few targets, smash the rucks, kick to the corners. The message to me all week was to play the game I'd been playing for Munster. But when the game started I couldn't do it. I couldn't control my nerves. I couldn't control my emotions. I was panicky. Jerky. Nervous. Unstable. I missed a few kicks to touch, I knocked on. Stringer wasn't coping either. The two of us were completely off the pace. Ireland went 10–0 down and if we didn't snap out of it our debuts were going to turn into a nightmare.

Then, all of a sudden, it clicked. I don't know how and I don't know why. I started feeling all right. I cut out the mistakes and found a bit of rhythm. We got a brilliant try and I converted it from the touchline. I landed another couple of penalties before half-time and we went in leading 13–10. All I felt was relief. That I had done something.

We got another try shortly after the break before Humphreys came on for me with half an hour left. In your dream debut I guess you play the full eighty minutes or come off to an ovation with a couple of minutes to go but it wasn't like that. Getting there was a dream come true but living the dream is another thing.

Gatty was asked to explain his decision to replace me at the press conference later and he was honest about it: 'We just felt that Ronan had made a few mistakes. He gave a bit of a Roy of the Rovers performance. He made mistakes but he also did some things brilliantly. David Humphreys played the corners intelligently when he came on. He was excellent driving us forward and keeping the momentum going. O'Gara will get better after this experience.'

That was the start of a debate that would go on for years. Me or him? Ireland had won handsomely on my debut, 42–22, and I had pulled myself together in time to play all right and had scored 10 points, but there was no guarantee I was going to keep my place. Humphs was class and that was the gun to my head.

That night, though, I wasn't worrying about it. The banquet on the evening of international matches is a black-tie affair but once the speeches are over there's nothing stuffy about it. The free bar stays open for hours and fellas do the dog on it. One of the traditions is that new caps must drink a short with every member of the squad – and with every member of the other squad too, if they get a tip-off. Claw is the kind of fella who would look after the tip-off. I was lucky that there were four other debutants that night but I still couldn't handle the pace. Jess drank some of my shorts and I had to slip off for a puke at one stage. After all the stress of the week it was like a pressure valve had been released.

We carried on to Annabel's nightclub next door and were ushered into the VIP area, ordered our bottles of champagne and thought we were cool. When you're young it's easy to get dopey notions about yourself. Delusions of grandeur I think they call it.

If the France game was next would I have been picked? Who knows? Italy were coming to Lansdowne Road and the management probably saw that as an ideal opportunity for me to find my feet a bit more. There was a lot of debate in the papers about who would get the number 10 jersey but in my own mind I was sure enough. I wasn't given any assurances, though, and I wasn't given much one-on-one feedback either. My dad would have watched the video a few times and taken notes and I would have watched it as well.

If you were to watch that video now you'd be amazed at how much has changed in a few years. Everything seems so much slower. The contact seems soft. When you go into tackles these days it bloody hurts. You're built to take it but it still hurts nearly every time.

I've learned the value of watching matches with the sound turned down. I used listen to the match commentator and pay attention to the analysis in the studio and that would have influenced my view of how I played. It was a crazy thing to do but so much about my approach was different back then. Out on the field you'd be conscious of people looking at you and conscious of what they must be thinking. Nowadays, there are matches when I feel like I'm out there on my own. I don't know how to explain it but on those days the game feels so easy. That feeling never lasts. You have it for a while and when it goes you don't know when it's coming back. It's like a golfer who shoots 64 one day and 74 the next. He's still the same player, with the same swing, but the outcomes are dramatically different from one day to the next. How do you control the outcomes? It's all in the mind. In this game that's the biggest struggle.

I believed I was ready for international rugby but the Scotland match challenged my convictions. I've always found it hard to accept people's opinions about things until I experience it for myself. Nobody could tell me anything, I had to find out for myself. I thought things would happen for me without doing my homework. Without me having to think a phase or two ahead, without me having to work out what I needed to do as an out-half. Humphs' tactical kicking was better too. I needed to work on that.

Myself and Stringer were both retained for the Italy match and we needed to get our act together. If I was kicking I needed an extra couple of seconds so we came up with calls to differentiate one from the other: '10' if I was kicking, 'Chilli' if I was running. At that level you need every second you can get.

The Italy match was better. Much better. We hammered them and I kicked 30 points, a championship record. Landed twelve kicks from twelve attempts. You could do that some days in training and be bollixed after it. I remember walking off the field thinking I'd arrived in international rugby. After the Scotland game I didn't have the comfort of that thought.

People looking at me during the week in camp probably thought I didn't have a care in the world, that nothing fazed me. A lot of that was a mask. With me confidence and insecurity sat side by side. People close to me would notice it. I don't suffer from mood swings but Jess knows that I get much quieter as the game gets nearer. Even now, on the morning of really big games, the nerves kill me. I'd be asking myself, 'Why am I putting myself through this?'

The Italy game was a huge relief. The way it is, you count your first few caps in ones. When you get to ten you can start thinking in blocks of caps but not at the beginning. The Italy game got me another start: France in Paris.

To this day the Stade de France is my favourite stadium. Going from Lansdowne Road to the surface over there was the difference between a farmer's field and a golf green. But it wasn't just that it was everything about the place. The walk to the pitch must be what it was like entering the Colosseum. You leave the away team dressing room and take a left. Then you hit the tunnel and the tunnel just keeps going. First you see the pitch, then the lower deck of the stand, then the next deck, then the top deck. Masses of people. You can't see the sky until you're out there. The bad experiences Ireland have had in Paris during my time never changed how I felt about the place. As a rugby player this is where you wanted to be.

That day, it was where every Irish rugby player wanted to be. Brian O'Driscoll scored a hat-trick and we beat France in Paris for the first time in twenty-eight years. I hadn't know Brian very long at the time. We've become great friends over the years and spent a lot of time together outside of rugby. That day, though, I was in awe of him. He produced a stunning performance in one of the great stadiums of the world against a team that usually murdered us in Paris. I had come nowhere close to that level. Anywhere in the world.

We were 8 points down when I was taken off after an hour. I thought I'd played all right but I couldn't argue with the decision. To win the game they needed to try something and it worked. Humphs kicked a good penalty with two minutes left to win the match for us, 27–25, and bury the demons of his miss in Lansdowne Road a year before.

I was happy for him. It's easy to say it now but I never bore any ill-feeling towards Humphs. Our rivalry was only starting and soon there was a pattern to the relationship for me. When internationals were coming up he'd always be on my mind. Ulster played a lot of games on Friday nights and I'd be glued to them. If the game wasn't on telly I'd check it on teletext. It was always in my head that he could do something outrageous like kick seven penalties and three drop-goals and that would be laying down a marker to me when Munster played later that weekend. A lot of our pack had rivals in Leinster but my thoughts revolved around Humphs.

The hype around Irish rugby was suddenly massive. Everyone wanted a piece of us. Munster were doing their bit to spread the game to non-rugby areas in the province and I remember one training session in Midleton, a big GAA town in East Cork, where we were swamped with kids. I must have signed a couple of hundred autographs. Brian O'Brien, the Munster manager, gave an interview that day where he compared me to David Beckham. That was a great help to me in the Munster dressing room.

The other big issue at the time was contracts. All of the Irish players were out of contract on 1 June. When the IRFU decided on that plan they probably weren't banking on our best performance in the championship for well over a decade, our first win in Paris for a generation and Munster storming the Heineken Cup.

Anyway, that's what they were stuck with. The papers were full of speculation about English and French clubs looking to pick up Irish players and the IRFU were under fierce pressure to keep everybody at home.

I didn't have an agent or a manager at the time but I didn't shy away from the wheeling and dealing. My existing contract was £25,000 and I had my eye on a decent jump up from that. When reporters asked me about my future I said that I had 'firm approaches' from two clubs. I explained that 'for obvious reasons' I couldn't reveal the names of the clubs. The reality is that I was hamming it up. I was happy with Munster and I had no real desire to go anywhere else but I couldn't let the IRFU think that I was desperate to stay put. They offered me £60,000 and I happily signed on the dotted line.

I kept my place for the final game of the season against Wales but we never got going and they deserved to beat us on a manky day in Lansdowne Road. It was a damp squib at the end of a good season. I wasn't great, I wasn't bad. I coped. The Six Nations was over and I wasn't a one-cap wonder. I was there. I had an international career.

Gerry Thornley in the *Irish Times* compiled end-of-term reports for every player. This is what he wrote about me: 'A sometimes mixed bag with his kicking and his breaks but overall an exceptional rookie campaign, marked by brilliant place-kicking, brave running and sumptuous distribution. Mentally tough and well worth the investment.'

Sometimes it suits us to believe what we read in the papers.

CHAPTER 5

> *'He's had three shots at goal and missed them all. This could redeem everything. A nation holds its breath . . . Is it there? Is it there!? Yes! Oh no!'*
>
> Jim Sherwin, RTE, Northampton v. Munster, 27 May 2000

Two weeks after Ireland played Wales, Stade Français came to Thomond Park for the quarter-final of the Heineken Cup. I was stepping from one new world into another world that nobody in Irish rugby had ever experienced before. Munster were no longer just a rugby team. People who had no interest in rugby were suddenly interested in us.

After the crowd that had packed the place for the Saracens game the quarter-final was all-ticket with the capacity set at 13,500 for safety reasons. People started queuing before dawn when the tickets went on sale in Cork and Limerick. I remember going to Munster games as a kid when only a couple of hundred people would bother to show up and I played in a good few Heineken Cup matches in Musgrave Park and Thomond where the ground wasn't packed either. That was the world we were leaving behind.

Munster have played a lot of huge games since that quarter-final in 2000 but in that season every game seemed to be bigger than the last one and the journey was taking us to places we'd never been before. That was the first day 'The Fields of Athenry' was sung by Munster supporters in Thomond and I remember the hair standing up on the back of my neck. Stade had a team of stars but like a lot of French teams in Thomond over the years they didn't really show up. We led by 9 points at half-time having played against the wind and in the second half all I had to do was keep Gaillimh and Claw happy: when they got up off the floor they wanted to see the ball down in the corner. Keeping them happy suited me fine.

When the semi-final draw was made a couple of days later we got Toulouse, away. Everybody knew it was the worst possible draw and even our biggest supporters thought it was the end of the road. I wasn't around for the 1996 match over there when Toulouse put 60 points on us but Gaillimh, Axel, Killian Keane and Dominic Crotty played that day and still had the scars to prove it. But we knew too that so much had changed since then. We had won all three meetings with French teams already that season and a gang of us were on the Ireland team that won in Paris. Why should we be afraid?

The weather in Bordeaux in early May was fabulous. We travelled with gallons of water to keep ourselves hydrated but some of us were still pretty green when it came to preparing for big games. Myself and Stringer decided to do a bit of sunbathing on the day before the match – a pair of pale Paddies lying out, having the energy sapped from us by the sun. As soon as we were spotted we were hauled in.

On Munster trips in those days there was always a big card school. Poker. Around the table you had the usual suspects: Claw, Woody, Frankie, Dutchy, Eddie Halvey, David Corkery before he got injured, David Wallace, Rob Henderson when he joined us and a few others. For a Saturday match I'd always play on the Thursday night and give it a skip on the night before the game. Other fellas, though, were animal for it. A couple of years later two of our starting 15 played cards until about six in the morning before a Heineken Cup quarter-final against Stade Français in Paris. One of them was nearly man of the match. If they were caught there would have been murder. The card games, though, were stopped a couple of years ago. The pots were getting too big and it was the same fellas winning all the time. Fellas were getting pissed off.

The day of the match was another scorcher. Everything seemed to be set up for Toulouse to kill us with their pace and their classy backs: a dry ball, a beautiful hard surface and more than 20,000 of their supporters making the short trip down the road to Bordeaux. Our attitude, though, was perfect: we weren't going to back down from anything. The Toulouse supporters who had come early booed us when we arrived on the pitch for our pre-match warm-up forty-five minutes before kick-off. So, once the team photograph was taken, we decided to do our drills in the corner of the stadium where the greatest number of Toulouse supporters were congregated – behind the try-line, right up against the perimeter fencing. They gave us more stick but we didn't give a shit. In our own minds we were making a statement. After a while they just stopped.

The pace of the game was savage. There wasn't a puff of breeze in the air or a second to catch your breath. They had most of the ball and we were doing most of the tackling. In the very first minute their number seven, Christian Labitte, caught an over-throw from one of our lineouts and ran straight at me: a big blond beast. I managed to get him down but I remember thinking, 'This is what it's going to be like now, these fuckers running at us all day.'

At half-time we were only 4 points behind but the sanctuary of our dressing room was 800 metres from the pitch, up a slope that felt like a hill in our distressed state. Inside there were iced towels and fresh jerseys and time to gather our thoughts. Woody's calf was gone. They strapped him up and he tried to carry on but as soon as he left the dressing room he knew he was shagged.

Losing Woody was a big disappointment but Frankie Sheahan

was a serious replacement and as a team we felt all right. We hadn't been blown away and we could see that Toulouse were struggling with the conditions as well. They hadn't bothered making the trek to the dressing room. Instead, they sat down in the tunnel and a couple of them still hadn't got to their feet by the time we passed them on the way back out. They were bollixed. Gaillimh got us into a huddle out on the field and made that point straight away: they were there for the taking.

Mike Mullins being sin-binned made things hairy for a while but we survived that too and we were only a point behind midway through the second half. Then, out of the blue, we nailed them. Two tries in the space of five minutes. Incredible.

I got the first of them. I still regard it as the best try of my life and probably one of the best tries Munster ever scored. The great thing was that it was so unlike us. It was a typically French score, on French soil, scored by a Munster team in the biggest game we had ever played up to that point.

The move started with a scrum on our own 22-metre line. I just said to Mickey Mullins, 'Let's have a go here.' I threw a simple wide, skip pass to him, he played a little reverse pass to Dominic Crotty and we were off. The ball changed hands seven or eight times and we kept it alive, eating up the ground. Inside their 22, Dominic ended up as first receiver. He ran a brilliant line that took two of them out and I ran a support line off him, screaming for the ball. He popped it to me and I had a clear run in. I touched down with a little roll. I don't know what possessed me to do that but I'll never forget the sheer fucking thrill. From start to finish the move was timed at 91 seconds. Dutchy got a brilliant intercept try a couple of minutes later and we were in the clear.

There were about 3,000 Munster supporters at the match and the scenes afterwards were unreal. We stayed on the pitch for a good while, soaking it all up, and at the same time I had a massive headache pounding inside my skull. When we got back to the dressing room I puked my guts up. I was wrecked. It was one of the greatest matches of our lives and one of the hardest things we ever had to do.

Over the years there have been some hard things that we failed to do and winning the final against Northampton was one of them. We got it wrong for that match and paid a huge price. We failed. I failed. I had a chance to be a hero and I blew it.

I think we dealt with the hype and the euphoria and the outside demands on our time in the weeks leading up to the match – I don't remember that being a hassle. But we didn't cope with being favourites. It wouldn't cost us a second thought now but back then we didn't know how to play that game. We always portrayed ourselves as outsiders, unsophisticated almost. We were like culchies going shopping in Dublin on 8 December, up to the big city, looking out of place – that's how we painted ourselves. Deccie knew all the things to say when we were underdogs but we couldn't pretend to be underdogs for this match. To get to the final we had beaten one of the biggest clubs in England – twice – and two of the biggest teams in France. We were favourites.

Our build-up in the twenty-four hours before the match didn't put us where we needed to be. On Friday we went to Twickenham for a run-out but we were caught in traffic on the way to the ground and caught in traffic on the way back. On match day we were so afraid of being delayed again that we arrived at the ground far too early. Players hate that. You might think it's a small thing but on the day of a big game time management and routine are massive. It's very easy to get pissed off and cranky when the schedule goes wrong. You're on edge, you need everything to be right – to feel right.

The biggest cock-up was our team meeting on the night before the game. None of us had ever experienced anything like that in our lives, before or since. It wasn't anyone's fault. The whole thing got out of control and nobody in the room had the cop-on or the experience to step in and call a halt.

We were sitting in a circle, not just the match 22 but all thirty players who were in the travelling party. Gaillimh asked the group what it meant to us to be here. I think he only expected a reaction from a few players but the thing took off and every player in the room said their piece in turn. The speakers were getting emotional and everybody listening was getting emotional with them. I remember Ken O'Connell pouring his heart out – an incredible speech. He didn't get near the Heineken Cup team that season but Ken was a good player who had been capped for Ireland. On the field he'd die for you. Everybody had fierce time for Ken and we all knew how much playing against Northampton would have meant to him. The minute it got emotional I was in trouble. I was trying to stare at the ground and switch off a bit because you couldn't listen to what fellas were saying without getting caught up in it.

Over the years I've only spoken when I had something to say. Other guys you expected to hear all the time in the Munster and Irish dressing rooms but I wasn't one of them. I like to think that fellas listened to me when I did speak because they knew I had thought it out and I wasn't doing it lightly. Other fellas only talk – or shout – for selfish reasons. To get themselves right. At this stage of my career I know who those players are and I don't listen.

At that meeting I was one of the last to speak. When it came to my turn my heart was racing. At that stage in my career addressing the group was still a big deal for me. By the end of the meeting we were all drained. It was as if we'd already played the match without a ball being kicked.

On the day I was as nervous as hell. I always had confidence in myself but, back then, some of that confidence was false. It wasn't built on achievement or experience. I thought I could perform at the very highest level but where was the evidence? Nowadays I sometimes think I'm better than I am and when I get like that I need a toe in the hole to go out on the field and back it up. The difference is that I know I can do it now. I know I can perform in the biggest matches because I've done it in the past.

Back then I didn't have that certainty. That day I didn't perform.

Years later the Northampton flanker Budge Pountney said that Northampton targeted me. 'We felt we could get at Ronan O'Gara and really have a go at him and really put him off his game,' he told Brendan Fanning in his book, *From There to Here*. 'We wanted to force him to make tackles, which is not the strongest part of his game. The plan was to do it in the first few minutes. "Let's get at him!" He was the guy who punched them around the park, so we wanted to make him think of other things apart from where he was going to kick the ball.'

Did they get to me? I don't know. I was used to having big back rows running down my channel. I expected it. I have never been a powerful player but I never shirked my tackles. I picked up an ankle injury in the first half but that was an accidental thing. My leg got caught between Pat Lam's legs, he kept running and my ankle was trapped and crushed. For a few minutes I thought I was going to have to go off and leaving the field then would have been a disaster, in my mind. That probably sounds bizarre given the way the game ended for me but it never once crossed my mind that coming off would have been a better outcome. I wanted to see it out.

My ankle was badly bruised but there was no serious injury. They strapped me up at half-time. I hate strapping on any part of my body but that's not an excuse. I can't say it affected my kicking because the knock was on my right ankle and there's a lot more pressure on your left ankle when a right-footer is kicking. I lost a bit of power pushing off for sprints but that wasn't the reason I played badly.

Did the occasion get to me? Yes. I wouldn't have admitted that at the time and I probably didn't realize it as clearly as I do now because I didn't have anything to compare it with. I know how it feels to cope in pressure situations now and that day in Twickenham didn't feel like that.

I had four kicks at goal and I missed them all. There was a swirling wind in the stadium and none of them were easy kicks but the conversion for David Wallace's try in the first half wasn't especially difficult and I dragged it. That was the first miss. Of the four kicks I felt I should have landed two of them. I've never watched a full video of the match but I've watched the last two kicks, with Jim Sherwin's commentary: 'He's had three shots at goal and missed them all. This could redeem everything. A nation holds its breath . . . Is it there? Is it there!? Yes! Oh no! It must just have slid away at the last moment . . .'

We were a point down with a couple of minutes left. A kick to win the European Cup. The biggest kick of my life. The last-minute kicks against Saracens? Different league.

If I was in that situation now I would have positive experiences to refer to in my mind. A bank of confidence to draw from. I didn't have that. It was just me and the kick. My homemade technique, my battered confidence, my doubts. The pressure.

It was a tough kick – out on the left, near half-way. I would back myself to get it now but I wouldn't be sure of getting it. And still, I struck it well. When I looked up and saw the ball in flight I thought it was going over but it was losing power the closer it got to the posts. The extra 10 metres of range that I have now would have pushed the ball through the breeze and between the posts. Instead, the ball died to the left. There was a minute or two left but that was it. Game over.

At the final whistle I stood in the middle of the pitch, surrounded by 70,000 people, yards away from friends and team-mates, completely alone. A boy got through the security cordon and ran up to me. I think he wanted me to sign his match programme but I ignored him. I wasn't even conscious of ignoring him. At that moment we weren't even in the same world.

After the match I was dragged in for a drugs test. Couldn't believe it. I was in a cubicle for about an hour, drinking water, trying to come up with a sample. The whole thing was a nightmare.

The lads were good about it. I knew they didn't blame me. They said all the right things but this was something I was going to have to deal with myself. You can cod yourself and go around saying that the rest of your game was all right. It wasn't. The bottom line is that goal-kicking cost us the fucking game. We could have scored another try and won and then my goal-kicks might have been brushed under the carpet, but for me, for my development, I had to take the lessons of the day head on. In terms of my mental development I was essentially a boy. That experience probably made a man out of me.

When we flew back to Shannon that night there was a huge crowd waiting for us in the airport. After that we went to Limerick City Hall for a reception. You could see by the way the place was set up that they were expecting to greet the European champions. More speeches. We needed all that like a hole in the head. The fans were great, everyone was decent, but when you lose a big game like that you just want to slip away with your buddies. Eventually, that's what we did. An all-nighter.

Ireland were playing the Barbarians in Lansdowne Road the following day and all of the Munster players in the Irish squad had to report to camp in Dublin that night. Ireland were preparing for a summer tour with Test matches against Argentina, USA and Canada. I was in an awful state: I was hungover, my ankle was killing me and I was still the guy who had blown a chance to win the European Cup.

There was no slagging from the Leinster or Ulster fellas but secretly I'm sure some of them were glad Munster lost. When we pull on the green jersey we're all united by the cause and over the years I've built up great friendships with Leinster and Ulster guys, but behind it all there's a huge rivalry. You can be fooled sometimes by appearances. Why would they want us to win?

My ankle was examined and I was passed fit to go on the trip but for the opening match against Argentina I was dropped. They said that my ankle wasn't 100 per cent and that I probably needed a rest but they could say what they liked. You know when you've been dropped. I finished the Six Nations as the Irish number 10 and now David Humphreys was back in for the most important match of the tour.

I don't remember being gutted though. Maybe after the Northampton match I was giving my emotions a rest. David Wallace won his first cap against Argentina and he was very wound up about it. Frankie Sheahan and myself were a bit giddy on the bus going to the ground, doing everything we could to make Wally laugh. Wally was always easy to distract but he reared up on us that day. I couldn't blame him. We were the muppets on the bench and he had his big chance.

I got on for the last couple of minutes against Argentina and nearly set up a try but they beat us fair and square by 11 points. The atmosphere that night was brilliant. The crowd were jumping and making a fierce racket, really hostile, just like a soccer crowd. I'd love to have played in that. Instead I got on for the next match against the USA in New Hampshire when basically the B team was given a chance. The USA were totally useless. We ran in thirteen tries and I converted eight of them: 83 points was a record total for Ireland but it was a worthless match.

I was back on the bench for the final game of the tour against Canada. This was the last week of what had been a ten-month season and a few of us took the liberty of going on the town.

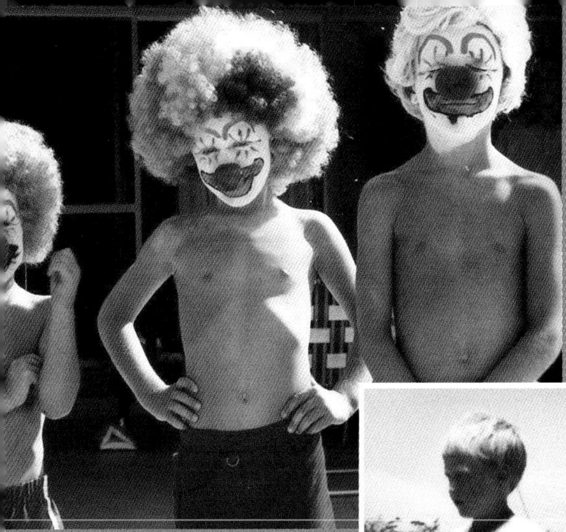

Early encounters with rugby (*above*), with Colin and my dad, and soccer (*left*).

Above and below: My brothers on holiday in the US and (*below left to right*) Colin, Fergal, Morgan and me.

Below: My first day at Pres.

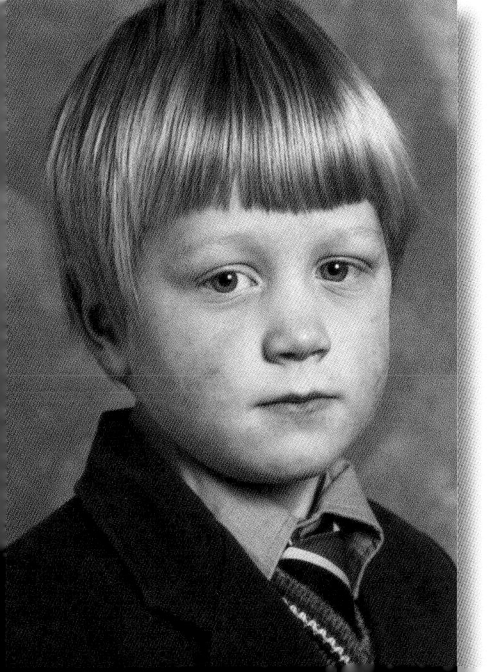

Below: Looking happier at my Confirmation.

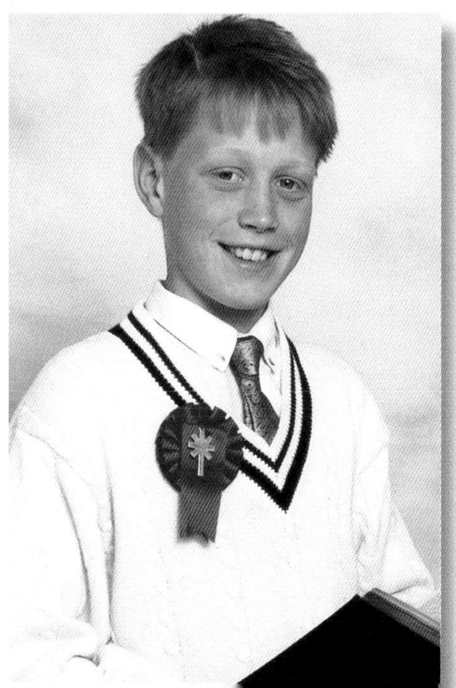

Above: Just friends back then. Jess and I have known each other since we were about ten; this is at a disco after Pres won the Junior Cup.

Below: Outside UCC after our wedding in the summer of 2006.

Above: Careful not to drop the bride! (*From the left*): my brother Morgan; my lifelong friends Eoin Walsh, Conor Howell, John Powell and Paul O'Mahony; and my brother Fergal.

Below: Our dog Tia is another part of the O'Gara home.

Left: O'Garas young and old. We have always been a close-knit family. (*Back row*): Colin and Dad; (*middle*): Grandad and Granny Langan, Mum and Morgan; (*front*): Fergal and me.

Below: My Granny Linda who lives in Sligo

Below: Graduating from UCC. My dad Fergal, on my right, is a professor there.

Left: On holiday with Jess and Mick and Joan Galwey.

Below: Sharing the good times with Alan Gaffney.

Below: Donncha gets shrimpy on a trip to Croatia.

In the USA with Wally and Aileen. People said we looked like the cast of *Dawson's Creek*.

Above: Team-mates in my early days at Munster included (*left to right*): Jason Holland, Mick O'Driscoll, Dominic Crotty and John Langford. John Kelly's wife Grace and Jess are in the centre.

Above: Me with the boy, Roy Keane.

Above: An O'Gara family gathering for Mum's birthday with (*left to right*): Morgan, Fergal, dad, Jess, mum and myself.

Homecoming, May 2006. Jess and I with the Heineken Cup after our win against Biarritz in Cardiff.

Wednesday was a rest day with a trip to Niagara Falls on the agenda so on Tuesday night we went out: myself, Frankie, Paul Wallace, Marcus Horan, Guy Easterby. We were drinking until about two or three in the morning and we might have got away with it if we had returned quietly to our rooms. You know yourself when you're drunk: you think you're capable of anything but the only thing you definitely can't do is keep the noise down. There was also some story that we'd been spotted in a bar by an Irish ex-pat in Toronto and a couple of emails later word had reached the IRFU in Lansdowne Road. I could believe it but I don't know how true that story is.

What really nailed us though was Guy Easterby's party trick. After the pubs closed we got into a student bar on a college campus where more drink was available. This was Guy's cue to step outside, take his clothes off and walk back in naked, holding his neatly folded clothes in one hand with his shoes resting on top. His brother Simon wasn't with us that night but normally they would do it together as a double act. Looking at the reaction on people's faces is priceless. In fairness to Guy he always had an amazing physique. Where most fellas are happy with a six-pack stomach he had an eight-pack. He must have done 250 sit-ups a day and when I was rooming with him he'd do sit-ups for ten minutes every night before he went to bed.

A woman at the college, though, witnessed this scene and wasn't impressed. She blew the whistle on us and we were marched down there the following day: myself, Guy, Gatland and Brian O'Brien who was on his first tour as the new Ireland manager. I kept my head down and Guy played a blinder. Like all the best defence lawyers he tried to create reasonable doubt.

'I'm 99 per cent certain that I saw you running around naked here last night.'

'But you're not 100 per cent.'

'I'm not 100 per cent, but I'm 99 per cent.'

The upshot was that we were in trouble. Brian O'Driscoll said to Frankie that Gatland wanted to send us all home. I don't know if he was playing with our minds or not but we were all worried for a while. In the end Gatland lectured us individually and our punishment was that we had to go to and from training every day in our number ones: jacket, pants, shirt, tie. The weather was beautiful and all the lads were in shorts on the bus. We felt like clowns in our rig-outs. The whole affair became a bit of a joke by the end of the week but for a couple of days I felt pretty small.

Then, on the day of the match, Frankie nearly got us in trouble again with his messing. We were standing for the national anthems and the television camera was panning the line, close-ups, like they always do. There was me, Guy and Frankie with our arms around each other when, next thing, Frankie starts tickling my ear. I got an awful fit of the giggles and I nearly erupted into the camera. Guy and Frankie started laughing as well and the three of us just got our heads down in time before the camera picked us up.

There was nothing funny about the match. Canada got stuck into us and we were 13 points behind early in the second half when Easterby and myself were sent on to replace Stringer and Humphreys. In fairness to Humphs his wife was about to give birth back home and he couldn't have been properly concentrated on the match. Anyway, I was just delighted to get on and make a difference. We got back level but they went ahead again with a penalty four minutes from the end. We created one last attack and in the final minute we were awarded a penalty.

It wasn't an easy kick. Out on the right, last minute, shit or bust. Losing to Canada would have been seen as a disaster back home but that was the position we were in. I couldn't pretend that the pressure was anything like the Northampton match and I couldn't pretend that landing the kick was going to take away any of the pain from Twickenham. But what if I missed it? Would people start thinking of me as a choker? How would I explain that one to myself? How many more doubts would it have created in my mind?

Lined it up. Nailed it.

CHAPTER 6

I knew I was going to spend some time living with The Kick. When people thought of me they were going to think of Twickenham too. I couldn't divorce myself from it or make people forget. Whatever I did in rugby or in life that kick was part of my story. How big a part? That was up to me. I was tormented by it for weeks, but I couldn't ever take that kick again. I had to believe that there would be other big days and other big kicks. And I did believe it.

Whatever people really thought they didn't say it to my face. In a situation like that people tell you what they think you want to hear or they say nothing at all. When I was out and about I didn't suffer any abuse apart from one night in a pub in Cork city. I was going to the toilet and this fella was smirking at me.

'How do I know you?' he said.

'I don't know . . .'

'Oh yeah, I remember, you're the prick that missed the kick against Northampton.'

I was a bit shocked for a minute. Why would someone do that? What kind of a langer gets a thrill out of abusing a complete stranger?

I can't say it upset me though. One of the things you develop in the Munster dressing room is a thick skin. The slagging is merciless. Fellas will sink to any depths to get a laugh. Paul

O'Connell is one of the wittiest guys you'll ever meet but some of his best lines are cruel. There are no limits or taboo subjects and if you can't take it your brain will be fried, simple as that. When we returned for pre-season training with Munster I knew I was going to be slagged about the miss against Northampton. There was hardly a day went by when Axel didn't bring it up. I think it helped me get over it. It would have been a lot worse if fellas were tip-toeing around the thing, concerned about my feelings and trying to pretend it didn't happen. It happened. Let's get over it.

Moving on was something we all had to do as a group. Keith Wood had returned to Harlequins, Eddie Halvey had signed for London Irish but John Langford had agreed to stay. Unfinished business was the reason he gave and that's the way we all felt. Keeping Langford was huge. Outside the group people wondered if we could get back to the level we had achieved the previous season, whether we could regroup and go again. That was the issue we had to confront. Deccie said something at a meeting early that season that summed up the challenge for us: 'Winners fall and they get straight back up, losers fall and they stay down.'

Our first big test was away to Castres. A week earlier we had beaten Newport at home in our opening Heineken Cup pool match but France has always been a place where we've measured ourselves. Deccie raised the bar for us. Our two previous wins in France had been at neutral grounds – we hadn't beaten a French team in their own stadium yet. He also came up with a stat that no club team had won three games on the trot on French soil in the Heineken Cup.

The Castres number 10 was the Scottish international Gregor Townsend. Was he on my mind? A little bit. When the opposition have a big-name number 10 I regard that as a challenge. Can I cope with this guy? Can I exert more influence on the game than him? There was a Lions tour coming up at the end of the season and if I was going to get on the plane Townsend was one of the guys I needed to beat off.

We made a shocking start: 10–0 down after six minutes, 20–6 down after seventeen minutes and then Alan Quinlan was sin-binned. Not for the first time, we were in the shit. We gave away a lot of penalties and we were chatting too much to the ref. Going in at half-time our blood was boiling. Deccie could see that and he did well to calm us down. Our composure in the second half that night was class. Gaillimh said later that the Castres game defined our season and he was right. To show that we were progressing as a team we needed to be able to deal calmly with a crisis situation and dig ourselves out of it.

We got three tries in the second half, two of them in the last five minutes. The clinching try fell to me. It was nearly a replica of the score we got in Bordeaux five months earlier, breaking out from our own 22 and running it the length of the field. Dutchy made a great break and off-load, Dominic hit me with a one-touch, finger-tip pass and I took off from just inside their half.

I had plenty of support runners and the Castres defenders kept backing off, expecting me to pass. I sold one dummy and went up a gear. At one stage I glanced around to see Gaillimh blocking one of their tacklers. This was the second-last minute of a really hard game, Castres had made a rake of changes in their pack during the match and here was Gaillimh, trying to keep up with a move that started deep inside our own half. Incredible. About 10 metres from the line I realized I was going to score. Axel roared at me to dive and, for once, I did what I was told.

I got the conversion to put us 32–26 in front and I felt good about my performance. My strike rate with the boot was only five from ten and I had missed a couple of easy penalties, including a bad miss when the game was level at 20-all. But I didn't let it affect my overall performance and I needed to be able to do that. To separate my goal-kicking from all the other things I had to do.

I was happy with my form, Deccie told me that he was happy and a week later against Bath I felt I went up another level. We beat them well in the end with a couple of late tries and I was cruising. Loving it.

The return match was over there the following weekend and I was brought crashing down to earth. Around that time I had a couple of nicknames. One of them was LA O'Gara because I had cleaned out Peter Clohessy at cards and the lame joke was that I'd won enough money to buy a flight to LA. That nickname didn't stick and you can be sure Claw got his money back the next time we sat down at the card table. The other nickname was AHS – Above His Station. That's still knocking around and after the Bath game at the Rec it felt appropriate. I had gotten ahead of myself. I thought I had this game cracked. The minute you think that you're in trouble.

Against Bath I was brutal. Crap. We lost by 13 points and I failed to score. I missed three penalties and a conversion, two of them from close range. 'The most damaging blow of all [for Munster] was Ronan O'Gara's normally reliable radar going completely off beam,' wrote Gerry Thornley in the *Irish Times*. 'This had been coming. A slight case of the yips.'

A few of the papers used the same picture of me being gang-tackled. Phil de Glanville has caught me by the legs and Steve Borthwick has grabbed me by the collar and it looks as if he's lifting me up like a kitten. That image summed up the game for me. Mike Catt played out-half for Bath and was man of the match. To cap it all the Lions manager Donal Lenihan and assistant coach Andy Robinson were sitting in the stand. Lovely.

By then I had a big thing in my head that I needed a kicking coach. The top teams were only coming around to that idea at the time. Ireland didn't have one. Mark Tainton was one of the few specialists in this area and Warren Gatland organized a one-off session for me and Humphs. He took us down to the back pitch at Lansdowne Road and the irony was that we kicked so well that Tainton didn't think he could do much with us.

Later on Mark became an established member of the Irish set-up but I knew from the beginning that he had a lot to offer me. On a couple of spare Sundays I flew to Bristol to do sessions with him. I had to take responsibility for that part of my game. It was too important. My homespun technique had taken me so far but I needed more structure in my kicking. I needed to understand the dynamics of kicking and have a formula in my head that I could fall back on. It's like a golfer: you need swing thoughts that you can trust, that you know will work under pressure. For me that was the next level I needed to reach and it wasn't going to happen overnight.

Before the Bath defeat we had won our first eight competitive games of the season. It was an off-day. No panic. We didn't have another game in the Heineken Cup for ten weeks but during that break we clinched the inter-provincial championship for the third year in a row. The inter-pros are gone now and nobody seemed to care very much about them in the years before the Heineken Cup but they were good for us when we were coming together as a team. No Munster team had ever retained the inter-pro title before we did. Now we had retained it again.

In early November, Ireland went into camp for the autumn internationals against Japan and South Africa. My overall form had been good since the start of the season but I couldn't be sure of my place. How much value would they put on the game against Canada? On the game against Bath? I was relieved to be picked against Japan but I also knew that if I cocked up I probably wouldn't be playing against South Africa. As it happened they were poor and things went well. We scored eleven tries and I was involved in a good few of them; I had twelve shots at goal and landed eleven. For what it was worth I got the Man of the Match award. I lasted the full eighty minutes too and when David Humphreys came on he replaced the full-back Geordan Murphy. All of that pointed to the probability of me getting a start against South Africa.

I needed days like that because in an Irish shirt I didn't have any security. It's easy to forget the things that were going through my mind all those years ago, the doubts and questions. Around the time of those internationals I gave a short interview to the *Examiner* for one of their lifestyle pages. The reporter was a friend of my sister-in-law and the column was about stress and how people cope with it. Back then I was in a different place and my worries were things that don't bother me now.

'This is my second season playing international rugby,' I said in the interview, 'and I have to say that, emotionally, I was a bit all over the shop when I started. I suppose the most stressful elements for me are team selection and reading the media reports. When the media analyse your past performances it can put pressure on you. Team selection is stressful because there is an awful lot of competition and you are always wondering if you are good enough.'

I was still far too conscious of what other people thought. And at the time people still thought that I was a bit flaky. That I could blow hot and cold. That I was a bit streaky. After the Japan match Tony Ward did his player ratings in the *Irish Independent* and expressed what I'd say a lot of people were thinking: 'A confidence-boosting performance from a pure confidence player.'

Every player trades on confidence. But when people say that you're a confidence player they're implying a weakness. They're saying that when your confidence fluctuates you can't manage the downswing. Was that a fair comment about me back then? I wouldn't have admitted it at the time but looking back now I'd say it was fair. It's all about having a high base-level of consistency and I was still searching for that.

I've always been a believer in sports psychology as an aid to performance. Other stuff, though, didn't do it for me. When we were in camp that autumn Gatty introduced us to transcendental meditation. This was supposed to help us deal with stress and give us better access to inner calmness. Outside people came in to talk us through it. We were all given a word to repeat to ourselves until we drifted into a meditative state. 'Ima' was my mantra.

The first session was compulsory and I think I went to one more session after that. It didn't push any buttons for me. I know Eric Miller got a lot out of it but he might have been in a minority. Only twelve players at a time were allowed into each session and they quickly banned groups of Munster players from going in together. After a couple of minutes there'd be a loud fart or a fit of giggling and the whole mood would be shagged. Juvenile behaviour I know but the Munster dressing room could be that kind of place.

The South Africa match was my first opportunity to play against one of the Tri-Nations teams. I relished the challenge but I didn't rise to it. I made a reasonable start but failed to keep it up. Too many poor decisions, too many mistakes. One of my last contributions was a skewed up-and-under that went out on the full. Humphs came on for me after an hour and made a good impact. With a few minutes left we were level with them, 18–18, and there was a real chance of taking a scalp. Then they conjured a try from nothing and we were left licking our wounds: 28–18.

I had blown a chance to consolidate my position as the Ireland number 10 and the debate was on again. Me or Humphs. Was I reading the stuff in the papers? Yes. Did I care? Of course I did.

Ward came down on my side, even though he wasn't blind to my faults: 'Humphreys was the more effective in his limited time on Sunday but such is the see-saw nature of this particular joust O'Gara will probably remain in pole position and I support that call. His only obvious weakness remains a tendency to attempt the half-break at the merest hint of an opening and subsequently lose possession because of his upright position and lack of upper body strength compared to those doing the tackling. In every other respect he is the genuine article.'

In the *Sunday Tribune*, though, Neil Francis gave it to me between the eyes:

'Ronan O'Gara, if he had played to his potential against the Boks, would have cemented his place in the side for the season. He underperformed. In the space of 60 minutes O'Gara made 13 forced and unforced errors. It was unacceptable . . . O'Gara must strive for inner calm, particularly in the big matches. In some of the recent big games – Scotland, Wales and South Africa – O'Gara hasn't recovered [from mistakes] and the drain of confidence has been obvious from his expression.'

I went back to Munster feeling like I had to prove myself all over again before the Six Nations. Our next game in the Heineken Cup was away to Newport in the middle of January. We were in a strong position at the top of the pool but Newport were right behind us. We had never won on Welsh soil in that competition and Newport had lost just one game at home in all competitions over the previous fourteen months. After twenty minutes we were 15 points down and it didn't look as if their record was going to be threatened by us. Our response, though, was as good as it had been against Castres three months earlier. This was another test of our bottle and we stood up to it. In the end we did them in the final quarter and won by 15 points.

For me, it was a dream game. I scored our first try and went on to kick four penalties, three conversions and two drop-goals: 29 points out of the 39 we raked up. The English papers were talking me up as a Lions player but Deccie knew better. 'O'Gara did OK,' he told the press, 'but it will be another two or three years before we see the best of him.'

He was right. The last thing I needed was to lose the run of myself like I did after the first Bath match. Deccie had known me long enough by then to understand my cocky side. It was important to my game as long it didn't get out of hand. Lions selection was a constant theme that season with more speculation after every weekend of matches – whether it was Heineken Cup or internationals. Pundits and commentators kept putting me in the picture and that's where I wanted to be. I made no secret of it. When I look back at some of the things I said to reporters I can't believe I was so frank but that's the way I was.

'I think at fly-half there are definite openings [in the squad],' I said to one reporter. 'You've got to wait and see how the Six Nations go but I don't see any other fly-half that I would particularly fear or would rate better than me to be honest. Wilkinson is playing with a dominant English pack. He's a good kicker and all that but there are other aspects of his game that aren't as good.'

No fear I'd keep all that to myself. Christ.

We needed to win our last pool match against Castres at Musgrave Park to be sure of a home quarter-final. They had nothing to play for and on a miserable evening we beat them by 10 points. Not for the first time that year the showers weren't working afterwards. We got on the team bus covered in muck. Beautiful. Professional rugby in Ireland had made a lot of strides but every so often you could see the cracks. For example, we didn't have a scrummaging machine when we were preparing for the Heineken Cup final a few months earlier. We'd been using a borrowed one all along but that wasn't available to us. That kind of thing.

That season the quarter-finals were held before the Six Nations and we had Biarritz in Thomond Park a week later. The hype was incredible again. All-night queues for tickets, massive media interest. We were loving it but we were also feeling the pressure. Nobody expected us to lose and that's always dangerous. Deccie did his usual trick of talking up the opposition but when he does that for every team the public are hardly going to take any notice.

Biarritz, though, weren't long opening everyone's eyes. They scored two tries in the first fifteen minutes and we had to work like dogs to be a couple of points ahead at the break. We pushed on in the third quarter but they wouldn't go away and when they got their fourth try near the end there was only a score between the teams. We held on to win 38–29 but Gaillimh said afterwards that he couldn't remember a harder match in Thomond Park. I thought we should have been a bit more ruthless. We were still learning I suppose. Maybe not quick enough for our own good.

I kicked 23 points, which took me past 100 points in the Heineken Cup for the second season in a row, but Axel Foley scored three tries and he got all the glory. He deserved it in fairness. A former Shannon player called Brian McGoey owns a Domino's place in Limerick and he said that any Munster player who scored three tries in a Heineken Cup match would have free pizzas in his place for life. He honoured that promise and it's still going. Axel is retired now and I'd say he'll nearly put yer man out of business.

Nine Munster players were named in the Irish team for the Italy match in Rome the following weekend with a couple more on the bench. Only twelve months earlier that would have been unheard of.

In those days we were based in the Glenview Hotel in County Wicklow, just down the road from Bray. We spend so much time in camp that you have to make it a home away from home and make the best of it. For craic in the evenings the place to be was Claw's room. Room 301, the biggest and best room in the hotel. That's what we always believed anyway.

Claw was probably sharing with Rob Henderson around that time because they were both smokers. In the privacy of that room they'd be horsing the fags and not a word said about it. Nobody was going to tell Claw to pack in the fags. Basically, Claw did what he wanted. Claw is the Law was his full title.

It wasn't unusual for Claw to have breakfast sent to his bedroom. Rala would bring it up: porridge, tea, two slices of toast and a fag. The pay-off for Rala was that he'd stay for a fag before he went back down. Claw's bedroom was where the card schools would be held and he'd organize the toasted sandwiches and refreshments. It was mostly Munster players you'd find in there and I don't know if other fellas felt welcome or not. For us, though, it was the place to be.

When Paul O'Connell came on the scene later he shared with Claw for a while and he tells a funny story about one night when Claw couldn't sleep. It was the small hours of the morning and Claw put on the television full blast. There weren't even any programmes being shown on the channel he was watching, only those long commercials for mail-order music CDs. Claw took a shine to one of the CDs on offer – *The Power Of Love*. He picked up the phone and rang the number on screen, gave them his credit card details and ordered two copies of the CD – one for himself and one for Paulie. In fairness to Claw, he was always fierce generous. All Paulie wanted at that moment was his sleep but instead he was getting *The Power Of Love* from Claw.

The trips to Rome are always class. Beautiful hotel, beautiful food, beautiful weather. For that match we went earlier than usual and had a Papal audience on Wednesday. We were sitting near the front of a huge hall in the Vatican, sweating in our number ones, waiting our turn, when myself and Frankie got a bit giddy. One of the IRFU past-presidents was sitting close by and we tried to convince him that Pope John Paul had sent a stand-in to meet us. We kept it going long enough that he was nearly convinced.

'Isn't that awful that the real Pope wouldn't come to meet us.'

'That is the Pope.'

'Mick, will you go away, I've seen the real Pope enough times . . .'

Meeting the Pope was a fierce buzz. We got a lovely group shot taken but Woody, as the captain, was the only one of the players who actually spoke to him. Being centre stage like that suits Woody grand.

Woody pointed out afterwards that the last Irish team to meet the Pope was the soccer lads in 1990 and they lost to Italy a few days later. We were never really in danger of losing but we were sloppy as hell in the first half and Gatty ate us at half-time. Diego Dominguez had to pull out at the last minute and he was crucial for them. His replacement had a nightmare debut and still we made trouble for ourselves. As usual they hit us hard and Mauro Bergamasco gave me an awful belt that put me down for a few minutes. When Italy are fresh at the start of the season they like nothing better than to kick the shit out of teams.

Hendo got the first of his three tries just before half-time and that gave us a bit of daylight. We came up with another four in the second half and I got the last of them, my first try for Ireland. You'd think that a moment like that would be branded in my memory for life but I think I've had too many bangs on the head. All I remember is that I sold a dummy close to the line and I found a couple of Italian buyers.

My try wasn't important to the outcome of the match but it was important for me in other ways. I had scored a few tries for Munster already that season and that was part of my game I needed to take to the international stage. I was perceived as a kicking out-half and I hated that because that label sold me short. Throughout my career kicking has been a key element of my game and with Munster over the years we usually played a game that required me to kick. It was nuts-and-bolts stuff. Highly visible and always associated with me. But I saw myself as an out-half who tried to create space for others and get back lines moving. I was involved in two of Hendo's tries that day and to me that kind of creativity was just as important as kicking.

There were only two minutes left when I scored. In an Irish shirt it was unusual for me to still be on the field so close to the final whistle but Humphs came on for Tyrone Howe that day and I took that as a sign of approval.

Beating Italy meant that Ireland had a winning start in the championship for the first time since 1988. We hadn't beaten France in Lansdowne Road for eighteen years and that's what we did next. As a team we were developing. Slowly we were moving on from the basic game plan of Gatland's early days: 'smash the rucks, set a few targets, kick to the corners.' That plan wasn't ditched, but it was expanded. We weren't playing a fifteen-man game but we were inching beyond ten-man rugby.

I wasn't involved in any of the strategic discussions but I suspect that Woody had a big influence. The perception over the years is that Woody and Gatland didn't get on particularly well but I never saw any evidence of tension between them. Gatland would have been smart enough to recognize the importance of Woody and listen to his suggestions.

We had a couple of new calls that season that indicated a little bit more ambition and variety. If one of the forwards was going to come steaming around the corner and take the ball off Stringer the call was 'Rambo'. If the runner was going to be off my shoulder the call was 'Turbo'. Outside of that we had O'Driscoll.

His try was the difference between the teams against France. When he got the ball from David Wallace he was 30 metres from the corner and that was the only place he might score. He was tackled as he got to the line but he had the strength to get the ball down. No other player on our team had the combination of pace and power to make that try possible. Very few players in Europe had those qualities to the extent that Drico had.

The Television Match Official took an age to decide whether he had got sufficient downward pressure on the ball before it squirted away. While we were waiting I took the ball and prepared myself for a conversion attempt. Christophe Lamaison clearly thought this was a bit cheeky and he followed me out to the 22, where we had a little chat that went something like this.

'No try,' he said to me.

'Probably not,' I said.

'Can I have the ball?'

'No.'

He didn't go away until the TMO made up his mind. They kept showing replays on the big screen, which was unusual for a controversial incident, and every time it looked dodgy. But the try was given and we were flying.

At one stage early in the second half we were 22–3 in front before they got their act together and made a charge at us. There was only a score in it at the end, 22–15, but we hung on. I was happy with my performance. I knocked the ball on three times in the first fifteen minutes and missed a handy penalty in the final quarter but I was able to bin the bad stuff and get on with making a good contribution. According to the stats I carried the ball more than any other Irish player that day. A kicking out-half?

In the press conference afterwards the French coach, Bernard Laporte, was very generous: 'O'Driscoll and O'Gara are two of the best players at centre and out-half in the world at the moment,' he said. Did I believe that? I knew I was confident and playing at the top of my game. I knew that I felt comfortable at this level after plenty of shaky moments. I knew I was getting better. And a part of me would have been happy to believe it.

Twelve months earlier Ireland needed Humphs to come off the bench and swing the game in Paris. This time he stayed where he was.

*

The foot-and-mouth crisis meant that the final three games in our Six Nations campaign were postponed until the autumn. We were in camp when the news broke and immediately we went into demob mode. It had snowed heavily that day and the first thing we did was have a huge snowball fight. Then we went into town and got hammered.

That was a night for drinking games. One of our favourites was a game involving peanuts. Somebody discovered that if you threw peanuts into a pint not all of them would rise to the top at the same pace. So we all had a racing peanut and two pints: one for sipping and one for racing. When the call came we all threw our racing peanuts into our racing pints. There was no prize for being first but whoever had the peanut that was slowest getting to the top had to sink his racing pint in one go. You also had to look after your racing peanut because if somebody else crushed it the outcome was the same as having a slow peanut: you had to knock your racing pint back your throat in one swallow.

In those days we used get out a bit more than we do now but not enough to prepare you for a session like that. The following day would be a write-off. You're dehydrated, you can't eat properly, you're puking, you lose a few kilos of body weight, your gym work is bad for a couple of days later in the week. Nowadays we'd only have a blow-out like that once or twice during the season. There are times when you feel like you're missing out by not going on the piss but they are surprisingly few. Attitudes changed and priorities were rearranged. When I started playing serious rugby the attitude to drink was a carry-over from the amateur days: match, drinking session, slow, painful recovery. The stakes are too high now. I play with fellas now who wouldn't even look at a chocolate muffin for fear of the damage it would do to their system.

Foot-and-mouth didn't do us any favours. The postponement

of Ireland's matches meant that I had three fewer opportunities to impress the Lions selectors. Jonny Wilkinson, Neil Jenkins and Gregor Townsend were all doing their stuff on the international stage while I was sitting on my ass. It was a few weeks before the ban on sport in Ireland was lifted and then we returned to our clubs in the All-Ireland League, a million miles from the Lions.

The bookies were quoting me at odds-on to be in the squad but that was just their opinion. Graham Henry, the Lions coach, had positive things to say about me in the paper but how much value could I place on that? My club-mate was the Lions manager but that didn't mean I was getting any reassurance from him. I bought my first house that year and I organized the mortgage through Donal Lenihan in the Irish Permanent. When we were sorting out the paperwork in his office the Lions inevitably came up. He just told me not to worry, that they were watching me, that he was happy with my progress and to keep it up. What else could he say?

Munster's Heineken Cup semi-final against Stade Français was fixed for Lille on 21 April, three months after our quarter-final. After the Six Nations was aborted it became the only focus of Irish rugby for a few weeks. *The Late Late Show* even did a special on Munster rugby. Gaillimh, Claw and myself were the guests. I was taking it all in my stride sitting backstage in RTE until they gave us the signal that we would be on in two minutes. I could see sweat appear on Gaillimh's face and I felt a bit sick in my stomach. We scrambled to put our ties on and they kept giving us the countdown: 90 seconds, 60 seconds, 30 seconds. In the studio I was sitting in the middle between the two lads and it must have been about four minutes before Pat Kenny asked me a question. I was as nervous as hell.

Eight days before the semi-final a match was organized against a Rest of Ireland selection in Thomond Park. Munster hadn't played together since January and I had played just a game and a half since the France match in Lansdowne Road. Trevor Brennan cut me in two in a League match for Con against St Mary's and I was out for three weeks with a badly bruised hip. I went on a blindside break and Trevor jumped out of a ruck to nail me. Murder.

Until the week of the practice match Munster had been together for just four training sessions since the Biarritz game. Looking back, it was shocking preparation for a Heineken Cup semi-final.

Donal, Graham Henry and Andy Robinson were all in Thomond Park and it was basically a final Irish trial for the Lions. The Munster players would have another chance in Lille but for other guys it was shit or bust. We managed to win 24–22 but I was fierce rusty. Started well and faded. Landed three kicks and missed four. I was desperate to find the form I'd shown two months earlier but I probably forced it too much. If the Lions selectors came to Limerick looking to be convinced about me they would have left unconvinced.

We had a lot of issues to deal with before the Stade match. Alan Quinlan and John Kelly were out and David Wallace was in a race against time to recover from a damaged medial ligament in his knee. Wally played but he wasn't right. They picked Donncha O'Callaghan in the back row but he hadn't played a minute of the Heineken Cup that season and for the biggest game of his life he was being asked to play out of position.

We never got going that day. The layoff had killed us. Our line-out was cleaned out, our back row didn't gell, I wasn't able to dictate the match. And still we nearly got away with it. When John O'Neill's try was disallowed ten minutes into the second half there was only 7 points between the teams. All the television replays clearly showed that his touchdown in the corner was good but there was no Television Match Official. The referee, Chris

White, looked over at the touch judge, Steve Lander, and he ruled against us.

We held them scoreless in the second half and brought it back to 16–15 with a couple of minutes to go but we didn't play well enough to win. John's dive in the corner was the only time we threatened a try. Somebody came up with a stat that it was the first time Munster had failed to score a try in a Heineken Cup match for three years but none of us ever felt like we were part of a try-scoring machine and in big games over the years that hurt us.

I've always felt that we had to work too hard for our tries. We've had great backs but we didn't have players who could get a try out of nothing just by whizzing off in pursuit of a loose kick or something. A handy try – we didn't get handy tries. All of our tries seemed to be big operations with huge teamwork. One try in the final against Northampton, no tries against Stade Français. We needed more tries in the biggest games. It was a serious issue for us.

I felt sorry for John too because that game was a big opportunity for him. He came into the team at short notice and played a blinder. I used to love playing with him because he'd go through a brick wall for the cause. The other lads would have him revved up for days beforehand and when match time came it was like releasing a caged animal onto the field. Some wingers have no interest in the ball. If it comes to them well and good but John used be roaring for it. We had a code – if he was on the call was '4 ball'. The match would hardly be started when I'd hear the call, '4 ball! 4 ball!' He'd take it any way it came. If you gave him a pass with six tacklers bearing down on him he wouldn't give a damn, he'd tear into them. Nobody had a work rate like John and that day he should have been a hero.

We got into a circle on the pitch after the final whistle and Gaillimh said all the right things. There was a running track around the outside of the pitch and we walked a lap to thank our supporters. In Twickenham a year before people had seen some glory in our defeat because it had been such an amazing journey. I didn't buy into that then and I don't think any of us were buying into it now.

Another one-point defeat? So fuck. We lost.

CHAPTER 7

I hardly slept for a couple of nights after the Stade Français match. Kept going over the game in my mind. Kept thinking about the Lions announcement on Wednesday. The Cork-based Munster players went on the piss in the Western Star on the day after the match and Donal Lenihan happened to be there. I tried to pump him about my chances. He played it dead straight. No clues.

At least Donal didn't make me wait until Wednesday. Late on Tuesday night he called. I was in. Brilliant. Brilliant!

I was with Jess in her mother's house and we went from there to see my parents. Woke them up to tell them the news. I knew they were suffering with me. You never realize how tense you are about something until the tension goes. I was desperate to be on that tour.

People said that Donal swung it for me because we were club-mates. I was clearly a borderline call and it was the obvious thing for people to say. Maybe he did nudge me over the line. I never asked him. Donal's no fool, he knew that people were going to come to that conclusion whatever he said. But he was a serious professional as well. If he didn't think I was good enough there's no way he would have batted for me.

Before I was even named, Stephen Jones in the *Sunday Times* had a pop: 'I am afraid,' he wrote, 'that if the selectors choose Ronan O'Gara, the lively but unmasterly Irishman, we will know that political decisions are alive and well.' Graham Henry said that it came down to kicking. It was between me and Gregor Townsend for the third out-half spot and Gregor wasn't a front-rank goal-kicker. The ins and outs of it didn't bother me. People could believe what they liked. I was on the plane.

I kept playing with Cork Con for a few weeks and we got to the final of the All-Ireland League. I kicked all our points in the semi-final win over Young Munster but the final against Dungannon was fixed for the following Saturday and that was the day the Lions went into camp. There was no question of being released to play. I was disappointed but I didn't argue. Con were beaten by 34 points. Whether I played or not wasn't going to make any difference to that outcome.

The Lions spent a week at Tylney Hall, a stately home in Hampshire, before flying to Australia. For the previous month we all had programmes to do in the gym and fitness targets to meet. I was getting better at that kind of stuff all the time but this was a whole new level for me. I found the week in Tylney Hall really demanding. I'd never trained so hard in my life. Most nights I was in bed at ten o'clock, shagged.

The main purpose of that week was team building. Whatever relationships we had with players from other countries would naturally have been distant. We arrived mid-afternoon that Saturday and when the formal introductions were completed we were marched to an assault course on the grounds of the estate and split into groups of four for various drills. No time to waste. Every minute planned. Every day we were repeatedly told about the importance of the Lions and the magnitude of the task that lay ahead. You were being made to feel that this was like nothing else you'd ever experienced in your life.

They employed a company called Impact, who specialized in group bonding and motivation. The same people had worked with the 1997 Lions too and we were exposed to them twice a day while we were in Tylney Hall. We'd dabbled in this sort of thing with Munster but that week was something else.

It was all about building trust. For one exercise you climbed to a small platform about 20 metres above the ground and let yourself fall backwards into the arms of your team-mates. Doing exercises that involved heights was a theme. Other stuff wasn't physical but I found it twice as hard. They organized a meeting where we had to stand up in front of the group and declare our good points and bad points, what's important to us, when we're at our best and when we're at our worst. You were baring yourself to a room of people who, for the most part, were strangers. Even the people I knew in that room wouldn't have heard me speak in those terms before.

It wasn't all daunting. On Tuesday they caught us from the blind side with a brilliant exercise. They teed it up by saying that for a successful tour we'd have to be fifty hearts beating as one. Then the double doors to the room burst open and a samba band walked in, playing their drums and shaking their tambourines.

'Lads, we're going to give you all instruments and you are going to start playing the samba.'

They split us into groups again and a short time later we congregated in the hotel courtyard to play as an orchestra: drums, tambourines, shakers, yo-yo bells, cow bells. It was an amazing sound. I was given a triangle. Not a major part. A sign of things to come.

My goal on that tour was to come back a better player. I knew I didn't have a realistic chance of making a Test appearance and that was made clear to me early on. It didn't stop me wishing and hoping and it didn't stop me getting frustrated at different times on the tour, but I knew there was much more in this for me than the honour and a jersey. The key to that was Jonny Wilkinson.

Jonny is a couple of years younger than me but in many ways he was ahead of me. He was the new superstar of English rugby and working with him on that tour opened my eyes. His work ethic was incredible. There were days when we were on the pitch from two o'clock in the afternoon until seven in the evening. The rest of the squad would be gone at five or maybe earlier but he would want to do another couple of hours after that. Neil Jenkins had dodgy knees so he didn't do the extra stuff. In that time it was just me, Jonny and the kicking coach Dave Alred. Those hours were gold.

With Jonny it was all about repetition, like a golfer on the range. He would practise the same kick over and over again – left foot, right foot. As kickers we were very different. He'd been doing it a lot longer than me, he had a system and he had much greater leg strength. I was still depending on what I had taught myself, more or less. Alred and Jonny had been working together for a while by then and their routine was the template for our sessions. I didn't have the confidence to speak up and say, 'This is what I normally do in training and this is what I need to do now.'

In that sense I was a bit like a rabbit caught in headlights. But I also didn't have such faith in what I'd been doing all along that I was going to stand up for it. My mind was open. I realized in time that if you try to copy someone you can only be as good as them. To be better you need to be different, but back then I was still learning and I needed that education.

Alred didn't try to impose his techniques on me, or tell me that what I'd been doing all along was wrong, but in a subtle way he wanted me to consider little changes. He had interesting drills and new ideas and he was very strong on theory. He wouldn't just say, 'This is the way to hold the ball for this kick', he would tell you why. To improve I needed that understanding.

Early in the tour there was a conscious effort to mix different nationalities in the rooming lists but also to build up certain relationships. Putting backs together, second row forwards together, half-backs together. In Tylney Hall I shared with Mike Catt, who I knew from a night out in Limerick after Munster played Bath. When we got to Australia I was put in with Rob Howley. I don't know how to say this without sounding like a voyeur but I'll never forget the first night when he stripped down to his Speedos to get ready for bed. The muscle definition was incredible. He was like an amateur body-builder or a sculpted greyhound. The feeling of inadequacy on my part was instant. Whatever muscles I had didn't look anything like his muscles. He told me about the supplements he took and that was another area where I was miles off the pace.

We played together in the opening match of the tour. Jonny had picked up a groin strain, Jenkins had a cut to his face from a collision with Jeremy Davidson in training and I was the only fit out-half available. We were told that everyone was going to get game time in the first two matches on tour anyway but I was glad to get in quickly. Western Australia were a team of amateurs but they were also useless – much worse than we thought they were going to be. But that didn't calm my nerves or take away from our focus. The hype about the tour was in over-drive and for the first game we were desperate to make a big impression.

We beat them 116–10, running in eighteen tries, thirteen of which I converted. I almost got in for a try too but I was stopped just short of the line. If I'd managed to get there the talk was that I would have broken the record for the highest individual score in one match by a Lions player. The fact is that I would still have been a couple of points short but that didn't matter to Austin Healy, who knocked great fun from this alleged near miss.

He made up a song to the tune of a rap hit at the time. The key line went something like, 'I wish I was a little bit taller, then I would have been the Lions' top scorer . . .' I didn't know Austin before the tour but, from a distance, he always came across as cocky. Meeting him, though, he was a fierce likeable guy and a brilliant entertainer. There was a spark to him, a bit of mischief. Over a seven-week stretch on a high-pressure trip guys like him are important.

I was the butt of some other slagging too. Most people call me Rog, pronounced Rodge, and have done since I was a kid, but with so many different accents in the squad this nickname was mangled in translation. So Graham Henry called me Roger one day, Phil Larder called me Rory and Dave Alred called me Rowan. The players got a great laugh out of this. They came up with a list of alternative names for me: Rupert, Ronnie, Reginald, Ramon, Robert, Roy, Rashid, Rex – basically anything beginning with an R. Hilarious.

A couple of weeks later everybody in the world of rugby knew my name. Nobody was laughing then.

The match against New South Wales Waratahs was the fifth of the tour. I hadn't appeared since the opening game and if it wasn't for a couple of injuries I was probably facing another evening glued to the bench, becoming more fed-up. Austin, who was also named as a replacement, injured himself in the warm-up and after twenty-seven minutes my new room-mate, Will Greenwood, did his ankle. Matt Perry was the only other back on the bench and he was a specialist number 15 so they opted for me to replace Will with Jonny moving to the centre.

Over the previous couple of weeks there had been a needle building. Not on the pitch but in the atmosphere surrounding the tour. There was still a lot of bad blood in Australia from the second Test in 1989, the so-called 'Battle of Ballymore', and all of that had been dredged up in the local media. Three prominent Australian coaches had criticized us in the press that week, accusing us of behaving illegally in the lineout, the scrum and the breakdown. We were basically being portrayed as bullies.

What we discovered at the Sydney Football Stadium was that the Waratahs had taken it upon themselves to sort us out. They made their intentions clear right away. Straight from the kick-off Danny Grewcock was flattened with an elbow to the jaw and Tom Bowman was immediately sin-binned. There were four seconds on the clock.

Fifty-three minutes later they did me.

We were attacking inside their 22, I passed to Woody and he took it up close to their 5-metre line. Two of their guys brought Woody down. One of them was Duncan McRae. As the ruck was forming I followed up and shoved him. Next thing I knew I was on the ground and McRae was pucking the head off me.

After the first dig I thought it was going to stop any second but they kept coming. Nine. Ten. Eleven. A frenzy of digs. One after another after another. I just lay there and took it. It was the weirdest feeling. Lying there I felt totally lost. Like I was in a daze. Even though he was on top of me I wasn't pinned down. I tried to protect my face with my right arm and after a couple of seconds I grabbed the back of his jersey with my left. Useless. Pointless. Why? Why didn't I try to push him off? Hit him. Something. Why did I just take it?

Two lacerations under my left eye needed eight stitches but the pain of that was nothing compared to the humiliation. Why didn't I try to defend myself? In the dressing room I was fucking raging. Raging with myself. Raging with McRae. When the game was over I wanted to go into their dressing room and have a cut off him.

Rage was useless to me then. Too late. Why didn't I hit him when he was pucking the head off me? I don't know. I still don't know.

My parents and my brother Morgan had just arrived from Ireland. That was their first match of the tour, their first sight of me in a Lions jersey. My Mum was in a heap up in the stand. Jess watched the game at home with her mother. I knew they'd be worried. It wasn't a bad injury but it looked bad.

Being thousands of miles away made it worse for Jess. Made her feel helpless. Watching the telly and sitting through the replays, looking at me leaving the field with blood streaming down my face, listening to the commentators going on about it. Waiting for me to call, knowing that she couldn't pick up the phone and reach me.

I wasn't concussed but I wasn't in my right mind either. I tried to go back on the field but that was out of the question. At least my parents could see me come out of the tunnel. Whatever state I was in at least they could see I was in one piece and raring to get back into it.

While I was being stitched in the dressing room the game had taken another turn for the worse. A big flare-up resulted in two players from both sides being sin-binned. McRae had already been sent off. For ten minutes it was 13 against 12. Farce.

When we got back to the hotel I went to my room. The lads were having a beer downstairs but I had no heart for that. Will was already in bed. His ankle was gone, his tour was over. We made small talk for a while. Dopey talk really for the sake of talking. That night we were both at a bad place in our careers.

The following morning I had to attend a hearing about the incident. Donal came with me. He said later that I looked like a Confirmation boy in my suit. Bob Dwyer was in there as well. They came up with some cock-and-bull story about McRae being provoked. The disciplinary panel didn't buy it. Donal said afterwards that they were trying to defend the indefensible and he was dead right. It was disgusting to listen to it.

McRae kept his head down for the hour that we spent in the hearing. Never once looked me in the eye. Never apologized. He could have been a man about it but he wasn't. He issued some kind of a public apology afterwards but that was worthless as far as I was concerned. The maximum suspension they could have given him was twelve weeks and they only gave him seven. There was uproar about that in the media back home but I wasn't too bothered one way or another.

Jim Williams joined Munster after that tour and he knew McRae. He said that he was a nice fella and what he had done to me was completely out of character. I have huge respect for Jim and I'd take him at his word about that. But the McRae I encountered that night and the following morning was a different person.

There was a big press conference that day and I was hauled out in front of the media. I'd done my share of media stuff over the years but this was on a scale I'd never seen before. The room was packed to the rafters: press, TV, radio, photographers. A propaganda war had been going on for a couple of weeks in the lead-up to the first Test and with the McRae incident that war had been taken on to a new level. They had accused us of being bullies and here was I with one eye nearly closed and a piece of my face swollen like a melon. For a couple of days my face was the story. For the only time on the tour I was in the middle instead of the outside.

Three days later I was named on the bench for the match against New South Wales Country. There was some talk in the papers of me wearing protective headgear but that was rubbish. I had a little patch to cover the wound under my eye and when Scott Gibbs got injured I was sent on in the centre. Jess was coming out on tour a couple of days later but she watched that game at home and she says she was terrified looking at the telly. It's always worse for the people around you. It didn't cost me a second thought and it didn't bother the Lions selectors either. They were preparing for a Test match the following Saturday and the muppets who weren't going to be involved were sent out for the Tuesday game.

I already knew my place in the greater scheme of things. When we played Australia A in Gosford two weeks earlier Neil Jenkins was taken off early in the second half and Matt Dawson replaced him. Austin Healy was moved from nine to ten and I stayed on the bench. Jenkins wasn't having a good tour and I was satisfied that I was playing better than him – even though the selectors didn't necessarily see it like that. In the pecking order of specialist out-halves Jonny Wilkinson was first and second was nowhere. In one press conference Henry said straight out that Austin Healy was the second choice out-half in the squad. Austin is a talented guy but he was brought as a utility back. I was pissed off to hear that but it wasn't a shock or anything. You always knew from the training pitch how things were panning out.

Dawson missed a couple of kicks when he came on against Australia A but his tour got a whole lot worse when he wrote a critical column in an English newspaper on the morning of the first Test. He was hauled over the coals and had to face the squad on the morning of the match. He apologized and said all the things you'd expect him to say.

The Lions won and a few days later I was picked to start alongside him against the ACT Brumbies – the Super 12 champions. Even though my goal-kicking had probably been the deciding reason why I was brought on tour in the first place it was made clear to me that Dawson was taking the kicks against the Brumbies. He was going to be on the bench for the second Test and he needed the practice. Alred has a big thing about having three front-line kickers in every match 22. In this case that was going to be Jonny, Jenkins and Dawson – regardless of what I did that night.

It was a tight match and given all the fuss over his column he was under a lot of pressure. When we were behind in the second half he missed a couple of kicks and when we got another penalty word came down from Andy Robinson that I was to take it. At that moment I could have been selfish but I actually thought of him. 'Daws,' I said, 'I'll kick it if you want but I know you can get this, come on, start concentrating.'

He took the kick and he nailed it. He comes across as a confident fella but all of us battle with doubts and he was no different. He thanked me after the match and he has said it to me a couple of times since over the years. It was the best thing I did on that tour, without doubt.

David Wallace had been called up to the squad as an injury replacement and he played in that match too. I set him up for a try with a half-break near the posts in the second half and we came flying at them in the end. Austin got over for a brilliant try in the final minute to level the scores and Dawson landed the conversion to win the match with the last kick.

I was happy with my performance that night and when the second Test was lost I thought I had a real chance of being on the bench for the decider. For the only time on the tour I went up to Henry to ask him why he kept picking Jenkins on the bench ahead of me. In fairness to him he gave me a straight answer. He said that if the Lions had a 45-metre penalty to win the Test match with a minute left he'd want Jenkins to take it rather than me.

I couldn't argue with that. Jenkins had done it on the previous Lions tour and had done it over and over again for Wales. I didn't have his record and I had yet to prove that I had his nerve.

The week of the final Test was a little bit chaotic. Howley got injured and was out of the tour, then Austin's back went into spasm and there was a huge doubt about him. Dawson was going to be in the team but if Austin didn't recover in time there was no cover for scrum-half on the bench. So they asked me if I fancied it. I was game for anything and they tried me out in training behind closed doors. As it turned out Jenkins was also crocked, which meant I was going to be on the bench one way or another. The Scottish scrum-half Andy Nicol was in Australia employed as a host with a tour operator and he was dragged onto the bench at a couple of days' notice.

In my IRFU contract there was a €10,000 bonus if I made a Test appearance for the Lions. I was slagging Hendo that he should go down injured in the last minute if we were miles behind or miles in front. No chance. The match went down to the wire and I stayed where I was. We lost.

The management took a lot of stick, not so much for losing the series but for the way the tour was handled. The perception was that we were a divided squad, over-trained, badly handled. There was a feeling that the mid-week team was not given enough attention and made to feel second-class. Some fellas did feel that, no doubt about it.

The only consolation was that we probably had the best anthem of any mid-week team in the history of the Lions. Hendo dreamed it up – one of the funniest fellas I ever met in rugby. He changed the words of the Travis song 'Driftwood' and came up with some beauties. He printed it off so that fellas could learn the words and one night in a pub in Manly he sang it with the backing of a band. Everybody thought the song was hilarious: 'We're driftwood, following the Lions, hanging on like leeches . . .'

I'm not saying the tour was perfect. I was frustrated at times too and I was glad to go home when it was over. But I never looked on it as a negative experience. This was a huge step up for me and I valued everything I learned. Looking at the English lads up close, their attitude, how they prepared, was hugely important. I came away from the tour with even more respect for them but at the same time training with them and playing with them stripped away some of the mystique too. The alternative for me that summer was playing for Ireland in Romania. What would I have gained from that?

Some fellas went to Australia with ambitions to be in the Test team and when those ambitions weren't realized they got sour and started giving out. Malcolm O'Kelly didn't enjoy it either but I had sympathy for Mal. The line-out on the midweek team suffered from neglect and I saw somewhere that his total game-time amounted to less than three matches on a ten-match tour.

The other thing was that he was picked on by the defensive coach Phil Larder. They reckoned that Mal wasn't buying into yer man's system and he was identified for special attention in a couple of video sessions. I thought it was unfair. Mal is a good friend of mine but I don't think I'm blinkered in my judgement on this one. They were over the top about Mal's so-called 'defensive frailties' and his tour was over from a long way out. He made the best of it and he was still great craic to be around but it was a long stretch when you knew there was no chance at all of being in the Test 22.

He aired some of his grievances in his *Irish Independent* column back home and then one day he arrived out for training wearing a long manager's overcoat. It was lashing rain and I followed him. Two of us doing the warm-up in a coat down to our shins. We were wearing our training gear underneath and after a while we took off the coats. I know it sounds like juvenile behaviour but long tours can do strange things to the mind and we were coming to the end of nearly two months in camp.

Nobody said anything to us. At that stage they weren't going to waste their time giving out to muppets.

CHAPTER 8

It must have been six o'clock on Sunday morning when we got back to the team hotel in Edinburgh. Jess, my half-back partner Guy Easterby and me. Working backwards the day had gone something like this: we got chips, we got drunk and we got a hiding from Scotland.

It was September 2001. The Six Nations matches called off for foot-and-mouth in the spring were being played. With two wins on the board there was a bit of hype and optimism. First up was Scotland away. Our record over there was brutal but we weren't buying into that. Then they stuffed us, 32–10.

In the hotel, thirteen hours after the final whistle, Guy had one of the Sunday papers. He turned to the match coverage and the player ratings.

'So, do you want the good news or the bad news?' he said.

'The good news.'

'We got five out of twenty between us.'

'Christ,' I said, 'don't tell me you got three!?'

At the time I thought that was hilarious. Six hours later I woke up to the grim reality with a shocking hangover. Not funny.

Guy had been taken off early in the second half and I was dragged ten minutes later. We were brutal. I was brutal. It's an awful thing to say but for once I wasn't too disappointed to leave the field. That's how bad I was. All the commentators who thought that I should never have been picked on the Lions tour ahead of Gregor Townsend had a field day. He didn't play that great either but he had a hand in their four tries and that put him way ahead of me.

The Irish papers weren't any kinder to me than the Scottish ones: Gerry Thornley in the *Irish Times* wrote that I'd had my worst game for Ireland, and probably my worst ever in a representative match. That bad. A week earlier the Irish rugby writers presented me with their Player of the Year award for the previous season. Great timing all round.

Peter Stringer had been left out of that game, dropped for the first time in his international career. In the lead-up to the match there was a lot of talk about how I would cope without him. I hated that. I always hated the suggestion that I somehow needed to play with Peter. That we had played together all our lives and couldn't be apart.

That was rubbish. I had played with a whole load of different scrum-halves at Con, UCC, Pres and Munster over the years. I'm a year older than Peter, which meant that we didn't play together that much when we were kids and hardly at all in school. I have a good relationship with Peter but we don't live in each other's pockets, on the field or off it. His absence wasn't the reason for my poor performance that day. That possibility never crossed my mind for a second.

Munster had a couple of back-to-back games in the Heineken Cup before Ireland played Wales and that gave me a chance to redeem myself. We beat Castres at home and Harlequins away and I played well both days. Really well. I got 23 points against Castres, including a drop-goal, and 16 points against Harlequins, including a flukey try and another drop-goal. I got the Man of the Match award in both matches. After the disaster against Scotland I couldn't have come up with a better response.

The only problem was that Humphs had an absolute blinder

for Ulster against Wasps just before we went back into Irish camp. He scored 37 points out of 42, an individual scoring record in the Heineken Cup. Not at Ravenhill either but over there. Unbelievable. Of course, he did it on a Friday night, as usual, which put the gun to my head the following day against Harlequins. I didn't back off the challenge but I couldn't get near him.

There was every chance that I was going to be dropped for the Wales game anyway but that put the tin hat on it. After touring with the Lions I probably believed that I was the number one Irish out-half and maybe I thought they'd give me the benefit of the doubt after one bad game. But you're only codding yourself thinking like that. With a player like Humphs around I couldn't afford the kind of cock-up I'd made against Scotland.

He's such a gentleman and such a gracious fella that you could never hate him for taking your place. In a way it would have been easier if I didn't respect him so much. In training you'd get the odd chance to tackle him and you'd try to wind him as best you could, knowing that he'd do the same to you. That was the only way I had of legitimately expressing my frustration against him.

We had kicking practice in the Millennium Stadium on the day before the match and it went badly for Humphs. He talked to me a little bit about it and I gave him as much encouragement as I could, but kicking is a personal thing and you have to find your own way around it. We went back the following day and he missed one kick from twenty-five in the warm-up. In the match he was nine from nine and we murdered them, 36–6.

After the kind of performance we had put in against Scotland there was always going to be a response. We simplified our game plan again and fellas were very fired up. If you're not one of the players involved in that response you've got a problem. For me, it lasted for the rest of that international season.

Myself and Frankie Sheahan came on for Humphs and Woody

with two minutes to go, just so the lads could get the acclaim of the crowd. Humphs had another blinder. How did I feel about that? Shit. If fellas tell you otherwise they're lying. It's a natural human reaction. We're all competitive by instinct and I'm sitting there, watching the guy who has taken my place playing out of his skin. It's not that you don't wish him well, it's not that you wish him any harm. I like him, I respect him. But when he's out there doing it you wish it was you instead.

A week later we had England in Lansdowne Road. They were going for the Grand Slam and we beat them. Woody got a great try in the first half and then after an hour Humphs got injured. I went straight on and the first thing I had to do was face a penalty. Woody came over to me, typically positive and bullish.

'You'll kick this.'

'Yeah, I will,' I said.

It was a good distance out but it was kickable. Apart from the shaking my legs felt dead. I went on with no warm-up or proper stretching. All I could do was concentrate on the technique and trust it. I dead-ducked it over the bar. An awful-looking kick. The divot went miles.

At least it meant I was straight into the match and I landed another penalty afterwards. The scenes at the final whistle were crazy. We hadn't beaten England since 1994 and the place was rocking. They blared out U2 over the public address and we did a lap of honour, lapping it up. I was able to enjoy it because I'd made a contribution. At the time I described it as the best moment of my international career, which probably sounds strange coming from a sub, but beating England was a really big deal back then.

The Taoiseach, Bertie Ahern, came into the dressing room afterwards to make a speech. Before he knew it myself and Quinny had him hoisted on our shoulders, giving him a king's chair. I don't know what came over me. We were all just buzzing.

We played Samoa a few weeks later, six days before New Zealand visited Lansdowne Road. I played well but I knew it didn't matter what I did. Humphs was going to start against the All Blacks and that was it. We blew a big chance that day. At one stage we were 21–7 in front and they still beat us 40–29. For the first time in my international career I didn't get on the field. Humphs started and finished. I was warming up at one stage, dying to get on. I understood their thinking but that didn't mean I was any less disgusted.

A few weeks later Warren was removed as Irish coach. People always think that players know about these things. That because we're on the inside we can see it coming or that we hear about it first. Most of the time we haven't a clue. I wasn't aware of any tensions between Warren and the IRFU or that he was making a bad fist of playing politics with them. I was just a player. They only tell us what they think we need to know. Most of the time that means they tell us nothing.

Warren gave me my break in international rugby and I was very grateful to him for that. We got on fine without having much of a personal relationship. He was a forwards' man and he probably saw me as a cocky young fella trying to make my way at international level. Those two things would have put a bit of distance between us. He was a lot closer to fellas like Claw and Gaillimh and Hendo, strong personalities and good characters. He enjoyed their company. Myself and Frankie would have tagged along with those boys but if Warren was with us he never let me believe that I was part of his circle. I had to serve my time and earn his respect. Fair enough.

He had a dry sense of humour but if he told a joke that wasn't remotely funny I still would have burst out laughing. A lot of fellas behaved like that with Eddie O'Sullivan in later years, but when Warren was around I was at the stage of my career when the coach's jokes were always funny. He also had a big thing about helping Rala, the bag-man. He said that if it came to a 50/50 call about team selection he'd go with the fella that helped out Rala. Did we think he was messing? Quinny and Frankie weren't taking any chances anyway. In fairness, I did a good bit of bag-carrying myself.

I got the impression that he was trying to harden me up, physically and mentally. At times he'd be cold towards me in camp and on the week of matches he always hammered it home that the other team were going to target me and I had to make my tackles. I didn't mind that either. Better for him to raise it with me before a match than for it to be an issue in the selection meeting on the following Tuesday.

They put me rooming with Humphs a couple of times as well and I think that was another test. It was funny when one of us was taking a call in the room and the question of team selection would come up in conversation. Even though it would have been the biggest single issue in our lives for those couple of days – and both of us knew that it was – you still couldn't answer that question when the other person was in the room.

You'd think it would be an impossible situation for us in match week when one of us was going to be out, but our relationship was strong enough to get over that. Humphs was a generous fella. If I was playing and he had some thoughts on the opposition or how I might approach the game, he'd share them with me. He was really sharp and I valued everything he said. He wasn't going around whispering in coaches' ears trying to advance his case. Humphs was straight up.

Then Warren was gone and Eddie O'Sullivan was in. You accept that and move on. By nature players are selfish. You might have liked the guy that's leaving or he might have been good for your career and on those terms you felt sorry for him. But you're not going to complain to the IRFU about his sacking. A new guy comes in and you start thinking of the consequences for yourself. That's the way it always is.

Eddie had been Warren's assistant with responsibility for coaching the backs. I knew him from the Ireland U-21s and from his cheeky approach to me when he was involved with the USA Eagles. The talk was that Warren and himself didn't get along. I would have known that without seeing any real evidence of it. They didn't hang around socially but there were no bust-ups in public or anything like that. Eddie's technical knowledge of the game was very good and I felt he had a lot to teach me. I never would have challenged anything he said in those days. All I was doing was listening.

The biggest knock-on consequence was that Munster were going to lose Declan Kidney and Niall O'Donovan to the Irish set-up at the end of the season. A few days before Christmas the lads broke the news to us in a room under the stand in Thomond Park where we used to hold a lot of our meetings. It probably wasn't a huge shock when you thought about it. After a few days you put it aside and get on with the matches. In this game there's always something to take your mind off the long term.

During those autumn internationals myself and Jess made an appearance in *VIP* magazine. We wouldn't dream of doing it now – for all kinds of reasons – but at the time it was harmless. Those kinds of glossy celebrity magazines were pretty new in Ireland and when they first came out they wouldn't have been interested in rugby players. But the profile of rugby was changing a lot and I remember the Wallace brothers – David, Paul and Richard – making an appearance around that time too. We shared the front page with Mary Kennedy from RTE, the TD Mildred Fox, the singer Samantha Mumba and the Irish soccer manager Mick McCarthy. We were down in the bottom corner. One of the supporting acts on the bill.

The approach came through Frank Quinn. He was handling any commercial stuff I was doing at the time and he thought it was a good idea. I had a couple of endorsement deals, including one with a clothing company called Club. The idea was that I would wear Club gear while Jess was given outfits from a boutique in Dublin.

We were photographed at the Rochestown Park Hotel and the interview was straightforward, but it's always funny to look back at old interviews and see the stuff that you were coming out with at the time. I said that I hoped to play until I was thirty. I reached that landmark in March 2007 and by then I had it in my head that I could make it to the 2011 World Cup. I also spoke about the pitfalls of being out and about in town as a well-known face.

'People are entitled to ask for autographs,' I said. 'As your profile rises you've got to be careful at times. You don't want to be caught or potentially embarrassed . . .'

Did I always remember that? No chance.

I got a bit of slagging about the photoshoot but it wasn't too bad. On the night of the Samoa match, though, Kevin Maggs caught me a beaut. At the post-match banquet players from both teams sit with each other and Jess was talking to one of the islanders at our table. Maggsy went out, got his picture from the match programme, cut it out and taped it on top of my head in one of the *VIP* photographs. Looking at Maggsy on the field you'd never think he had that creative streak in him. Another great laugh at my expense.

We hammered Wales at home in the first match of the 2002 Six Nations and I got five minutes at the end, and scored a try. Humphs came off to a standing ovation. I felt like I was a million miles away from the team and in that position you have a different perspective. More selfish.

Against England at Twickenham two weeks later we shipped a couple of injuries and I got on for Hendo at half-time. They were destroying us and the game was already over as a contest but I scored our only try and I remember coming off the field feeling quite happy. That's something you'd never say in public after the match or share with your team-mates but I can't deny the feeling. We've all trotted out the line about the team being more important than everything else but that's not the whole truth. You think of the team and you think of yourself but not always in that order. I needed to find a way back into the number 10 jersey and in that context I could look beyond the result and see a positive.

It's strange how things can pan out. Two years earlier England beat us 50–18 in Twickenham and if I hadn't hurt my knee I could have made my international debut in that game. That was a record defeat and the 2002 match was a new record. In different ways, neither match turned out badly for me. Am I not supposed to think like that? Don't be fooled. There are times when every professional player thinks like that because there are times when you must watch your own back. That's a law of the jungle.

We destroyed Scotland at home in the next match but I only played a bit-part. For the Italy game Woody was injured and Gaillimh wasn't in the squad so Humphs was made captain. That's where he stood in the estimation of the management: a senior man, a key player. I got some game time in the first half as a blood sub for Humphs and again at the end and I was happy enough because I felt I made an impact. What pleased me most was helping to set up a try for John Kelly on his international debut. Rags got another one after half-time and all the Munster lads were thrilled for him. You meet some bluffers in this game but John wasn't one of them. For years he was a huge presence in the Munster dressing room and one of the finest men I ever met in rugby.

The Italy match was also Claw's last international appearance at Lansdowne Road. In his career he played a lot of great matches on that pitch but I'll always remember something he did on the day before a Test against South Africa. Both teams were having a captain's run and we were scheduled to go on second. The South Africans, though, were late finishing their session. They were in a circle having a team talk when Claw started throwing balls in their direction. When that didn't work he walked right up to them and told them to move on, their time was up. Only Claw would have had the neck to do it and only he would have gotten away with it.

When he was taken off in the second half against Italy I was still on the bench and we made a big deal of him as he walked towards the touchline. He waved to the crowd in the stand with a grin on his face, half taking the piss out of himself. I grabbed his arm and raised it up but all that stuff wasn't his scene. There was a presentation to him at the banquet that night and he sang 'My Way' with his own words thrown in. It was obviously a party piece of his but in all the sing-songs over the years I'd never heard it before. The way it was with Claw – if he didn't want to sing he'd just tell you to fuck off and nobody would be able to twist his arm.

There were tears in his eyes when he was singing. Over the years he crossed a lot of fellas on the pitch and there's probably no point in telling those fellas about Claw's big heart. If I was packing down against Claw and meeting him in rucks I'd probably feel differently about him too, but as a team-mate he was a diamond.

Our last Six Nations match was against France in Paris. A beautiful April day, just the way they like it. They killed us. We had big expectations for this campaign but none of them were met. We won our home games but didn't play well in two of them. After Warren was shafted one of the criticisms was that we didn't have a defensive coach or a modern defensive system and that had been exposed against New Zealand. Eddie brought in Mike Ford but we still ended up leaking 45 points against England and 44 against France.

That wasn't Mike's fault. His system was very good and we were all impressed with him. He had a clear picture of every defensive scenario, he gave us print-outs for different situations, he knew what he was talking about and he was good at communicating his thoughts to the players. But this was the first time that any of us were involved in a sophisticated defensive system and the calls were all double-Dutch to us at the start. Bringing in Mike was the way forward but there wasn't going to be improvement overnight. There was no mystery to the hidings from England and France: we weren't as good as we thought we were.

The international season had been a big disappointment for me but Munster were having another good season and whatever happened with Ireland that was always my platform. There was a summer tour to New Zealand and I had to speak up and make my case. But apart from that the Munster cause stood alone. The Heineken Cup had become a huge thing in all of our minds. Not an obsession but an absolutely massive driving force. At the end of that season Deccie and Niall O' were leaving the Munster set-up, Claw was retiring, Gaillimh was coming to the end of his career and was finishing up as captain. Very soon our dressing room was going to be a different place and you couldn't be sure how different. All of that focused our minds for another push. We allowed ourselves to think that it was now or never. Rationally, that makes no sense because there will always be another campaign, but you use what you can and for the first few months of 2002 that thought fed into our motivation.

We had suffered a dip either side of Christmas and people wondered about us. It was the first year of the Celtic League and we reached the final against Leinster. The competition didn't have a sponsor and nobody was paying it much attention until that day when nearly 30,000 people turned up in Lansdowne Road. It was the first big Munster–Leinster occasion of the professional era and they beat us.

From our point of view it was a desperate cock-up. Eric Miller was sent off fifteen minutes before half-time and we went into a 9-point lead early in the second half with the wind at our backs. We couldn't lose. I remember joking with Denis Hickie, inviting him to chase one of my touch kicks into the stand. Denis is a good friend of mine and he didn't take any offence but that was our frame of mind. Half relaxed, half cocky. There was a needle in the game but that wasn't new for Munster–Leinster matches and it didn't bother us.

Then they came up with two brilliant tries and knocked us back on our arses. I'll never forget the Leinster coach, Matt Williams, going mental after the match, running up and down the side of the pitch. Rubbing our noses in it. We wouldn't have done that but I suppose it was a big deal for them at the time to win a trophy. It also prompted people to start doubting us. We'd lost another final. Some people said we were slipping – going backwards. I remember being pissed off but I don't remember being worried.

A few weeks later, in the middle of January, we played Castres away in our final pool game in the Heineken Cup and we gave our critics some more ammunition. We had beaten them by 5 points in Thomond Park and to top the pool we only had to avoid losing by more than 5 points over there. Five minutes into stoppage time we were three behind. In the last minute of stoppage time they got a try. Instead of winding the clock down and playing it tight we tried to run the ball out of our own half and they hit us on the counter. It was a brutal mistake for us to make. For an experienced, battle-hardened team it was unforgivable. We hadn't played well but we were grinding out a result and we've always prided ourselves on being able to do that. Our punishment was a quarter-final draw away to Stade Français.

They had beaten us in the semi-final the year before and there was a bit of bad blood hanging over from that. On the day before the match the tension increased. We were scheduled to have a private training session at the ground where we'd go through our lineout variations but they were slow to leave the pitch and when they finally did we spotted a guy hanging around the stand, talking into a mobile phone. Claw asked our press officer Pat Geraghty to go over and hunt yer man away. Pat had a small bit of French but it was obvious from where we were standing that lines of communication were never established. Eventually Pat grabbed yer man's phone and next thing a punch was thrown. On the bus back to the hotel we sang the theme tune from *Rocky* in honour of Pat but there was a serious side to it as well. Stade Français had tried to jerk us around and we weren't going to take it.

There was an incredibly strong wind the next day. I remember one of the dug-outs being blown away before the match started and both teams struggled in the lineout because the ball was moving so much in the wind. We had the benefit of it in the first and led 16–3 at the break after a great try from Anthony Horgan. None of us thought it would be enough. To win the match we agreed that we would need to score 14 points in the second half.

As it turned out we didn't score again and we still hung on to win by a couple of points, 16–14. Our tackling and the discipline were unbelievable. Diego Dominguez was their out-half and with that wind at his back he was liable to land penalties from 10 metres inside his own half. We sat in the dressing room for nearly two hours afterwards, totally shattered. Every year we seem to have one monster performance in January and that year that was it.

Because the quarter-finals were played in January and the Six Nations were more drawn out than they are now there was a three-month gap to the semi-final against Castres at the end of April. It was crazy when you think about it. The Celtic League was over, so without any competitive matches they organized a friendly against Leinster in Musgrave Park a week before the semi-final. On a miserable evening they held us to a draw and we were poor.

We were also dealing with the possibility of not having Claw. A couple of weeks earlier he was burning rubbish in his back garden and, basically, set himself alight. A few days later he came into training, probably looking for sympathy and got a desperate slagging for his trouble. He should have expected that. Maybe he did and he just wanted to get it out of the way.

This was our fifth time playing Castres in the last eighteen months so we had a lot of history with them. Some of it was nasty baggage. In the pool match over there one of their guys bit Claw on the arm. You could see the bite marks clearly. We brought a citing against them and on the back of video evidence Ismaela Lassissi was charged but the whole thing turned into a farce. They made a contemptible, groundless claim of racism against Claw and in the end Lassissi was cleared of the charge. Claw was desperate to play and a couple of days before the game he was passed fit. For us that was huge.

I had my own personal duel with Gregor Townsend to think about. Back then I thought about my opposite number much more than I do now because I was always measuring myself against other people. Is he better? Where am I coming up short? Over the years I had fewer worries about those questions. Fewer doubts about my ability. Back then I still had stuff to prove, to myself and to everybody else.

Between Ireland and Munster this was our third meeting of the season and by everybody's count the score was 2–0 to him. Gregor was a very talented player and on his good days he could be brilliant, but on other days he could be pretty average. I was never spooked by him. Against Castres we were going to be playing for territory a lot and trying to pen them back. Playing that game gave me an advantage.

On the bus to the ground Deccie put on the *Lion King* DVD. He showed us that film a couple of times that season. It was one of Deccie's notions. There was one scene which was basically about leaving the past behind. I think that was the message Deccie was driving at. Not all of Deccie's innovations connected with me. I didn't pay any attention to the film, although I liked Elton John's theme tune. I sang along to that all right. I have my own way of getting my head right on match days. I don't need external stuff, I don't need to shout and roar in the dressing room. A lot of fellas listen to music on the bus but I don't bother with that either. There's no right and wrong with a process like that. Whatever works.

It was a bloody tough match and we did really well to win. They were 9–0 ahead coming up to the break, having played with the wind, but then they conceded two penalties in the space of a minute. Going in at half-time only 3 points behind gave us a massive boost.

Early in the second half, I made shit of my knee. I tackled Norm Berryman in the middle of the field and ripped it on a sprinkler head. I could see the bone through the cut on my right knee. Mick Shinkwin, a man well used to stitching me, got out the staple gun and patched me up. Thirteen stitches. The pain was serious but I was able to play on. When you're pumped up in the heat of a match it's amazing what the body can take. The lads said I was roaring with pain going into a tackle late in the game. Roaring, they'll accept. Shirking they won't.

The first thing I had to do when I came back on was face a long-range penalty. I looked over at Jason Holland, who was our back-up kicker. Dutchy looked at me as if I had two heads. When the referee turned his back I moved the ball forward a metre or two and nailed it. I got another one shortly after. There was a tricky wind but I had a good kicking day: six penalties and a conversion. We were 18–12 in front when Rags sealed it with a try at the end. I got the better of Townsend too.

Job done. Another final. Leicester.

In the build-up to the final I had to answer a lot of questions about the Northampton match and the penalties I missed. I didn't duck any of the media interviews and I answered all the questions. I had already dealt with that stuff in my head a long time before. Fellas chose their words carefully when they brought it up but I knew what they were asking. Was I still haunted by it?

I said I wasn't and that's what I believed. I had performed well in a lot of big matches and pressure situations in the two years since the Northampton match. But I also knew that this was different. This was a Heineken Cup final. The questions that I had failed to answer in 2000 could only be addressed in another final.

As a group we made mistakes in the build-up to the final in 2000 and we learned from that. Our team meeting on the night before the match was short and controlled, not the emotional mess that had drained us two years earlier. And still, you can't plan for everything.

Two days before the match Anthony Horgan broke his hand and was out. It was the freakiest accident you ever saw. After arriving in Wales we had a short training session which finished with a game of tip rugby just to bring up a sweat. It was backs against forwards and it finished level. The tradition in those games is that the winners form a guard of honour to clap the losers off the field and as the lads go through they get slapped around the ass and the legs. The forwards would have considered a draw as a moral victory for them but we weren't having that so there was a race to set up the guard of honour. As he was running Hoggy swung his arm and made contact with Claw. Whatever way he did it he broke two bones in his hand. How can you explain something like that?

Hoggy was devastated. We were in school together and we've been friends for a long time. I really felt for him but what can you say to a fella in a situation like that? Words are useless. John O'Neill came in on the wing and we had to get on with it.

As has so often been the case over the years there was a big selection call to be made in the back row. Jim Williams was in his first season with us and his contribution had been immense. He was a serious player and a massive leader. An injury had kept him out of the semi-final but he was fit again and Deccie decided to keep him on the bench. I've no doubt that Jim was disgusted but in our group you have to take it. Sulking isn't tolerated. You can be disappointed for a day but anything longer than that and you're looking for trouble.

In the end the make-up of our team made no difference to the outcome. Leicester were better than us, simple as that. They got two tries and could have scored one or two more. We scored no tries and in a really big game that failure hurt us again.

Everybody made a big deal out of what happened at the end. We had a scrum under their posts and Neil Back got his hand to the ball just as Strings was about to put it in. Our supporters called Back every name under the sun but if one of our players had done that in a similar situation he'd have been a legend. In rugby cheating goes on all the time and fellas are always pushing the limits to see what they can get away with. Back did what he needed to do for Leicester to win the match. If I was in his shoes I might have done the same thing. He caught us a beaut. What people forget is that Lewis Moody tried it in the previous scrum as well and didn't pull it off. We should have been alive to it.

That wasn't the reason we lost and anyway there was no guarantee we were going to score a try from that position. We had called a back-row move that had worked for us once earlier in the season. It was an inside-outside move with Wally coming flying through the middle. It suited me because the last thing I wanted was a conversion from the sideline to win the match.

I knew Back from the Lions tour. He was very intense about his rugby and spent a lot of time in the gym but he was a good fella and we kept in touch for a few years. He asked me to write an article for his testimonial programme and only laziness stopped me from doing it. I didn't hold any grudge against him.

I played all right that day. Not brilliant – all right. I landed three penalties and I remember the relief when the first one went over. I hadn't scored in the 2000 final and the last thing I needed was a bad start. But when we were chasing the game in the last quarter I missed a couple of kicks. The roof was closed in the Millennium Stadium that day. No wind. No excuses. They were poor misses and basically my fitness didn't hold up. I remember standing over one of those penalties in the last twenty minutes feeling really tired and my technique fell apart on that kick. In a high-intensity game like that you're under completely different stress. When you're kicking, everybody else is getting a breather. You don't even get a breather at lineout time because everyone is barking at you for calls. You can go from a situation where your heart rate is up around 180 and you need to bring it right down to kick a goal. That's where fatigue takes over and that was a huge lesson for me.

By then I had also missed a tackle on Austin Healy for their second try. He was playing at number 10 and he came down the channel between me and Dutchy. I half thought that Dutchy would take him and he definitely thought I was going to take him. It was a bad breakdown in communication and Healy got through very easily. I was fingered for the cock-up and I accepted that.

Losing again was a killer and it hurt like hell but it didn't hurt like it did in 2000. Playing the way we did we had no right to win. In those situations you take consolation wherever you can find it.

Did I answer all the big questions? Not emphatically. Not in a way that made all the questions go away.

CHAPTER 9

In every career there are big turning points. Stuff that tests your character and challenges you to respond. Make or break. For me the summer tour to New Zealand in 2002 was one of those times.

Bluntly, this was it: in two Tests I kicked one penalty from eight chances. Not all of the kicks were easy but at least three of the misses were bad, pure and simple. In the first Test the All Blacks were there for the taking. We had them on the rack. They were getting cranky with each other and their body language was all wrong. I missed three kicks in that match and they got a late try to beat us by 9 points. People said my overall game was good and that was fine. The lads said they didn't blame me for losing the match and that's what you'd expect them to say. But the truth is that my missed kicks were the difference between winning and losing. I'm the kicker. I didn't do my job.

There was a lot of fuss about the ball on that tour. New Zealand had a contract with Adidas and they had brought out a new brand of yellow Torpedo ball. In the northern hemisphere everybody used the Gilbert but we knew well in advance what ball would be used on tour and we started to practise with it after the Six Nations.

I hated it from the beginning and I expressed those feelings publicly before we left Ireland. There was a huge problem with consistency: some of the balls were round and fat, others were long and thin. It wasn't just me either. The All Black out-half, Andrew Mehrtens, described the ball as a 'pig'. Woody said in one press conference that it was a 'bar of bloody soap'. But we were stuck with it for the tour and I never got to grips with it. I didn't use it as an excuse over there and I didn't criticize it once we left for home. My misses were a bigger issue than that.

I had plenty to drink on the night of the first Test. I needed to be detached from reality for a while. You know it will make tomorrow worse but you're just trying to get through today. The management tried to build me back up for the second Test a week later but in those situations you must repair yourself. I don't think I did. I didn't have the tools for that process. Mental strength is something that I always felt was part of my nature but I wasn't able to keep negative thoughts out of my mind for the second Test. I didn't back myself to pull it around and when you don't think you can do it you definitely won't.

I had four shots at goal and missed them all. In the first Test I wasn't taken off until six minutes from the end but in the second Test Humphs came on midway through the second half and some commentators felt I should have been replaced at half-time. We were 10 points down at that stage and I'd already missed two kickable penalties. By the time Humphs came on we were 20 points down. Game over.

Quinny came on just after I was taken off and was sin-binned within a minute. He was trying to get his Ireland career going at the time but indiscipline was an issue for him and he was in despair coming off the field. He sat next to me on the bench. I looked at him and started laughing. I was at one of the lowest points in my career and I just started laughing. A dopey laugh. It was totally irrational but I was too shattered and beaten up at that moment to have a rational response to my situation. New Zealand were killing us in Eden Park and we were sitting there like a pair of orphans. Quinny still talks about that. He says he could have killed me that night. He wasn't laughing. His despair hadn't got to that point.

When we got home I went to Crete with Jess for a couple of weeks but I couldn't rest. I couldn't get the tour out of my mind. I had to talk to someone about it so I rang Woody. He was strong on the mental side of the game and he told me I had to confront it. If I tried to forget it or sweep it under the carpet the demons would come back. My dad is a big believer in sports psychology and he had given me books down the years. I understood that the mental side of the game was vitally important but I felt I could handle it myself. I did one session with Dr Aidan Moran in University College Dublin years before and I thought it was very interesting but I didn't go back for more. After New Zealand, though, I knew that I needed help.

I raised it with Eddie O'Sullivan and he put me in touch with a sports psychologist in Limerick called P. J. Smith. We met for three or four sessions and I poured my heart out to him. Goal-kicking was occupying all my thoughts before matches and it was draining my confidence. I had to get on top of it. I had to find a way of separating it from the rest of my game. I had to find a way of controlling it.

We talked a lot about the power of visualization and I really embraced that. My pre-shot routine was home-made and pretty basic. This was something more sophisticated and solid. A big part of it was picturing a smaller target behind the posts and visualizing the ball passing through that. It meant that if you didn't strike it sweetly you still had 3 metres either side of your imaginary target to get the ball through the posts. When I was practising I would make the imaginary target quite small so that on match days the real target would seem a lot bigger. I adapted the techniques to suit myself and then I settled on a routine. The structure gave me comfort and over the years I've stuck with it. I go through it now in fractions of a second. I don't have to stop and consciously follow the steps. When I'm getting ready for a kick my mind slips into auto-pilot.

I never believed that nerve was the issue. I suffered in the Heineken Cup final against Northampton but I didn't shirk it. I wasn't a bottler. I didn't buy everything that P. J. said to me because I didn't think I needed all of it. I wasn't mentally weak. But I needed something. Something new, something extra. Like a dietary supplement, except that this was feeding my mind.

In the first week of September Munster had a Celtic League match against Llanelli in Stradey Park. It was my first game since the New Zealand tour and Ireland had a Test match against Romania a week later. Humphs had scored 14 points for Ulster the night before and Eddie was in Wales to watch our match. Of course, he was looking at other players too but I knew he was watching me.

I was under pressure to deliver a performance and I did. I landed five penalties from five attempts, played a 50-metre cross-kick for Mossy Lawlor to score our try and narrowly missed the conversion from the touchline. My punting was good and I controlled the game. Ticked all the boxes. I looked nothing like the haunted figure that tormented Quinny on the bench in Eden Park. The relief was enormous. I was back.

It was twelve months to the 2003 World Cup in Australia and I was facing into a season-long battle with Humphs. He turned thirty-one that month but he was playing as well as ever. Because we had to pre-qualify for the World Cup we were scheduled to play fourteen matches that season. Eddie knew that he didn't need to commit to me or Humphs and that's the way he liked it. He wanted us to compete for the jersey and drive each other on. He kept saying in public that there was nothing between us and what he said to us in private was no different. The stats backed him up: in the previous three seasons Humphs had started in thirteen Tests and I had started twelve. Both of us had a crap record of finishing games that we'd started and that pattern showed no sign of changing.

A week after the Llanelli match I was named for the Romania Test in Thomond Park. I took it as a vote of confidence. New season, blank page.

The place was only half-full, the atmosphere was dead, we couldn't get the ball off them in the second half and nobody was excited about a 39–8 victory. Nobody was excited about what was coming next either: a 6,000-mile journey across seven time zones to the Siberian city of Krasnoyarsk for a World Cup qualifier against Russia. Nightmare.

Martin Murphy, a good man who works for the union, was the liaison man and he had been over there on a recce mission during the summer but everything about the trip was the opposite of what he said it was going to be. He said the food would be lovely, our mobile phones would work, we wouldn't suffer from jet lag: wrong, wrong, wrong. It was so bad that it was funny. He got some slagging. One of the lads made up a song but I can only remember a line from the chorus: 'There's only one Martin Murphy, walking along, getting it wrong, walking in a Russian wonderland.'

They were a tough outfit and they had a butty little centre who ran straight at me all day. He was wearing flanker's boots and he was the shape of a table, about three foot tall and three foot wide. He had no intention of passing the ball and Maggsy let me at it. After about an hour I roared at him, 'Maggsy, will you fucking hit him.' He just laughed at me.

A week later we had Georgia in Lansdowne Road and it was the same caper. They had a monster centre who could also play second row or flanker. We murdered them but he went through me for their only try. Maggsy didn't want to go near the beast and my tackle was weak. The technical term for my body shape in that tackle is 'the toilet position' because I was sitting back.

Criminal. Yer man steamrollered me. I was doing a lot of work with Mike Ford on my defence at the time and that try didn't do me any favours.

In fairness, Maggsy apologized straight away. I used to love playing with him. He was a brilliant bloke, great craic, and his heart was incredible. Like John O'Neill with Munster you could throw him any kind of ball and he wouldn't complain – he'd make the best of it and bosh it up the middle. I can remember about a dozen team meetings on the night before an international when there were tears in his eyes while he was speaking to the group. You don't see much of that any more and I think we're poorer for it. Maggsy grew up in England and he spoke with an English accent and probably because of all that he used get fierce wound up for matches against England. Every last ounce of his passion came out in those games. We're still in touch but I miss him around the place.

He played against Australia when they came to town for the autumn internationals a couple of months later and that was one of the best days we shared in an Irish jersey. People have probably half forgotten the thrill of beating them that day. As the years went on we kept raising the bar for ourselves and the public's expectation got bigger. But when Australia toured with a full-strength squad in 2002 Ireland hadn't beaten them for twenty-three years. The conditions were desperate that day in Lansdowne Road, which would have suited us more than them. They had lost over in Argentina and they seemed a bit beaten up and tired when they got to Dublin. But we still had to go out and do it.

It was a dream game for me. I landed six penalties from six shots at goal and I kicked really well out of the hand. I felt like I was in total control. In the rain the plan was to punch them around the park and keep them on the back foot. It was like playing for Munster and we won 18–9. I had produced other good performances for Ireland but this was against the world champions and I had played with authority. It felt like a step up.

I didn't reach that level against Argentina two weeks later but we won again and I landed four kicks from four shots. In ten competitive games since the start of the season my stats were 54 from 66.

New Zealand was buried. Moving on.

With Munster we were starting all over again. Deccie was gone and Alan Gaffney was the new coach. Gaillimh was still in the squad but he had stood down as captain and Jim Williams took his place, elected by a secret ballot of the players. Claw was gone. Marcus Horan and Donncha O'Callaghan were stepping up.

I welcomed the change. I was twenty-five now and Deccie had been my coach since I was fourteen. On the way up he had been a huge influence on my development and I'm forever grateful to him for that. He backed me, challenged me, promoted me, improved me. But it had reached the stage where I needed to hear a new voice and a different perspective. After eleven years there was nothing new Deccie could say. We might not always agree but underneath there's a respect. When somebody has been your schoolteacher first I suppose there'll always be a certain distance. I can be a cranky bastard at times and that contributed to a few arguments between us but we never had a falling out. His biggest strength was getting a team in the right frame of mind for big games but over time that was something I managed myself.

Alan came in and looked at us differently. He felt that our ball skills needed to be improved and he was right. We did a lot of drills in training that gave us the confidence to play a different game. More expansive. Not mad expansive but more varied, more ambitious. In the previous three years Munster's success had been based on cup rugby. We had a big man at 12 who set targets for our forwards to run off and then we drilled the ball to the corners.

That way of playing had gotten us to two Heineken Cup finals but it wasn't good enough to win either of them. In the knock-out stages of the 2002 competition we had scored two tries in three matches and one of those was in the last minute against Biarritz when the game was virtually won. We weren't going to win the Heineken Cup if we didn't score more tries.

We couldn't keep on doing the same thing and coming up short. We had to try something different. The transition was going to be difficult and a lot of our supporters didn't like it but there was no dissent among the players. We had to find a way of playing a more rounded game.

Alan was very strong on video analysis too and I felt the benefit of that. Back play was his speciality and he suggested things to me that made my game better. He was good on passing techniques and the kind of detail that makes a difference.

I enjoyed working with him but during his three years with us feelings towards him in the Munster squad were divided. Our pool of players wasn't as deep then as it is now and when the internationals were away in camp Munster struggled for results. Those players left behind felt that Alan took out his frustrations on them. They were beasted in training during the week and then given a really simple game plan at the weekend because he didn't think they were capable of executing anything more complex. The morale of the Celtic League team became poor after a while. Then we'd come back from Irish camp and it was all smiles again. All I could do was take him as I found him and he was good for me.

We had a tough pool in the Heineken Cup, which made it difficult for us win matches while trying to redefine the way we played. We lost to Gloucester at Kingsholm and put in a shocking second half away to Perpignan in our second-last pool match. There was silence in the dressing room for twenty minutes afterwards. Those two defeats meant that we went into our last game against Gloucester needing to score four tries and win by 27 points.

We were made aware of the maths early in the week but all we were doing was aiming to win. A lot of our thoughts that week were about saving face. The Perpignan performance had been embarrassing, Gloucester were top of the English Premiership and there was a real fear that we could lose our unbeaten record at Thomond Park in the Heineken Cup. It turned out to be one of the greatest days we ever had.

The forwards were really pumped up. One of the Gloucester pack had said in an interview during the week that he was looking forward to playing in Thomond Park. He probably thought it was a harmless remark but the lads chose to take offence. As far as they were concerned it was disrespectful.

We didn't go looking for tries straightaway. Instead we went back to basics. Thomond Park Terrorism. Henry Paul was their full-back and the plan was to bomb him with garryowens. I had studied videos with Alan and we thought their back three were vulnerable so that was our first route of attack.

Do you remember when you were a kid the sound you made when you were playing Indians? Whoawhoawhoa!! That's how Quinny describes the noise in Thomond when a garryowen goes up and the charge is on. Before we went out on the field against Gloucester that's the last thing he said to me: Don't forget the Indians. Plenty of Indians.

I miskicked the first one, which made it worse for Paul. It was a horrible kick that wobbled and shook in the air. He couldn't get his bearings and made the huge mistake of allowing the ball to bounce over his head. Normally a miskick wouldn't give the boys time to get up on the full-back but Paul was in such a mess that Mickey Mullins and Jason Holland hammered him the second he gathered possession. Paul was rattled and we didn't let him off the hook.

For me that match summed up the challenge of playing out-half for Munster. We needed tries but we needed to win the match first and we needed to keep the crowd revved up. I've always had to strike a balance between pleasing the forwards and not pissing off the backs. When I kick it to the corners Hayes or Frankie or Quinny or Axel or somebody from the pack will come over and say, 'Well done,' and then two seconds later I'll hear a shout from Mickey Mullins or Shauny Payne: 'That was on outside…' I like spinning the ball out to the backs but the thing I've enjoyed most is pleasing the forwards. Without them we're going nowhere.

We had two tries in the bag by half-time and then we turned to play towards the scoreboard end. Nobody talks about a scoring end in Thomond Park but if there is one that's it. The breeze is usually blowing that way and whatever little slope there is in the pitch falls to that end. Maybe it's all in my head. The third try came after an hour but the fourth try didn't come until the last minute. The usual panic.

For us to win by 27 points I needed to land the conversion but I wasn't clued into that. We had discussed the numbers at the start of the week but it didn't really come up after that. We didn't want that to be a distraction. There was such pandemonium after the fourth try that I thought we were home and dry. Because of a sloppy article in the match programme there was a certain amount of confusion in the crowd about what we actually needed to do to qualify but plenty of people were on the ball too. Jess was sitting next to her granddad in the stand and the whisper around her was that I had to get the conversion. She couldn't look.

I treated it like any other kick. In my new regime every kick was equal. Earlier that season I had missed a couple of second-half kicks against Romania in Thomond when the game was over and my concentration had dipped. I took some criticism for that and people were right to raise it. Giving every kick the same attention was a mental issue and when I settled on a pre-shot routine that year I didn't change it from one kick to the next. That was my creed from then on. That conversion mattered to me and my standards. I can't claim nerves of steel on that one because I was oblivious to the wider consequences.

Anyway, over it went. Mayhem.

We stayed in Limerick after the match and had a right session. Claw's pub was the usual venue for those big nights and then we went downstairs to his nightclub, the Sin Bin. Inside, I met Henry Paul. Even though I had a few drinks on board I had enough cop on not to rush up to him. Enough of his day had already been spent dealing with Munster players rushing up to him. I was a bit cagey but he was friendly in fairness. We had a nice drink together and a chat. It was a cool end to a perfect day.

A couple of weeks later we played Neath in the final of the Celtic League at the Millennium Stadium. The competition wasn't a big deal in itself but at the same time we couldn't afford to lose. Between the Celtic League and the Heineken Cup we had lost three finals in the previous two seasons. If we lost again the people who believed we were chokers would have been able to shout it from the rooftops. As it turned out Neath were useless and we stuffed them by 20 points.

About twenty-five minutes into the game I had to go off. Brett Sinkinson stamped on my ankle at a ruck. Really did me. I was disgusted. I had already landed four penalties and I was flying. The Welsh Rugby Union banned Sinkinson for six weeks and in the end I was out for nearly as long. An hour and a half after the match I was carted off to hospital for an X-ray. They put me in an ambulance, which was totally over the top and a source of great amusement to the lads. There was nothing broken. It was badly bruised and back home later they discovered some ligament damage, but I didn't think I'd be out for any more than ten days or two weeks.

The first game of the Six Nations was only a fortnight later and that should have been uppermost in my mind. Instead, I behaved like an amateur. I was given crutches at the stadium but when drink took over back in Limerick later that night I discarded the crutches and joined in on the dance floor. It was reckless carry-on for a professional rugby player and I paid the price. I missed the first two games against Scotland and Italy, Ireland won handy both days and Humphs was outstanding.

I made a comeback with Cork Con in early March but I didn't get a run when we beat France the following weekend. On the weekend after that I found myself in a strange place. Rephrase that: I put myself in a strange place.

The papers were full of a story that I had been approached by the Miami Dolphins to be their kicker. The *Evening Echo* in Cork had heard a rumour and rang me for a comment. I didn't deny it. In fact, I threw coal on the fire. I was trying to be cute. Smart. I was in the final year of my IRFU contract and I knew Humphs was on a good bit more money than me because he had turned down offers from abroad. Without thinking about it too deeply I saw this as a chance to up the ante.

How did the rumour start? Probably with a handshake and a bit of banter in the restaurant of the Old Head of Kinsale Golf Club. Jess's Dad is a director of the club and most of the members are overseas residents. Wayne Huizenga, the owner of the Miami Dolphins, is one of them. I was in the restaurant with Jess and her dad and we were introduced to Mr Huizenga. There was a bit of small talk and that was it. Obviously, though, somebody saw us and jumped to conclusions. Cork is a small place and starting a rumour is the easiest thing in the world. Back then, I suppose, I didn't have the same appreciation of that as I do now.

On a Saturday morning a couple of weeks later I got a phone

call from the *Evening Echo*. They had heard that the Miami Dolphins were interested in me and instead of telling them the truth I told them what they wanted to hear: 'I have spoken to them on the phone,' I said, 'and I am expecting further contact. There is a lot to be discussed, including their set-up and how many kickers they have on their panel.'

The *Echo* hit the streets of Cork at lunchtime and I was playing a home match for Con against Carlow in the All-Ireland League that afternoon. When the match was over I was collared by a reporter to comment further and, stupidly, I kept the story going.

'I was flabbergasted when I received the call,' I told him. 'This happened a few weeks ago and I am very surprised that news has gotten out. I haven't given it too much thought but you can never say never. The World Cup is my goal but you can never rule anything out. It's something that I may consider later in my career. Things are very hectic for me right now. My discussions with the owners of the Miami Dolphins were very basic and they're only in the initial stage. I was born in Sacramento and I watch the sport on television but I've never played or kicked a ball. There might be discussions at a later date. It may be an option but I want to put it aside for a while.'

All of the Sunday papers picked up on it and some of the tabloids put it on their front page. They went to town. One of them said that the Dolphins had offered me $12 million a year. Another one said I'd be on $100,000 a week. The whole thing had gotten out of hand. Madness.

When I turned on my phone after the Con match there was a message from Eddie O'Sullivan. 'What's this shit I'm hearing?' was the gist of it. I called him and he held his fire on the phone but I guessed that he was steaming. The Irish squad were going into camp the following night and I was summoned to Eddie's room. The manager, Brian O'Brien, was there as well and they weren't happy. I told them exactly what had happened and we agreed that we needed to put out the fire quickly. A statement was pulled together and issued to the media. The story limped on in the papers for a few days, as if they didn't entirely believe the statement or they didn't want to believe it. I could have stopped all of it before it started. My fault. Lesson learned. Stupid. End of story.

Then came the slagging. A golden opportunity for the comedians. They started calling me Flipper, as in Flipper the dolphin. It didn't stop there. At the end of training later in the week they set up a line of scrimmage, like in an American football match, and made me stand behind it to kick the ball. Beautiful.

Back in the real world Ireland were chasing a Grand Slam. Our fourth match was away to Wales and they were having a brutal season. Nobody expected us to lose but we nearly blew it. Humphs was picked to start again. His form was good and I was coming back from an injury but that didn't stop me from feeling frustrated. When I came back into the squad for the France match Eddie told me the deal straight out: he regarded the matches against France, Wales and England as a series, Humphs was the man in possession and unless he got injured or lost form badly I was going to be back-up.

As far as I was concerned I'd done enough in the autumn internationals to consider myself the first choice out-half. Had those performances been forgotten? Did they not count for anything? Did that contribute to the whole Dolphins thing? Yeah, probably. One way or another we all like to be wanted. I'm not proud of that.

I didn't express my disappointment to anybody but by the Wales match I was starting to feel a little bitter. There was no harm in that as long as it didn't get on top of me. Bitterness was an emotion I could control.

The match was a cliffhanger. When I came on with ten minutes left Wales had just scored a try and we were only a point up. I was dying to get on. I remember feeling giddy on the bench that day. Not joking or fooling or anything but really pumped up. I had a sense that something good was going to happen. There's no point trying to explain a feeling like that. Donncha was sent on at the same time as me. It was his first cap and he was planking himself on the bench with nerves. He sprinted across the field to a line-out on the far side. There wasn't that much of a hurry but he was all fired up. It was eighteen years to the day since his father died and it was a hugely emotional thing for him.

It looked like we were going to hang on until Stephen Jones dropped a great goal in the first minute of injury time. I looked over at Brian O'Driscoll and he was so exhausted he couldn't talk. I went up to Steve Lander the referee and asked him what was left. I had to badger him for an answer and eventually he said two minutes.

Malcolm O'Kelly asked me what I was going to do with the restart but it wasn't really a question because he was going to tell me anyway. He said stick it on the 15-metre line. We needed to recover the ball and to give the boys any chance I needed to get three or four seconds of hang-time on it. I was so pumped up that I over-cooked it by about 10 metres but Mal made a brilliant surge to get there and tap it back on our side. Donncha secured it, then Strings picked it up and flung it out to me. I was expecting the Welsh back row in my face but they weren't. I was 40 metres out but I was in space so I chanced the drop-goal. It felt like a good connection but when I looked up it was an ugly, wobbly kick. Somehow it got there. My first drop-goal for Ireland.

I don't normally celebrate when I score but I jumped up and punched the air. It wasn't just the importance of the score. It was weeks of bottled-up frustration pouring out.

It still wasn't over. Justin Bishop deliberately knocked on a Welsh pass in front of our posts and the referee played advantage instead of giving them a match-winning penalty. Jones attempted another drop-goal but Denis Hickie made an unbelievable block and by then Lander had called advantage over.

Game over. Out of jail.

The upshot was that we had England in Lansdowne Road eight days later in a shoot-out for the Grand Slam. There was a lot of debate in the papers about who should start at out-half but I didn't get the impression from Eddie that he was agonizing over it. He had made his mind up. Humphs was the man in possession and he kept the jersey.

The hype that week was unreal. I don't think it got to fellas. When you're a sub you don't feel the same anxiety anyway but I didn't see any tell-tale signs in fellas' faces. That was the day England lined up on the wrong side of the red carpet to meet the President and the English captain Martin Johnson refused to move. He got massive stick over it but if I was in his position I'd have done the same thing. Their attitude that day was, 'not an inch'. If he moved it would have looked like they were backing down before a ball was kicked.

After that they killed us. I came on for Humphs after an hour but there was only one out-half on the pitch that day and he was wearing white. Wilkinson was awesome. Two drop-goals in the first half, one with either foot. Class. I was only on the field a minute when Will Greenwood steamrollered me close to our line. Half a dozen English lads piled in behind him and Denis Hickie threw himself in with me. You can guess the outcome.

That English team were at the peak of their powers. We were after having a good season but we were nowhere near them.

Getting back with Munster was like beginning the season again. The prize for cheating certain death against Gloucester in our last pool match was more certain death, away to Leicester in the quarter-final. They were going for three titles in a row in Europe and in domestic competitions they had lost only once at Welford Road in sixty matches. Stack all that on top of the memory of losing to them in the final the year before and you had a perfect Munster cause.

Like England at Lansdowne we didn't take a backward step. Leicester had class players but they also traded on aggression and intimidation: physical and verbal. We were prepared for that and ready to confront it.

My old pal Austin Healy was at number 10 for them. I liked Austin from the Lions tour but you had to know him. After Leicester beat us in the Heineken Cup final in Cardiff there was a reception for both teams in the stadium afterwards. Myself and Jess were walking down the corridor towards the reception room when we bumped into him. You'd imagine that he'd be sensitive in a situation like that – we were after losing for the second time in three years and, naturally, we were devastated. Instead he came out with some smart comment that probably would have been funny in different circumstances. Jess couldn't believe it but that was just the way he was. He was an in-your-face kind of guy. That's the way he played and that's the way he behaved. For all that I liked him.

He had a hard time against us in Welford Road. He had struggled with injuries that season and wasn't himself. To make things worse Rob Henderson smashed him in a tackle midway through the second half that left him in bits. They had just scored a try and Hendo had been at fault. He was fuming. They had a scrum and we half expected Austin and Leon Lloyd to do a switch. Hendo said to me he was going to nail Austin if they tried it and he was true to his word. Hendo's tackle was so violent that Austin collided with Lloyd and they both hit the floor. Austin was groggy, his knee was hurt and they called for a stretcher. Next thing he got up and insisted on continuing. Typical Austin. Even when we put him down he refused to accept that he'd been put down.

It was a big mistake. We had a scrum just inside our half and we had a move designed to target his area. We went straight for him. He missed a tackle on me and when I made the break there was plenty of support. Hendo, Mickey Mullins, Axel, Frankie, Quinny and Marcus were all involved before the ball returned to me for the try. Austin missed two tackles in that move. Once we scored they took him off. I landed the conversion to put us 13–7 in front and after that we were in control.

A few minutes later Strings got another try at the end of another lovely move. Beating them was great but doing it in style was really satisfying. Eleven months earlier we never looked like scoring a try against them in the Heineken Cup final; now we'd scored two at Welford Road.

For the semi-final against Toulouse in Toulouse we were going to need more tries. And they just weren't there. Over the years the south of France was where we learned our lessons and earned our spurs. Beating them in Bordeaux in 2000 was one of the best days Munster had ever had but there was no repeat. Only familiar bloody heartbreak.

They didn't take the lead until five minutes from the end, when Jean-Baptiste Elissalde got over in the corner and landed the conversion from the touchline. We had fought like dogs to get in front and stay in front and Toulouse had made a lot of mistakes, but we needed a try and we needed a bigger cushion going into the last few minutes. We pounded them in the first half but we couldn't get over the line. Same old problem.

I had landed two penalties and two drop-goals and we suddenly needed another one to save the match. But we didn't have a set move that was designed to create a drop-goal opportunity and Alan gave out to himself about that afterwards. As the clock wound down I had a couple of pot-shots from long range. No good.

Beaten again. By a point. Again.

Jim got us into a huddle on the pitch afterwards. Usually I don't remember much about what goes on in those huddles. You're half listening but you're not really taking it in. Jim, though, was really impressive. He grabbed everyone's attention and held it. In other years there would have been a lot of tears in the circle but Jim made sure we didn't feel sorry for ourselves. He was incredibly positive. By nature he's a fairly quiet fella but when he's wound up he's got a booming voice that can be frightening. He was roaring at us to keep our heads up, that we'd come back better.

Nobody was going to lose the faith. That faith is a big part of what we are. People were asking how we were going to come back from this. What else were we going to do?

CHAPTER 10

Me and Eddie had words. I was talking, he was listening. On our summer tour we had just beaten Tonga, 40–19, in desperate conditions. The heat was mad, the pitch was like a car park and it was coated in powdered coral. That stuff was lethal. Somebody said it was like taking a cheese grater to your skin. They got a brilliant start, the crowd was going bananas and when they had their blood up playing at home they were hard to beat. We had about half of our first-choice team and I thought we did really well to come back from 11 points down and put them away.

Fellas were pretty shattered in the dressing room. We'd broken our balls out there and next thing Eddie comes in and gives us a bollocking. In his eyes that performance wasn't good enough. Everybody was stunned. I was pissed off.

I held my tongue in the dressing room but when we went back to the hotel I asked to speak to him. I'd never done something like this before with Ireland but I was around long enough now and I would have regarded myself as a senior player on the team that took the field that day. I decided that I should behave like one. Over the years I'd had a pretty open relationship with Eddie. Plenty of fellas had difficulty talking to him but I never did. I didn't eat the head off him or anything but I told him that I thought he was wrong to say what he'd said in the dressing room. I told him that it was over the top and bad for morale.

In fairness to him he didn't argue. He accepted my point of view, called a team meeting in the hotel and apologized to the players. It was a big gesture from him and the right thing to do. Everyone's mood picked up straightaway. We had one game left against Samoa and that wasn't going to be comfortable either. At the end of a ten-month season everyone needed to be on board and in the right frame of mind.

The first match of the tour had been against Australia. My form for Munster in the knock-out stages of the Heineken Cup did nothing to change Eddie's mind about the number 10 jersey. Humphs started for the sixth game in a row and in Woody's absence he was the captain too.

We were only a point down at half-time when Humphs went off injured and I came on. In the second half, though, Australia killed us: 45–16 was the final score, six tries to one told the full story. We folded a bit in our patterns and they got a couple of breakaway tries. Soft. We weren't the same team away from Lansdowne Road and that reflected badly on us. O'Driscoll was missing too and the brutal reality was that Woody and Drico were our only world-class players back then. We had plenty of good players but we didn't have the strength in depth of the top teams. Nowhere near it.

With the World Cup only a few months away Eddie was wrapping players in cotton wool. Eight lads went home after the Australia game and I had the option to join them. I stayed. Eddie's mind mightn't be changed by anything I did against Tonga and Samoa but I needed to believe that it could be.

I had broken the scaphoid bone in my hand against Tonga but that's a weird injury because it doesn't show up for about ten days. There was no sign of it on the X-ray after the match and with a week of ice-baths and good physio I started against Samoa.

The biggest problem that day wasn't my hand but the heat:

98 degrees with crippling humidity. The red-haired lads were in fierce trouble. Hoggy got heat stroke and he had to go off early in the second half. Jonny Bell was struggling with it too. Of course, Psycho O'Connell lasted the distance. They'd have had to shoot him to get him off. At half-time I was incredibly cranky. I was freaking at the thought of having to go out again in the second half. It felt like there was no oxygen and we were only a couple of points ahead. Murder. We had a recovery session in the pool later on and I couldn't stop myself from puking. I probably took liquids on board too quickly and my system was all over the place. Fried, probably.

We stuck at it well in the second half, though, and pulled away to win 40–14. I ended up with 32 points: two tries, two conversions, five penalties and a drop-goal. Guy Easterby made up a story that I shouted 'Bingo' when the drop-goal went over – as in a full house. Complete lie but the lads loved it. Guy was brilliant for taking the piss.

I'm glad I stayed. The tour had been good for me. Those games against Tonga and Samoa were a real mental challenge in hostile conditions and we came through it. I felt like a leadership figure for probably the first time in my Ireland career and I enjoyed the responsibility.

Humphs, though, was still in pole position for the World Cup and I failed to put any pressure on him in the warm-up games. After the tour I needed to have a pin inserted in my scaphoid, which meant that I missed the matches against Wales and Italy at the end of August.

The Italy match was in Thomond Park and I watched it from the terraces with Quinny. The comedian Pat Shortt was near us and I goaded him into saying something funny. He turned the tables on me a beaut, torturing me about Humphs. The crowd around by us were in stitches. Ireland hammered them and

Humphs played a beautiful reverse kick for Denis Hickie's try. As a professional player being injured is the loneliest place in the world. Watching that didn't improve my humour.

I got back for our final warm-up game against Scotland at Murrayfield but I didn't get up to the pace of the game until about the last twenty minutes. By then Geordan Murphy's World Cup was over before it started, destroyed by a broken leg. The squad was being announced the following morning and other fellas were going to be shattered in a different way.

David Wallace was touch and go. He played well against Scotland and I thought they had to bring him. We flew into Dublin after the game and there were a couple of carloads of Munster players going south. We stopped off in Naas for a couple of pints and we kept telling Wally that they couldn't leave him behind. But they did. The following morning he got the news. It's hard to believe it now with the rugby he's played for Ireland in the last few years.

I've known Wally since we played for Munster schools. As friends we've gone on holiday together and as rugby players I'm his biggest fan. I've always rated him. He has freakish power when he gets those legs pumping and his pace over the first 20 metres is incredible. It's a matter of opinion of course but I haven't seen a better number 7. When the All-Ireland League was a much bigger deal than it is now there was talk of trying to lure Wally to Con and I definitely encouraged it. Frankie Sheahan used wind it up as well every chance he got but that was more slagging. I was serious. Garryowen was his club but his parents live in Cork and that's where he spent part of his childhood. I think he enjoyed the courting and flirting and at one stage a signing on fee of ten grand was on the table – which was huge. It might even have been more than his Munster contract at the time. He didn't bite though. He stayed loyal to Garryowen. They looked after him too.

I said once that to get the best out of Wally I needed to dominate him. He doesn't accept that. We would discuss what needed to happen in certain situations on the field and sometimes those discussions would get a bit heated. My nickname for him now is NW – 'Never Wrong'. He doesn't like that but he can't have it every way. If he's wrong some of the time why can't I win some of the arguments? He should have been picked for that World Cup but I guess I'm biased.

In professional rugby four years is a long time. Preparation keeps changing, which doesn't mean that we get it right these days and got it wrong in the past. We had three matches against Test nations in the space of four weeks before the 2003 World Cup and all of our front-rank players were exposed to those games. There was no question that we were going to lack match practice or match sharpness.

Our stated goal within the squad was to reach the quarter-finals and then reassess. Ireland had failed to get that far in 1999 and we weren't getting ahead of ourselves. Four years later that level of goal-setting would have been unacceptable but in 2003 we didn't even have a Triple Crown to our credit.

Another big difference between 2007 and 2003 was that we had a brilliant team base in Australia. We were in Terrigal, a coastal town, and the hotel was fifty yards from the sea. That was our playground. After training we'd cool off with a dip and we chanced our arm at surfing. We got lessons but Paulie O'Connell couldn't wait to master it. He took off in search of the big wave and after half an hour he'd broken his surfboard. The instructor couldn't believe it: 'I've been surfing thirty years,' he said, 'and I've never broken a board. This guy has been surfing for thirty minutes!'

There was a good gym on site and lovely cafés and restaurants up the street. We must have been there for three weeks waiting for the games to start but it never felt tedious. We were fresh and relaxed and happy. If those things are missing no amount of technical back-up or physical preparation can make up for them.

Humphs was picked to start the first match against Romania. We won well and he played well. I got my chance against Namibia in the next pool match. Our plan was to play a quick rucking game and spin the ball out but it lashed out of the heavens and those plans were shelved. Eddie said he wanted Munster cup rugby, punching the ball around the park. We won handy again. Argentina were next.

From the second the pools were announced everybody knew that was going to be the pivotal game of our World Cup. The defeat to Argentina in Lens during the 1999 tournament was a massive low point in the history of Irish rugby and that was hanging over us too. Everybody expected Australia to qualify as the top team from our pool and the second quarter-final spot was going to be decided between us and Argentina.

Humphs started for the tenth time in thirteen Tests that year. I had convinced myself that I had a chance, that I had done enough against Namibia. After the team was announced I was in a world of my own for that training session. It took me a day to get over it, which is a long time on tour. I was sick to my stomach of being a sub and fed up of telling myself that I was better than him. I put real pressure on myself for the Argentina match. I wasn't nervous in the usual way: I was psyched. If I came on – when I came on – I had to deliver. I had to prove to myself all the things that I was tired of telling myself. The way I saw it I was going out there to defend my reputation.

Watching the game from the stand you could see that the tension had gotten to us and some fellas were going around like zombies. We were nervous, edgy. When I came on sixteen minutes into the second half we were a point in front and the game was in the balance. I thought we were doing things in slow motion. There wasn't enough intensity or pace, there wasn't enough talking. It looked to me as if we were waiting for Lens to happen all over again. Humphs didn't look happy about coming off. I know how that feels too.

I was wound up. I called the backs into a huddle. I thought they'd been lifeless. I said whatever happens just make sure we can look each other in the eye after the match. I started shouting at everybody. Most of it was the usual stuff that you hear all the time but I said a strange thing to Victor Costello: I told him that his dad was watching, do this for your dad. I'm not sure when his dad had died but I remember reading an interview with Victor when he spoke about what an influence his dad had been and how much he missed him. I don't know how that came into my head but it probably shows how emotional I was. I apologized to him afterwards because I was worried that I had gone too far and caused him offence, but he was cool about it. He said that it was a great thing to hear.

In play the first thing I did was lose the ball in contact. The second thing I did was fail to find touch. Their full back, Ignacio Corleto, gathered the ball and dropped a goal from 45 metres out, near the touchline on a wet night. Unbelievable strike. That was my initial impact. All talk.

A couple of minutes later we got a penalty. It was a pressure kick and I nailed it. Five minutes later I got another. We were hanging on by a point at the end but we won. I was happy with myself. I knew I'd made a difference.

The big downer was Quinny. He scored a brilliant try in the first half but dislocated his shoulder in the process and his World Cup was over. I remember him sitting in the dressing room afterwards with a blanket draped around him. He wasn't crying or anything but he was fierce quiet and everybody could tell from that how upset he was because Quinny's never quiet.

He's a great friend of mine and he was my room-mate at that World Cup. Sharing with Quinny wasn't everybody's cup of tea

Above: Celebrating the Ireland U-21 Triple Crown in April 1998 with head coach Brian McLaughlin, David Wallace (*left*) and Cian Mahony (*centre*).

Left: A first senior call-up, and mother wolf Mick Galwey has a pair of little cubs under each arm during the national anthem. The photographers loved it.

Left: Strings and I didn't start well in our Six Nations debut on 19 February 2000 against Scotland, but all of a sudden, it clicked.

Below: Rala is a key man in the Ireland set-up.

Below: The five new caps that day, with (*left to right*): Shane Horgan, Simon Easterby and John Hayes forming a front row. Hayes and I have shaken hands before each Ireland game ever since.

Above and below: Lansdowne Road, 20 October 2001, and a first win against England since 1994. Drico and I lap up the atmosphere, then Bertie Ahern joins in the party.

Above: The result of Duncan McRae's work for the NSW Waratahs against the Lions on the 2001 tour. Why didn't I defend myself?

Right: With Eddie O'Sullivan after beating Australia in November 2002. It was a dream game for me, landing six from six.

Below: Another fierce encounter. Serge Betsen caught me a beaut at the 2003 World Cup.

Cooling off in the Tongan sea in 2003. The heat was mad and the pitch was coated in powdered coral.

Left: My cheeky try to beat South Africa in 2004. It drove them bananas.

Right: My 'Yahoo' moment against Argentina two weeks later led to more bad blood.

Above: 27 March 2004. Hayes and I raise our arms to a first Triple Crown. Two more would follow in 2006 and 2007.

Below: First try by an Irishman in Croke Park, 11 February 2007

bove: Humphs and I were rivals
or so long, but there was never any
ension or bad feeling between us.

ight: Bull may have saved my
fe after I lost consciousness at
Murrayfield in March 2007.

Left: The closest I'll ever get to the World Cup?

Above: Going out for kicking practise before the World Cup game against France in September 2007. It was the toughest week of my life.

Right: Looking so young in 2001. Playing with Drico has always been an honour; this was on our Lions debut.

but I've always enjoyed it. On the field he's a smart player and a hard bastard but as a room-mate he's like your mother. There's a real caring side to him. He'd nearly pull the blankets back and tuck you in when you're going to bed.

At that stage Quinny was down to about four or five fags a day but he couldn't do without them and he had his routine. The rooms were non-smoking but he'd always try to wear me down. I wasn't having any of it. Out to the balcony. He told me that he'd sit on my bed and smoke when I was out of the room but with Quinny you had to be prepared for the psychological warfare. Drico was in a single room next to us with a door linking the two rooms. He'd come in for his daily chat and Quinny would nab him to go for a fag. If it wasn't Drico it'd be somebody else. He'd always nail somebody.

The biggest problem we had was that I liked to go to bed early and Quinny liked to stay awake until one or two in the morning. When he was awake I wasn't getting much sleep. We didn't survive as room-mates for much longer after that World Cup. Quinny was in and out of the team and then he was in and out of the squad. When you're on the team you're better off rooming with somebody who is on the team as well, which is how me and Donncha got paired together. Quinny still accuses me of breaking us up. I'd have to speak to my lawyer before I answered that one.

My heart went out to Quinny when he got injured. I was in that situation with Will Greenwood on a Lions tour and when that happens to your room-mate there's nothing useful you can say. He hung around for the rest of the tournament and made the best of it. He went to the Melbourne Cup with Frankie and Paul Collins from Today FM, another Tipperary man. From what I heard Frankie and Quinny were using Paul's microphone to wind people up, pretending that the interview was going out live on air. Typical Quinny.

Then you start thinking about yourself again. The final pool game was against Australia and I knew I'd given the management a decision to make at number 10. By Wednesday night I'd heard nothing so I rang Humphs at about half eleven. He'd heard nothing either. The following day they told me I was in.

I was bullish about it. My intention going into the game was to play flat and get our back line moving. We hadn't done it at the World Cup and as far as I was concerned we hadn't really done it all year. In fairness to Humphs he was probably limited by the game plan against Argentina, but Eddie gave me licence against Australia and I was determined to use it.

We rattled them and we should have beaten them. They were there for the taking but we didn't believe it enough. After the Argentina game it should have been drilled into us that a win against Australia was crucial but we let ourselves off the hook. We looked on it as a bonus situation. Beating Argentina meant that our World Cup couldn't be classed as a failure and a win against Australia would be a bonus that nobody was expecting. Our standards should have demanded a win but we didn't have those standards back then.

In fairness to Woody, his standards were different to most guys'. With twenty minutes to go we were 4 points down and we had a penalty chance to close the gap. We had them on the rack and Woody decided to kick to the corner and go for a try. He was criticized for that decision later. Was it the right thing to do? He wanted to go for their throats and I respected that.

The other factor was that maybe he didn't trust me to land the kick. I don't know. He didn't say that to me but maybe it was in his mind. My kicking was dodgy that day – my tactical kicking was bad early on and my kicking off the ground was patchy all day. From kicks at goal my success rate was 50 per cent, not nearly good enough. But in general play I was happy. I really got into the game and I got our back line moving.

With ten minutes to go Humphs came on and I was disgusted.

I didn't try to disguise it either. Over the years there were plenty of games when I expected to be taken off or I was looking over to the line wondering if Humphs was getting ready. Against Australia the referee had to tell me that my number was up. I was so wired into the game and I felt so good about it that it didn't cross my mind that I'd be leaving it any minute.

They beat us by a point and it's a huge regret. That could have been one of the great days.

I kept my place for the quarter-final against France and it turned into one of the worst days. An absolute nightmare. They killed us. A couple of our fellas might have escaped with their lives but I wasn't one of them. Tactically, we got it wrong. Our plan was to play a zig-zag pattern: attack here, attack there, keep it very narrow, suck them in and create space for our backs to sweep round on the outside. The problem was that we were being smashed in the collisions, we couldn't get on the front foot and we were trying to force passes that weren't on.

Serge Betsen caught me a beaut early in the game and more or less put me away. I was concussed but I refused to go off and I must have convinced our medical boys that I was only dazed. Playing on was a stupid thing to do but I guess I wasn't in a position to make a wise decision. I've played with concussion a couple of times and it's the weirdest feeling. Everything seems smaller. The pitch seems like the size of a matchbox.

I half got away with it but I didn't really. They scored a breakaway try after a breakdown between me and Mal O'Kelly that was mostly my fault. Very little right. By the time I was taken off nine minutes into the second half we were 37–0 behind. For one of the few times in my life I was glad to leave the field. I had spent months trying to get back into the number 10 jersey and this was the way I was leaving the World Cup. Chewed up and spat out. We got a couple of tries near the end to take the bare look off the scoreline but nobody was fooled by that.

After the match we were called into a huddle out on the pitch. Woody was very emotional. That was his last game for Ireland. Throughout his career he had objected to the give-it-a-lash mentality of Irish teams and during his time we had moved on from that. But that performance against France was a desperate way for him to bow out. We didn't give it a lash and we didn't believe we would win.

I returned home to the same challenges. Humphs wasn't going away. The Heineken Cup was a mountain standing over us.

CHAPTER 11

In the Munster dressing room the slagging is relentless and merciless. Nobody escapes. Some things are off-limits but very little. You might make the mistake of thinking that an issue was being ignored because it was too sensitive and then realize that they were just biding their time. When Duncan McRae thumped the head off me on the 2001 Lions tour they wouldn't have slagged me about it straightaway. But they didn't wait for long and, to this day, they haven't grown tired of it. In their eyes it's a classic.

After Toulouse beat us in the 2003 Heineken Cup semi-final there was a delay in the airport on our way home and we were ushered into some kind of waiting room. John Fogarty and Donncha saw this as an opportunity to put on a show for the lads. The piece they chose was a full, all-action re-enactment of the McRae incident. Fogs played the part of me which meant that he delivered the punchline: my finger-wagging. This is what cracks them up. I've taken eleven blows to the head and my reaction is to finger-wag McRae to within an inch of his life.

For a couple of weeks in January of 2004 all that stuff was dragged up again. Gloucester were in our pool in the Heineken Cup for the second year in a row and McRae had signed for them. He gave an interview in which he claimed that he got death threats after the incident and was abused in the street. It was the first I heard of that. Was he looking for sympathy? Forgiveness? Did anybody hold him down and give him eleven digs in the head? We stood in the same room at a hearing and he nodded in agreement when his coach Bob Dwyer claimed that I had provoked him with a swinging arm. Every camera angle in the ground showed that this was false. Complete baloney.

In the week before we played Gloucester, McRae said that he wanted to apologize to me face to face. He had that opportunity in Sydney and didn't take it. I didn't duck the media or the McRae issue in the build-up to that match. I said that if he wanted to shake my hand I wouldn't turn him away. Sure enough he came over to me after the match. It was a cold handshake. Anything else might have transmitted the wrong message. I didn't have any respect for him and that's where we stood.

They beat us in Kingsholm. We were shocking. Our discipline was bad, our lineout didn't function. Because of the World Cup the pool stages of the Heineken Cup were played off quickly either side of Christmas and we had games on four weekends in a row during January. The return match against Gloucester was seven days later, which was a good thing for us. Our blood was still boiling.

We weren't in a bad position in the group. We had beaten Bourgoin in France early on and to take control of the pool we basically needed a bonus point win over Gloucester in Thomond Park while also denying them a losing bonus point. That was the first season of bonus points, which made the equation more straightforward than the Miracle Match of the year before. They got an early try but we kept our heads and got our fourth try with eleven minutes left. No heart attacks, no panic.

McRae was booed throughout the match. There was all kinds of reckless talk about what might happen to him on the pitch but that was stupid stuff. Everybody held their discipline. Alan Gaffney knew him from Randwick in Australia and we targeted him with our runners because Alan thought he was a weak tackler, but that was the only place he figured in our game plan.

At the final whistle the crowd invaded the pitch and McRae made a burst for the tunnel. There was a big post-match function under the stand and two of their biggest players never left his side for the night. Alan tells a story of inviting him to go on the piss in Limerick and McRae couldn't believe what he was hearing. He said he had even booked into Jurys Hotel under an assumed name. Alan didn't know if he was being serious or not but it could have been true.

Treviso made us work bloody hard for our bonus point in Italy a week later and then we wiped out Bourgoin in our final pool game in Thomond Park. For once we got out of our pool without walking a tightrope. We finished top as well, which meant a home quarter-final against Stade Français. But getting out of the pool was something we knew how to do. The big climb would start again in April.

On the Thursday night before Ireland played France in Paris, Stade Français sent a car to pick me up at our team hotel in Versailles. A Merc. I didn't tell anybody that I was going or who I was meeting. I had dinner with the team and then disappeared for the evening, dressed in my Irish training gear apart from an unmarked black fleece. It wasn't much of a disguise and it was a totally unsuitable rig-out for a nice French restaurant.

I guess the courtship had been going on for about a year but this was our first date. I had a chat with Diego Dominguez after a match during the previous season and he asked if I had any desire to leave Munster and play abroad. He was reaching the end of his career with Stade Français and he said that they were interested in signing me. I was happy where I was but I'd have been a fool to dismiss the possibility of going elsewhere without first seeing what was on the table. My phone number was passed on to

Max Guazzini, the president of Stade Français. We had some conversations during the year but nothing heavy. One of the things Max insisted on was absolute privacy. If any word of our contact reached the press that would be the end of it.

Waiting for me in the restaurant in Paris were Max and Pascal Fourni, a big agent in French rugby who was also a business partner of Diego's. I had enough French from school and first year of university to conduct the conversation in their language. The French always appreciate that and the evening went well.

A few Irish players still hadn't agreed new contracts with the IRFU and I was one of them. I didn't have a firm offer from Max but I had food for thought. He painted a lovely picture about the facilities at the club, the area of Paris where the players live, their ambition and their resources. He didn't say what they would pay me but he left me in no doubt that it would be a generous offer. He wasn't going to play his hand until he knew that I was seriously interested.

I never had any wish to play in the UK but the thought of joining one of the big clubs in France always seemed attractive. Just the idea of a completely new challenge in a totally different culture. Stepping out of my comfort zone and seeing if I could cope. Jess loved the prospect of living in Paris. She had taught English as a foreign language before and was well up for it. My dad didn't dismiss the idea but he wanted me go slowly, don't commit to anything, weigh it up.

Deep down in my heart I probably knew that I wasn't going anywhere. I wasn't turning in my bed at night agonizing over it. Munster was too important to me. We were still chasing the Heineken Cup and winning it with somebody else would never compensate for not winning it with Munster. The buzz of those European campaigns lifted every season. Our dressing room was a unique place and when I togged out with Munster I was playing with friends. Loyalty was a huge force in our group and I had no wish to break away from that. I always admired people like Steven Gerrard, Ryan Giggs, Paul Scholes and Gary Neville who played all their careers at one club, maintaining high standards and constantly pushing. At Munster we had a lot of guys like that.

Max didn't put me under any pressure and I respect that. I continued my negotiations with the IRFU but I didn't mention Stade Français and never tried to use them as a lever. I had a ball-park figure in my mind of what the Stade Français offer would be and I was prepared to stay at home for less. But not a whole pile less. The IRFU came back with a deal that I thought was acceptable and in early March I signed for another three years. I rang Max and he was cool about it.

We've stayed in contact over the years. More often than not it would just be a text after a match but our relationship was good and their interest in me continued from a distance. Early in 2007 when my IRFU contract was up for renewal I sat down with Max again. Munster had won the Heineken Cup, I was hitting 30 and one way or another this was the last big deal of my professional career. I had to get it right and make myself consider all options. The IRFU, though, made it easy for me to stay put and I was glad of that.

After a World Cup people are always talking about the next four-year cycle and building up to the next World Cup but players don't think like that. People wondered if we'd be flat for the 2004 Six Nations because the World Cup had ended badly but that kind of thinking makes no sense. For us to be competitive in the Six Nations every year we have to be full-on and fielding our best teams. There's never any question of Ireland experimenting or making wholesale changes with a view to getting it right for a tournament that's four years down the road. There can't be. Our pool of players isn't deep enough. Ten years ago you probably had about eighteen Irish players who were really good enough for Test rugby. Now you've got about twenty-eight. Compared to the top Test nations in the world that's a fairly small number.

Look at the players that came in for the France game in Paris who hadn't started against France in Melbourne: Shane Byrne, Tyrone Howe and Axel. All of those lads missed out on the next World Cup by a couple of years but they were the form players at the time.

Starting the season against France in Paris after the drubbing they gave us in Melbourne was like that trick for toilet training a puppy: rubbing our nose in the poo. France weren't at their best and we hung in there for what was regarded as a respectable defeat, 35–17. We didn't go there for that and whatever people might think we weren't settling for it. We were challenging ourselves and trying to move on. Drico was injured so Paulie was captain for the first time. He was only on the team a wet week but that showed the respect he commanded already. Can you imagine him settling for a respectable defeat? He gave a brilliant speech before the match and called a rake of lineouts on himself, leading from the front like he always does. We just weren't good enough.

It was a big game for me after the disaster in Melbourne. Straight after the World Cup my form for Munster had been up and down. I came good, though, against Bourgoin in the last pool match and maybe that swung the selection for me. And maybe, in my case, Eddie was thinking about the next World Cup. In a press conference before the France match he said that I was 'the man for the future'. Humphs was thirty-two and still playing well but he was five years older than me.

If Eddie had come round to a decision about his first-choice number 10 he didn't share it with me but the signals were positive. For that Six Nations he gave me more freedom on the pitch to express myself. We still had our structures and patterns but I wasn't a slave to them if I thought something else was on. I started and finished against France and started and finished against Wales in Lansdowne a week later. I had 40 caps by then but it was the first time that I had started and finished two games back to back in my Ireland career. One of the papers worked out that I'd been taken off seventeen times for tactical reasons. Think about what that says: 'We need the other guy to change this match for us.' The challenge still for me was to change Eddie's thinking.

For a kicker, playing against France poses different problems to any other team. Their back three play as a close unit and they sweep across the pitch in a pendulum motion. The full-back really bosses the 11 and 14 and they cover the space well. Mark Tainton, our kicking coach, would have analysed them and given me a print-out of his thoughts early in the week. To have any chance of kicking to the corners against them you need to drag their wingers out of position and that means going through the phases, having our wingers and full-back run decoy lines. And patience. Half the time people are probably saying, 'Why didn't he kick there?' but against France you have to be smart and wait. If you kick at the wrong time or to the wrong place against them they'll kill you. I kicked one bad ball down the middle that day and they turned it into a try.

I played well and at the time that meant more to me in defeat than it would now. I wasn't as concerned with the overall team performance as I was in later years. I wanted to consider myself one of the leaders on the team but while I was still fighting for my place that was difficult. Eddie named five vice-captains for that season and I was one of them. But so was Humphs. What did that say about my status? It was a mixed message.

I had huge faith in my ability but it wasn't enough that I believed in myself. I had to show it. In different situations, in hostile environments. With Munster over the years we put a big emphasis on producing the goods away from home because we believed that's where the true character of a player comes out. To perform like that in Paris on a losing team was a higher level for me. I was conscious of making that jump.

After we steamrollered Wales in Dublin eight days later I gave an interview in the *Irish Times*. It's hard to remember what you were thinking exactly at different times over the years but I recognize these thoughts. 'With Jonny Wilkinson out [injured] there's a huge opportunity in this Six Nations to make a mark as an out-half and the first two games have gone very well. The likes of Frédéric Michalak aren't playing particularly well so I'd like to think I can lay down a marker, step it up a level.'

I wouldn't have spoken like that in public if I didn't feel confident in my game. For the first time in my Irish career I was looking beyond Humphs.

Two weeks after the Wales match we had England in Twickenham. The World Champions. It was my first start against them over there. It was a big deal for me and a big deal for us if we were going anywhere as a team. We had the wrong plan against France but we came up with a plan that we all believed could beat England. Attack them out wide, play from side to side and force them into penalties. But a game plan isn't worth a curse without the composure and the guts to execute it.

Maggsy wasn't in the starting fifteen but his feelings about these matches weren't dictated by the number on his back. During the warm-up at Twickenham he was roaring like a bull. Most fellas seemed calm but appearances don't tell you everything. After a few minutes I missed a handy penalty from in front of the posts. It was my easiest kick of the day and I belted it high against the left-hand post. Eddie described it as a shank. I said afterwards that I hadn't given the kick 'due respect' but that answer was a whitewash. It was nerves, pure and simple. I had taken about 100 kicks in practice since the previous Wednesday and missed about three but you can never re-create match conditions on the training field.

I didn't miss another kick though. I took a couple before half-time that were pressure kicks and they sailed over. I landed another from distance, probably at the limit of my range after Richard Hill had creamed me in a tackle. After the assault he rubbed my face in the muck. At the banquet that night I had a friendly go at him over that. 'You hardly expected me to do nothing,' he said. Wing-forwards don't have the words to compliment an opposition out-half. Rubbing your face in the muck is as close as it gets. I knew I was worrying them a bit. When I picked myself up it was important to slot the kick. In every match these are the little battles that decide the war.

All around the team everything clicked. We hammered them in the lineout and pinched or spoiled eleven of their throws. Martin Johnson had retired and his loss was enormous but that was no excuse for their collapse out of touch. Our lads destroyed them.

Our defence was really good too. Mike Ford had been working hard with me. I expected Lawrence Dallaglio to run down my throat every chance he got and I didn't have to wait long. They wheeled their first scrum just enough to give Dallaglio a clear path down my channel. In moments like that early in the match you have to stand up and make a statement. If he went through me there was 40 metres of open field in behind before Girvan Dempsey would get him. I managed to get him down. No tackle of mine would ever make a wing-forward think twice about coming again, I didn't have that physical power, but if they think they can blow you away you're finished. In the stats I showed up with nine tackles. I'd say fourteen is my best tackle count in an Irish jersey but that performance came a good bit later. Nine was good for me back then.

Our try was a training ground move, too, which was sweet. Eddie spotted that Josh Lewsey shoots up out of the line and we exploited that. Drico played a brilliant pass and Girvan slid into the corner. I landed the conversion from the touchline. Right over the black spot. With a 6-point lead we had to defend like lunatics for the last ten minutes but nobody cracked.

They were on a 22-match winning run at Twickenham going back four and a half years. It was hard for England after the World Cup with big players missing but that day was a watershed for us as a team. With the exception of France in 2000 all of our best performances and biggest scalps had been in Lansdowne Road.

Italy were next and then Scotland for the Triple Crown, both at home. We hadn't won a Triple Crown since 1985 but I said in an interview that with the squad we had we should be looking at winning the World Cup. Straight out. I'm pretty sure I beat everybody else into print with that thought. In fact, I'm certain. Was I shouting my mouth off? Was that a good thing or a bad thing? It was just me. Expressing ambition is something that never caused me embarrassment or a second thought.

The Italy match was a dogfight in a swirling gale and we eventually got on top of Scotland in the second half after a shaky start. They got it back to 16-all at one stage after the break and I had made plenty of mistakes in the first half. A couple of commentators said they were surprised that Humphs didn't come out for the second half. The possibility never crossed my mind. I was having the best Six Nations of my career and for the first time in an Irish shirt I wasn't looking over my shoulder. I knew Humphs was there but I couldn't feel his breath on my neck. Eddie gave me the chance to pull it around on the field and I'd have been disgusted if he didn't. Humphs came on in the last minute when all the scoring was done and we were 21 points clear. To me, that was a clear indication of where we stood.

I missed a couple of kicks that day, which reflected my season in another way. My stats for the Six Nations were 8/9 in Paris and Twickenham, 10/20 in three games at Lansdowne Road. I loved a lot of things about that place but I hated the wind. On the stillest of days there'd be a breeze in Lansdowne. On the day we played Italy you wouldn't even put out the washing the wind was so bad. Of all the major rugby stadiums in the world there was nowhere like it.

The story of my dad leaving the ground with me and my brother before the end of the 1985 Triple Crown match had appeared in a couple of newspapers and there was bound to be a bit of slagging. Only the source was unexpected. Two days before the game I got a text from Donal Lenihan, who had set up Michael Kiernan's winning drop-goal that day. The one I only ever saw on television. 'At least I'll do you the courtesy of staying until the final whistle this time around.'

I'm not sure there was the same national euphoria about our win as there had been about Donal's Irish team but for us as a group it was important. We had made progress and we needed some tangible reward for that. We celebrated hard that night and again the following day. People regard the Triple Crown now like the League Cup in English soccer and over the last few years Irish rugby people have grown increasingly cynical about it, but we hadn't won anything for years and we were entitled to be pleased about it. That day everybody was.

We finished drinking in the team hotel at about six o'clock on Sunday morning and I resumed at noon with Maggsy and Guy. Smirnoff Ice got us going again, nice and easy. I was in bed about seven. Shot to pieces. Lights out. When it comes to drinking I have plenty of heart but I get exposed at the top level.

I was sitting in the stand at Musgrave Park on the night that Christian Cullen made his debut for Munster. It was during the Six Nations, Ospreys were in town, Munster were missing their Irish internationals and it was a low-key match except for his presence. Among rugby people the excitement in the city was unreal. Here was the leading try-scorer in All Blacks history coming to play for us. For soccer people it would have been like David Beckham coming to Turner's Cross and signing for Cork City. Musgrave Park was electric. I was thrilled about his signing because it was a massive statement of ambition. He was a special player and to win the Heineken Cup we needed something different. Ten-man rugby wasn't going to do it for us.

He arrived in Cork in November 2003 and my mum invited Christian and his girlfriend to have Christmas dinner with us. Mum is great for stuff like that. Munster have a lot of overseas guys now and they support each other but back then it was only Jim Williams and another new signing, Shaun Payne. His arrival wasn't greeted with the same fanfare but Shaun was a brilliant player for us over the next few seasons.

Christian was hurt in his last provincial match in New Zealand and needed an operation when he arrived in Ireland, but those first twelve months were probably his happiest with Munster. He was hammered with injuries over the next two and a half years and he never seemed to get a long clear run. It was frustrating for us but it was incredibly frustrating for him. His professionalism, though, was unreal. I watched him in the gym doing rehab for his shoulder and his knees and he could spend four hours a day pushing through the pain barrier. In the end his body just gave up on him.

His first Heineken Cup appearance was the 2004 quarter-final against Stade Français at Thomond Park. It was a perfect day to play the kind of game that Alan had been shaping since he took over and we didn't hang around. We spun the ball wide off the first attacking lineout, I put in a skip-pass to Mike Mullins, he put in a skip-pass to Christian and Shaun scored in the corner. Hendo got over for another try shortly afterwards and after ten minutes we were 17–0 in front, cruising.

The problem, though, was that we seemed to believe the game was over and in the second half our concentration dropped badly.

They came storming back at us and I needed to land a couple of penalties at the end to put a bit of daylight between the teams. It finished 37–32 and we'd scored four tries, but we'd conceded four too and that was a freakish thing to happen at Thomond Park. According to the stats we missed three times as many tackles as they did and conceded three times as many turnovers. All of that was sloppy and worrying.

I only missed one from eight shots at goal and my kicking that day was probably better than at any time in the Six Nations. For that I got the Man of the Match award and praise from Stuart Barnes, the Sky Sports pundit and former England out-half. He said afterwards that with Wilkinson injured he would pick me as the Lions number 10 if the tour was that summer. Barnes had always been a Humphs fan and never disguised that opinion. I respected that: I was a Humphs fan too. But he thought I had moved onto another level in my game and that tallied with my feelings.

The semi-final against Wasps in Lansdowne Road was an incredible occasion. The crowd of 49,000 was a record for any Heineken Cup match outside of the final and the Munster support was unbelievable: it must have been ten of ours to one of theirs in the crowd. On the bus going to the ground there were red jerseys all over the place. I don't get emotional at times like that but some of our guys did. This was our fourth semi-final in five years but our first on home soil, and after Ireland's good season the hype was massive.

It was a beautiful day. Top of the ground. Just what I love. I was confident and mad for it. Then, twenty-nine minutes after the first whistle, my game was over. It was reported afterwards that I'd pulled a hamstring in contact and at first that's what I thought it was. It was the weirdest feeling. I got out of a ruck and it was like a temporary paralysis of my right leg. I tried to continue but I couldn't run it off. It turned out that there was nerve damage in my lower back.

I heard years later from one of their players that Wasps spoke about getting me 'off the park'. In rugby you can achieve that without going outside the rules and even without malice. Over the years with Munster we often targeted the opposing number 10 and tried to get into him. They didn't do anything illegal to me. I expected traffic in my channel – I always do – but that day it was rush-hour. Dallaglio led the charge and the rest followed. In the *Irish Times* Gerry Thornley described me as 'road kill'.

It was an amazing match. Early in the second half we were 7 points down; with twelve minutes left we were 10 points up. They had two guys sin-binned before an hour was played. We had two guys sin-binned at the end and finished the game with thirteen men. That's when they twisted the knife. At the final whistle we were out on our feet, and we'd lost 37–32.

Jason Holland came on for me and did a great job from placed balls but inside centre was Dutchy's best position and he was being asked to take over at 10 in a match that was already flying at 100 miles an hour. He was a really smart player but that was a big ask. When Toulouse beat us in the semi-final a year earlier they introduced seasoned internationals off the bench and we all agreed that our squad needed to be deeper. It was, but not deep enough. Quinny still hadn't recovered from his injury at the World Cup and the night before the match Wally was diagnosed with chicken pox. All of a sudden we were throwing young Stephen Keogh into the back row to make his first start in the Heineken Cup. In fairness to Dutchy and Stephen, they both stepped up to the plate, but Wasps were too good.

We had played our part in a brilliant match but there was no honour for us in defeat. No consolations, no excuses. We had come up short again. There were tears but we weren't feeling sorry for ourselves. To come back we needed to be even harder on ourselves and whatever we lacked we never lacked the guts for that process.

*

I've toured the world with rugby and I feel like I've hardly been anywhere. My memories are mostly of hotels and stadiums. There were weeks when I may as well have been in camp in Dublin for all the difference it made to me. I regret that now. On tour there's always a free day in mid-week when the lads would go sight-seeing. For me and Humphs that was our day for kicking practice at the stadium. Did I feel we were missing out? I didn't think of it like that. We had kicking practice to do. As far as I was concerned we were on tour but we weren't tourists.

Mark Tainton, our kicking coach, would be there, and so would Rala and the Doc, Gary O'Driscoll. Mark was doing his job with Humphs and me but the other lads probably never realized how important they were. When you were practising the last thing you needed was to jump into the stand and go searching for balls in the seats. The lads would keep the balls rolling out onto the grass and have a water bottle handy if you needed a drink. I can be grumpy sometimes after a kicking session and that's when I needed their company. Kicking is a solitary thing but it's also a selfish thing. The lads recognized that and accepted it.

That summer Ireland toured South Africa. According to the IRB rankings we were number five in the world and they were number six. Before we left home there was a lot of talk about winning an overseas series against one of the big southern-hemisphere nations for the first time since Australia in 1979. They seemed to be in transition and we were on the up. They lost six players from their original match 22, they had four players making their international debut, a new coach and captain, and three guys who had been brought back into the team after five years in the wilderness. Anthony Foley had four times more caps than their back row put together. They should have been there for the taking.

How good were we? Still not as good as we thought we were.

In the first Test, at Bloemfontein, we didn't get enough points on the board in the first half when we were playing well, and when we hit the front just after half-time we couldn't build on it. I was getting onto Drico to rev the lads up a bit but we were dead. For the first time in a long while our pack was cleaned out. Without at least parity up front we haven't a chance against anybody. South Africa pulled away in the last fifteen minutes to win by a couple of tries. Conclusive enough.

It was my first time playing a Test match at altitude. I was warned about the ball flying further but in practice during the week I didn't see much evidence of that. What I didn't take into account was the adrenalin of a match day. Early in the game I tried to bounce the ball into touch and overshot the line by 30 or 40 metres. Comically bad. Kicking is a bit like hitting the ball in golf: without timing, power is useless. Sometimes you can try to put force into a kick and it'll travel like a dead duck, 15 metres into touch. The ones that fly are never forced. That one took off without permission.

In the second Test a week later we finished strongly but by then I was on the bench. I was shockingly bad and I can't explain why. Strings inside me struggled as well but that doesn't explain my performance. One of their forwards gave me a right good box on the head but I can't blame that either. The only good thing I did was drop a sweet goal just before half-time. My old mate Neil Francis in the *Sunday Tribune* gave me 3.5 out of 10, the lowest-rated player on the field. That kind of rating brought me back nearly three years to the disaster in Edinburgh in the autumn of 2001. I had travelled miles since then. Where did that performance come from? I haven't a clue.

Myself and Strings were dragged together seventeen minutes into the second half. How often do you see a half-back pairing replaced at the same time? That's how bad we were. Humphs came on and did really well. Without winning Ireland had a storming last quarter and a lot of the credit went to him.

To me that was a kick in the ass. I had shut him out since the start of the year. He didn't even get a run in the first Test and he was only given scrap time in the Six Nations. It looked like I'd nailed the argument once and for all. I wasn't even worrying about him. Now he was finishing the season on a high and I had cocked up in a major Test match.

Murder.

Like all tours it ended with a court session. Court sessions are an institution in rugby that probably sound silly and juvenile when you try to explain them to the outside world. Basically this is the deal: judges are appointed and they issue fines for various offences, usually announced on the bus coming home from training. The offences can range from being late to nodding off during a team meeting to wearing gear that conflicts with our team sponsors to all kinds of even more trivial stuff. If fellas had a row at training the judges could insist that they kiss and make up on the bus. Sometimes a kiss on the cheek wouldn't be acceptable to the court and the lads would have to pucker up full on the lips.

Then you have other offences that are just made up by the judges for the amusement of everybody. If you try to argue the fine will be doubled. Witty fellas like Quinny and Frankie would be the judges and in his role as the enforcer John Hayes would collect the fines. The money would go into a kitty and we'd blow it on drink at the end of the tour.

For some reason Colin Farrell was in South Africa at the time and he joined us in the team hotel on the night of the second Test wearing his Irish jersey. There was some savage drinking but Farrell didn't blink. I remember in one round a few of the lads were tackling pint glasses that were full of spirits and God knows what. It looked manky. Farrell drained his glass. No bother.

For me and a few of the lads the other mission on that tour was the purchase of diamonds. We were told that we'd save a packet buying them out there. When we got home and compared the prices we realized that we probably needn't have bothered but at the time we thought we were being very sharp. We took advice about the best place to buy them in town and a gang of us piled into the shop. Marcus, Simon Easterby and Frankie were in long-term relationships and they were in the market for engagement rings. So was I.

I didn't know Jess's ring size and it didn't cross my mind that it would be an issue so I had to ring her mum from the shop. In the circumstances I had to tell her that I was buying an engagement ring but I swore her to secrecy. I get on great with Judy and I knew I could trust her. I didn't propose to Jess for another eighteen months. Judy must have been tempted to ask what the hell was keeping me but she never opened her mouth.

CHAPTER 12

The first time I proposed to Jess was at her sister Katie's wedding in the summer of 1996. We had only been going out since Christmas, we were both teenagers and I had a few beers on board. Katie goaded me into it and in my vulnerable state I caved in. I went down on one knee and asked for her hand in marriage.

It was nearly ten years before I asked again. I made my plan carefully: the ring was sorted, I rang her father Dom to ask his permission, and I waited until January 2006, just after the tenth anniversary of our first date. We were living together in Rochestown and I arrived into the kitchen with the ring beautifully wrapped. I'm sure I rehearsed my lines but that didn't stop me from fluffing them.

What I meant to say was: 'Jess, here's an anniversary present.'

What I ended up saying was: 'Jess, here's an engagement present.'

Snatched at the kick from under the posts.

We've known each other since we were around ten. We both used go to Dooks in Kerry on our summer holidays. Jess's family had a house down there and I used go with the Cahills, a family I knew from Con. The Dalys were friendly with the Cahills too but Jess had no time for me. She thought I was very cheeky.

One of the games we played down there was Kiss and Torture.

The boys would chase the girls, trying to grab one they fancied and then give them the choice: kiss or torture. I never chased Jess. Not back then. She says that I fancied a friend of her sister's from Germany. Sophie. She's right too. Sophie was lovely.

During secondary school we didn't come across each other much. Jess went to Scoil Mhuire on Patrick's Hill, which was close to Christians', our big rivals on the rugby field. Some of the girls from that school would drop into the gaming arcade on MacCurtain Street where I could be found after school now and again. Jess didn't pop in there very much but for some reason she showed up at the Pres victory celebration in Jurys after we won the junior cup. We had mutual friends and there's a picture of us sitting together at a table during the disco. Pure coincidence. I was tiny in those days. Jess was towering over me.

When we got a bit older my gang and her gang used go to a pub on the Mardyke. This would have been fifth year or sixth year in school when we were both underage. Jess had no problem looking 18 but even with fake ID I was in trouble. Sneaking in wasn't a big problem and once inside I used put on a black woolly hat. Another of my friends used do the same thing. I guess we thought it made us look older. It sounds a bit desperate now. Anyway, I was rumbled plenty of times and kicked out.

At the end of sixth year there was the usual round of Grads Balls and Debs Balls. Jess was invited to the Pres Grads by a guy in my class and I invited one of her best friends, Diana. Diana was a bridesmaid at our wedding later but that night Jess and I spent a lot of time talking for two people who didn't go as dates. We hadn't really got along very well before that night and that's probably when our friendship began.

We started our Arts degrees at UCC in the autumn. Psychology was a subject that we both chose in first year and we used sit together in those lectures. Jess sometimes had her mum's car in college and if she was going to town I used invent reasons to go with her. Then we'd go to Victor's Sandwich Bar on South Main Street for lunch. The rolls in there were massive.

It went along like that for a while. She says that she only regarded me as a friend in those days but she came to Cashman's Bookies with me a couple of times which, when you look back, was a big romantic gesture on her part. I fancied Jess but I hadn't the courage to ask her out. I tried to act cool, talking to her about other girls and listening to her stories about other young fellas, but the bottom line was that I wanted us to be more than friends.

She was snapped up very early for the UCC Rugby Club Ball but then we finally got it together on St Stephen's night. I played for UCC that afternoon in the annual fixture against Con and then there was a big disco in the clubhouse that night. It took off from there.

Over the next few years we spent a lot of time together and some long stretches apart. We didn't go away on a summer holiday until after third year in college and then Jess went to study in Dublin. After that she went to Australia for seven months. I was profiled in the match programme for a Heineken Cup game at the end of 1999 and one of the questions was, 'Who would you most like to meet?' The answer I gave was: 'My girlfriend Jess when she comes home from Australia.' In the Munster dressing room I hardly need to explain the risk I was taking with that answer.

Jess worked in PR and marketing for a while and then she changed direction and spent eighteen months in Limerick training to be a primary school teacher. On weekends in Cork she spent more and more time staying over at my house and when she finished in college she moved in.

We were married in the summer of 2006 at the Sheraton Hotel in Fota, ten miles outside Cork city and that was probably our first experience of bitchy rumours. The Sheraton was a new hotel and when we got engaged it was still a building site. We were looking at a place in Killarney because we needed a big room for the crowd and the options in Cork were limited. But we also wanted to get married in the Honan Chapel at UCC and that was sixty miles from Killarney.

Then we were approached by the marketing person from the Sheraton. She was friendly with John Kelly and she wanted us to consider their hotel. We went down for a look in late January and it was hard to believe that it would be finished before the summer. We agonized over it for a while but we didn't have great alternatives and eventually we made a commitment. In the end the hotel opened with two months to spare.

The rumour that went around Cork later on was that they gave us the reception for free because of the publicity our wedding would generate for them. Another rumour was that they paid us to have our wedding there. Absolute crap. They did a brilliant job for us and we paid our money like everybody else. Pure and simple.

We knew that there would be a certain amount of media attention on our wedding but we tried to control it. We've always been very conscious of keeping our private lives to ourselves. We made a decision years ago that we weren't going to be a celebrity couple around town, having our photograph taken at functions and launches and dos. I did plenty of publicity shots over the years but that was either rugby business or private business. Jess wasn't dragged into any of that.

We were approached by a couple of glossy magazines who wanted to buy exclusive access to the wedding and we wouldn't even consider it. I like a deal but I'm not going to sell my soul. One magazine cobbled together something later on where they gathered all the photographs that were available from the day and made it look like an exclusive. It appeared to me to be a cheap, grubby marketing ploy and I've no doubt people looked at that and thought they'd paid us.

We were conscious of our privacy that day but we weren't

going to turn it into a war either. Pat Geraghty, the Munster press officer, did a brilliant job on our behalf. His thinking was that if we played ball with the media they wouldn't be intrusive. All media enquiries and requests were routed through Pat and he did his best to keep everyone sweet.

There had to be limits though. RTE and TV3 both asked if they could do a quick interview with me after I came out of the church but I thought that was inappropriate. We allowed photographers and television cameras in the churchyard but it's not a big area and we didn't want them in our face. So barriers were put up and they had to stay behind them. Jess's brother Philip was our wedding photographer and he did a great job of keeping them back. The Sheraton had security people on the gate of the hotel too in case any photographers tried to sneak in.

That might sound over the top but this was going to be one of the happiest days of our lives and we were determined that it wasn't going to turn into a circus.

In my experience some people don't think twice about invading your privacy. Mass is a great example. I have a very strong Catholic faith and I'm a regular mass goer. I don't always get a chance to go on Sundays because of matches and travelling but I always make a point of going during the week. I don't go out of habit and I don't go to be seen. It is a conscious part of my life. I feel I've been very lucky in so many ways and I go there to pray and say thanks.

I like it when the church is quiet and I can slip in and out with my baseball hat pulled down over my face. It probably sounds odd but it's harder to be anonymous in a crowd. When I go on Sundays there's always a chance of being spotted and approached. I've had people come up to me in church looking for a chat about rugby. One young fella asked me to autograph his mass booklet during mass. I don't blame the kid so much but what were his parents doing?

A mass I loved going to over the years was at teatime on Sunday at St Patrick's near the train station. It was usually given by Fr Christy O'Shaughnessy and I loved his whole approach. His sermons were humorous, interesting and down to earth while still making a serious point. He had a great way of connecting with people. Jess and I didn't know him but we very much wanted him to say our wedding mass and we were delighted when he agreed.

I had my own speech to worry about too. Going back over the years I was slow enough to speak in team meetings or dressing rooms but I got over that. There were 240 guests at our wedding but I wasn't terrified at the prospect of standing up in front of them. For sing-song purposes I only have a couple of numbers, one of which is the Chris de Burgh song 'Lady in Red' and I incorporated that line into my speech about her never looking so lovely as she did that day. I'm a brutal singer so my strategy in sing-songs is to sing the first couple of lines and hope everyone joins in. I couldn't claim to be a solo artist.

The wedding reception went like a dream and the party continued at the Old Head of Kinsale Golf Club the following day. That was a much smaller affair for family and close friends. To shorten the journey from Fota we took the car ferry across Cork harbour and Drico ended up driving the boat for a while, a bottle of beer in one hand and a fag hanging out of his mouth. Even in the off-season he couldn't resist being skipper.

Our wedding was on Thursday but we didn't set off on our honeymoon until Sunday evening, when we flew to Manchester en route to Sandy Lane in Barbados. At Cork airport they invited us into a private lounge. It had never happened before and we didn't organize it but it was really welcome.

The France v. Italy World Cup final was on telly and we sat back. At half-time in the match there was a knock on the door and one of the airport staff popped his head in: 'Do ye mind if this gentleman joins ye?' The gentleman in question was

Roy Keane who was travelling on the same flight to Manchester.

Jess didn't recognize him at first in his beard and baseball cap. I'd know him anywhere. It's strange to have a hero who is only a few years older but hero is the best word to describe my admiration for him. I always loved his drive. His attitude. The way he turned himself into a great player with less talent than other top players. The way he kept going for it, regardless of the challenge or the obstacles.

I had met him briefly a couple of times before but now I had him cornered in a room. He was trying to watch the match but I kept coming at him with questions. He had quit playing at the end of the season and I asked him about his plans. I knew from his answer that it was a no-go area. Sunderland was never mentioned. He was good company for the time we spent together although he'd probably say that I annoyed the hell out of him with my constant chat.

Sandy Lane was everything you'd expect it to be: totally luxurious with pampering beyond belief. If you wanted something while you were sunbathing on the beach you stuck a yellow flag in the sand and somebody came to take your order. They couldn't do enough for you: cold towels, fruit, drinks, whatever. It was a fantasy place where you left the real world at the gate.

What I couldn't leave behind was my nature. Jess and I play tennis and one day we were challenged to a game of mixed doubles by another couple in the hotel. They were older than us by at least ten years – maybe fifteen years – and in the baking heat our youth should have been a match-winning advantage. This is the way I was thinking. We won the first set but they won the second and at some stage during that set my competitive instincts took over. There I was, on our honeymoon, getting revved up about a dopey tennis match and trying to get Jess revved up as well: 'Come on, Jess, we can't lose to these!'

Then, with the match level, they called it a day and that made me even more angry. Yer man was going around the place boasting about taking a set off us. There was only one thing for it: a rematch. This time there was no mistake. We kicked their asses.

If Jess and I had been married after a whirlwind romance and a quickie ceremony in Las Vegas this behaviour might have come as an awful shock to her. But she knew well what she was getting with me.

I'm blessed that she accepts me for what I am. Blessed beyond words.

When did the rumours start? I can't remember exactly. Jess thinks it was October, which would mean that less than three months after our wedding people were saying that our marriage was over. Why did the rumours start? I don't know. We don't know. We haven't a clue.

I've thought about it a lot but I haven't come to any conclusions. We could never trace it back to a source and we didn't even have real suspicions. There was nobody that we could confront about it or take action against. Somebody told us that rumours like these usually start close to home but we couldn't think of anybody we knew who would want to bring this tripe into our lives.

How do you fight a rumour? You can't. That's the problem. It's not like a libel in a newspaper where you can get a retraction or an apology or sue for damages. If you come out publicly and deny them you're giving the rumours more status and maybe some credibility. Denials only throw petrol on the fire. The bottom line is that people are happy to believe the worst about others. If that wasn't true malicious rumours wouldn't exist.

The best strategy is try to ignore them but that doesn't necessarily make them go away either. At least not quickly. Once they start they take on a life of their own. They get arms and legs and travel for miles. Dutchy returned to New Zealand for a couple of years after he finished with Munster and he called me to say that he had picked up the story down there. He wasn't asking me if there was any truth in it because he knew the ordinary, everyday reality of our lives. We were never concerned about what our family and friends might think because they could see the reality for themselves. If there was any tension in our marriage we wouldn't have been able to hide it, simple as that.

In the beginning I used hear the latest version of my marriage break-up from other players. They used laugh about the stories because they knew how ridiculous they were and I guess I used to laugh along and try to put up a front. But it was annoying me. The only good thing was the feeling that all this was going on in a parallel universe. After training I was returning to a happy home telling my wife the latest story I'd heard about our split. It was a totally unreal situation to be in. But the crucial thing was that I was returning to a happy home.

I'm sure we didn't hear all the rumours but some of the ones we heard were unforgettable. I was supposed to have run off with one of Jess's sisters – not sure which one. Jess was supposed to have kicked me out of the house. I was supposed to be living in an apartment in Tralee – with somebody else, but not one of Jess's sisters. Strings was supposed to be living with Jess. Take your pick.

The funny thing was that the people repeating these stories were always convinced about their accuracy. There was never a doubt in their vicious minds. They were usually quoting 'friends' of ours. Which 'friends'? One of Jess's brothers-in-law is a Garda inspector and he was told 'on good authority' by another Garda that I was gone from Jess and away from the family home. Jess's brother-in-law was able to put him straight but how many times were those stories passed on, unchallenged?

Jess was really hurt by some of the rumours. Then I went along and made it worse.

*

It started out as a good night. We were in camp before the 2006 autumn internationals and we were off the leash on what are known as bonding sessions. In plain words that means going out on the town, having a few pints and having a laugh. We started off with a lovely Chinese meal and the wine was flowing. Eddie O'Sullivan would be a restrained guy and wouldn't drink very much but even he had entered the spirit of the occasion.

Later on we went in town to a nightclub and in those situations people start coming up to you. People who would leave you alone walking down the street during the day lose their inhibitions with a few drinks and they want to say hello. Years ago they looked for an autograph. Now they want a picture. Every second person has a camera phone so they want you to stand in and smile. If you say no you're an asshole in their eyes and if you don't take cover at some stage your evening will be ruined. Cover was hard to come by that night.

I don't remember the picture being taken. I was absolutely pissed and I looked it. They were strangers, like all the others, and I stood for the picture like I was asked. The problem was my pose. One of the girls was wearing a top with thin straps and I put my right hand under one of them, just below her shoulder. Why did I do it?

I wish I knew. It wasn't funny. It was stupid. Unacceptable. It looked desperate. I had crossed a line and put myself in a crazy position.

I rang Jess when I heard the picture was going around on an email and I asked Wally to send it on to her. Some of the pictures on the net were doctored and in one of them my wrist is huge. But the original picture wasn't a mock-up and I never attempted to say it was.

Jess was upset. I could feel the hurt in her. She knew that nothing had happened between me and the girl because she had seen this scene a million times before on nights out. Strangers and pictures had eaten into plenty of our evenings together and there were nights when it tested her patience. What really annoyed her, though, wasn't just the location of my hand in the picture but the look on my face. That blank appearance of somebody who had had too much to drink. She couldn't understand why I was posing for pictures with strangers in that state. And that was the heart of the problem. I was in no fit condition to make a good decision. I had done thousands of harmless photographs over the years but I had turned this one into a bloody mess.

Drinking isn't my strongest suit. I don't have hollow legs like some fellas. We drink so little nowadays that whatever tolerance I have is less than it used to be. If we were on a rare two-day session with, say, a Saturday night followed by a Sunday I'd be better on the second day. I'd be well able to keep going but I'd be under pressure before a lot of fellas. What sometimes happens then is that I nod off in the pub before the night is finished or in the chipper afterwards.

I don't know if it was a reaction to that night or not but the IRFU send three minders with us now when the team is on an evening out. That's a good thing. As international rugby players we know that we're public figures and we have a certain responsibility to people who follow rugby and support the team. There aren't any prima donnas in the squad who want the public to be kept at arm's length. But we're entitled to a bit of privacy too and when you're letting your hair down with your team-mates you don't want the whole world watching or taking pictures on their camera phones.

The photograph added another twist to the rumours about our marriage. The timing couldn't have been worse. People who believed we had split up had the confirmation they needed. You can imagine what they were saying: no smoke without fire. It's the easiest thing in the world to say. Most of the papers ignored the photograph but a couple couldn't resist writing about it. Everybody seemed to know about it regardless of the media.

Jess probably felt it more than I did. I was disgusted with myself for being so stupid and helping to make our situation worse. She didn't deserve that. In all the years we've been together she's been a rock for me. I hated the thought that all this stuff was causing pain to her and my parents.

At least there was a lot of good stuff going on in our lives at the same time. In November of 2006, while the picture was circulating on the internet, we moved into our new home. It was on a site we had bought a couple of years earlier on the outskirts of Cork city. Building a house always has problems and stresses but getting it finished was a massive kick for us. My good friend Michael O'Flynn was invaluable with his advice and did a brilliant job. It was our dream home. Perfect. Everything we wished for.

But the people who were dragging our names through the mud knew nothing about our life inside that house. We couldn't put names and faces on them. And they didn't know us.

They hadn't a clue. That was the bottom line.

CHAPTER 13

There were five months between the second Test against South Africa in the summer of 2004 and their visit to Lansdowne Road in November. Over the previous couple of years we knew we'd made progress but where did we stand in the world? Had anybody taken any notice? Did any of the top nations give us a second thought? During the tour it was clear from his comments that Jake White didn't rate us and we didn't have what it took to ram his words down his throat.

So he came to Dublin and, in different words, the South African coach repeated himself. He said that Drico was the only player who would get on the Springbok team and he felt that one of our second rows would push for a place in the squad. White didn't even refer to Paulie or Malcolm by name, which added to the insult. In his eyes we were no different from all the other Irish teams that South Africa had beaten in the previous thirty-nine years.

Eddie said after the game in Lansdowne Road that White's comments weren't the source of our motivation. Eddie was being diplomatic. For all the giant strides that have been made in sports science and sports psychology the power of wounded pride is still huge. At his captain's meeting on the night before the game Drico made a big play about White's lack of respect for us. I said my piece too. 'He'll remember our names tomorrow night' was the gist of it. Malcolm said afterwards that there were fifteen bitter men going out onto the field and that's how it was. Raw. During the national anthem there were tears in the eyes of Drico and John Hayes. The England game in Croke Park three years later was the only other time I'd known John to cry before a match.

It was a big game for me. I had cocked up badly in the second Test down there and I had to come up with a response. I hadn't given Jake White any good reason to know my name. Eddie picked me to start for the tenth match in a row, which reflected where I stood in his eyes. But Humphs hadn't gone away and I had to keep delivering on Eddie's faith. That day, I did.

We beat them 17–12 and I got all of our scores. The try was cheeky and it drove them bananas. We were awarded a penalty 10 metres out and the referee, Paul Honiss, called over their captain John Smit. In his mouthpiece he said, 'Time off, Malcolm,' telling the television match official to stop the clock. He told Smit to talk to his players about repeated offences and then I heard him say, 'All right, Malcolm,' and he started his watch again. Smit turned away and started calling his players in but the ref seemed ready to carry on.

I put the ball down, looked to the touchline and allowed them to think that I was going to kick to the corner. It was an unbelievably windy day, the angle wasn't great and going for 3 points wasn't the percentage call. They looked a bit slack and I said to Paulie, 'We could be on here.' I had tried a quick tap and go with Munster a few times without getting over the line but I knew by their body language that this was a big chance.

I shouted, 'Let's go' to Paulie. He was just to my left and Bakkies Botha would have expected me to give him the ball. That distracted his attention long enough for me to get in. They were furious. Smit looked for an explanation from the ref but 'Time's on' was as much as he got out of him. If it had happened to us we'd have been livid too.

The only frustrating thing afterwards was that we should have won by more. We had chances to bury them. Instead we won by 5 points, which allowed them to go on about my try. The emotion, though, was unreal. In the life of this Irish team that was one of the best days. It didn't matter how good we thought we were without the scalps to prove it. They had won the Tri-Nations that summer, they travelled with a full team and the talk was of a Grand Slam tour of the northern hemisphere. That was the scale of the challenge we faced.

The other satisfying thing was that we stood up to them. In the summer they had really bullied us down there. Averaged out they were nearly 8 kilos a man heavier than us. We came home from South Africa knowing that we had a big power deficit to make up. Addressing that was going to take time but we had to make strides in that direction. At the end of that summer we had our first ten-week pre-season with Ireland. The decision to take us away from the provinces for such a long stretch caused a lot of controversy but it was the only way forward. Power was just one element of what we were trying to improve but I put on 3 kilos during the pre-season and with my metabolism that was a significant gain.

Our other big visitors that autumn were Argentina. Against them power was always an issue. And needle. We hadn't played them since the World Cup fourteen months earlier and that was a dogfight. Two of their guys were suspended for eye-gouging but that didn't reform their behaviour. In Dublin they were filthy. Simon Easterby needed stitches after he was gouged in the mouth and they gouged or tried to gouge another five of us in the eyes. I was one of their targets and I was lucky that yer man just missed. I ended up with a gash next to my right eye. A lot of cheating and rule-bending goes on during a rugby match and nobody squeals about it afterwards, but gouging is beneath contempt and we had to speak up.

In spilling rain and a swirling wind this was another war and they nearly caught us. We were 10 points down early in the second half and were still a point down with less than two minutes on the clock. I had kicked all our points without playing as well as I had against South Africa. My tackling was dodgy and I fluffed a couple of touch kicks but confidence was carrying me through every match that autumn.

We mounted one last attack and a drop-goal was the only way out for us. For those situations we had a zig-zag pattern. 'Marmalade' was the code name. Don't know why. The forwards take it up in pods of four, over and back, but keeping it pretty central, inside the two 15-metre lines. The weather was so bad, though, that we couldn't afford to go through too many phases in case the ball was spilled. When Strings spun it to me I was about 40 metres out, but it was a lovely pass and I was in a decent position. Over it went. 21–19. Sweet.

In my celebration I jumped up and clicked my heels together, like that scene in *The Wizard of Oz*. Tom Tierney used to do it in training if he pulled off something classy. He'd shout 'Yahoo' and the practice kind of caught on. None of us had ever done it in a match, though, and a few of the Argentinians didn't like it. I had my back turned to them, running towards my own goal when I did the knack. A couple of them had just picked their faces up out of the muck and my 'Yahoo' was the first thing they saw.

I didn't mean any disrespect to them and it wasn't meant to be a provocative gesture. Anyway, compared to gouging it was a pretty minor irritant but it didn't stop them from getting thick about it. Before the banquet in the Shelbourne Hotel that night I was standing at the bar with their captain Agustín Pichot, having a perfectly pleasant conversation. Next thing their hooker, Mario Ledesma, came over and started shouting the odds. He was speaking in Spanish so I didn't understand what he was saying but it was clear that he was having a go and everything about his demeanour was menacing. From where I was standing it looked like he wanted to kill me and I wasn't hanging around to test my hunch. I slipped away before anything kicked off and let his team-mates calm him down.

That night was different to any post-match banquet I've ever attended. Normally both teams bury the hatchet and leave behind whatever happened on the field. But too much had happened in that game – and other games before that. There was a bad atmosphere around the place. At one stage one of ours and one of theirs got into a full-scale row with accusations flying in both directions. That's the way it was between us and them. Bad blood.

I was due to meet Ledesma again a couple of weeks later. He was at Castres and they were Munster's next opponents in the Heineken Cup. In the end he pulled out with a calf injury but his absence didn't necessarily improve my enjoyment of the match. Instead I spent the evening listening to foul-mouthed abuse from their number 8, Paul Volley. He joined them from Wasps, having played against us in the Heineken Cup semi-final the previous season. I wasn't on the field very long that day but he was on my case from the start and caught me with a forearm into the jaw. He wore number 8 for Castres that night but he played like an open-side wing-forward. The only thing on his mind was getting to me any way he could.

Most of the time, in most venues, kickers are given a respectful silence. In Thomond Park that silence is an institution that nobody dares violate. Over the years, though, every kicker encounters fellas who try to mess with their mind and insert a bit of doubt. 'Watch the wind' or 'I've this post covered.' Harmless stuff that wouldn't cost you a second thought. When you go to France you don't expect silence for the kicker. The crowd will make a racket and do their best to put you off. But what I got from Volley went beyond that. When I say that it's unprintable you can imagine how bad it was.

The physical stuff was routine enough. He hit me with a late tackle early on and kept pushing his luck with the referee but you can accept that. It's his job to hit me as often as he can. And he was cute too. When I was kicking at goal he was doing his best to block my view of the black spot on the cross bar. He stood right in my line of vision. You're supposed to be 10 metres away but he was only about 8 metres away and he'd make the ref push him back. That's gamesmanship which happens in rugby all the time. But the stuff that came out of his mouth was way over the top and unacceptable. They beat us 19–12 and we just hadn't been good enough, especially in the first half.

Afterwards Sky Sports were doing post-match interviews in a long bar at the back of the stand. I went up with Pat Geraghty, our press officer, and waited my turn. Volley was due to be interviewed just before me but he arrived into the room just after us. As he walked past he came out with a smart comment and I snapped. I unloaded a pile of abuse that had been building up inside me since the first late tackle about two hours earlier. Like all these fellas he was well able to give it but he couldn't take it. He walked over with his chest out as if he was going to knock the head off me, still mouthing.

'Mario was right,' he said, 'you're only a fucking prick.'

At that point Pat walked over and stood in between us. Volley went down to do his interview and next thing Paulie came steaming into the room, as if he knew there was something going on. 'Where is he?' The cameras were on Volley at the time but while he was doing his interview Paulie was pointing at him. I'm glad that finger never pointed at me.

The return fixture was eight days later and Volley's last words to me were that next Saturday couldn't come quickly enough. Over the following few days he obviously had time to reflect on that remark because a different Paul Volley showed up in Thomond Park. He changed from a monster to a mouse. It was unbelievable. He even complimented some of my kicks during the match. 'Well done, mate' – this sort of stuff. I never witnessed anything like it. Mr Nice Guy.

That match was my fiftieth Heineken Cup appearance and I marked it with a yellow card. There was a bit of jostling going on and I paired up with one of their props, Justin Fitzpatrick. It was mouthing more than anything. Just as well probably. Anyway the ref sent both of us to the sin-bin.

We hammered them that night which put us in a strong position in the pool with three wins from four games. Getting out of the pool, though, was something we were able to do every year. Winning the competition was a different problem.

At the start of every season we spend a day at the University of Limerick setting our goals and thinking about how we can make ourselves better. The Wasps defeat had a massive impact on everyone and we knew that it wasn't a case of tinkering with our approach: we had to be radical. Paulie was adamant that our fitness hadn't been good enough against Wasps, in terms of both power and speed. That was addressed in pre-season. Paulie's opinions carry massive weight. When he drives something it usually gets done. Defence was another area that had to be addressed. We missed too many tackles in the semi-final. So Graham Steadman was hired and we put a new defensive system in place.

After that there was the annual issue of training being split between two centres, Cork and Limerick. That had been coming up for years. Jim Williams felt it was killing us and Alan Gaffney agreed. Too much time was being spent on the road. It was bad for recovery and it was a waste of time. They were right. The obvious solution was that we all move to Limerick, where the training facilities were better, but the Cork lads didn't want that.

I had bought a site in Cork to build a house and I certainly didn't want to move. The compromise was a training schedule that reduced everyone's travelling. For gym and speed work the Cork and Limerick players would train separately in their own bases and some of the group sessions would be done halfway in Charleville. The Cork-based players still spent more time on the road but that was fair enough because the resources for training were better in Limerick.

All of the changes were welcome but it didn't make any difference to the bottom line. We won our final two pool matches in January but we weren't one of the four best pool winners and the price for that was an away quarter-final against Biarritz in April 2005. We played all right and lost by 9 points. Not good enough. Still not good enough.

As it turned out the Castres game was my last appearance in the Heineken Cup that season. I broke my hand against Leinster over Christmas and that kept me out of the January matches and then my knee was banjaxed for the quarter-final.

In between I was fit for the Six Nations. With England and France at home people were talking about a Six Nations title or a Grand Slam. We weren't shying away from those goals. After a Triple Crown it was the logical next step. In the squad a Grand Slam was our stated goal.

We started off in Rome and I had a nightmare. For their home matches Italy started using the new Mitre ball that season. Eddie ordered a dozen of them in good time so that myself and Humphs could practise, but it was a lot different to the Gilbert and I really struggled with it. I missed touch seven times in the first half and two of those kicks went out on the full. When I got it right for the first time after about twenty minutes there was a big ironic cheer. Killer.

We got out of there with a win and then we had Scotland at

Murrayfield a week later. Mentally, it was a draining week for me. I couldn't go three minutes without visualizing drilling the ball to the corner and finding touch. If that part of an out-half's game isn't functioning he's a liability, simple as that. My last start in Murrayfield was in 2001 and that had been a disaster. In the first couple of minutes Jason White came down my channel and that's the last thing you want. I made a bad job of stopping him but things got better for me after that and we ended up stuffing them.

John Hayes scored a try that day and that was a massively popular score. In the Munster set-up he still gets slagged about his try against Toulouse in Bordeaux in the 2000 Heineken Cup semi-final. The heat was unreal that day and he took forever to lift himself off the ground. In a video meeting a few months later we counted him out like a boxer: One, two, three . . . I think we got to about twenty-eight before Hayes was on his feet.

Hayes is a great fella to have around the place. Good craic. Christy Moore and his brother Luka Bloom came in to the team hotel to play a gig for us during that Six Nations and they came up with a brilliant song about 'The Bull Hayes'. It was a great gig but that was the highlight for everyone. Coming home from training one day after the Scotland match we had a competition to find who had the biggest head. Not the biggest ego, but actually the biggest head. Hayes was doing the measuring which is exactly where you'd expect him to be: right in the thick of it. Donncha, Frankie, Shane Byrne and Marcus Horan were the shortlist of nominees and Marcus won. Now, there's something about Marcus that you didn't expect to find out.

I've no doubt that sounds a ridiculous carry-on for grown men but when you're in camp you're not living in the real world and this kind of stuff helps to keep boredom at bay. Another tradition for years with Munster and Ireland was that fellas were stripped at training on their birthday. Right down to their socks and their boots. Gaillimh and Claw led the charge and it was pointless to resist because that only increased the suffering. They made up the rules and they were law. Once your gear was off you'd be drenched in Lucozade and covered in sticky spray that the forwards use for grip at the lineout. That spray was applied in the most uncomfortable places. You can use your imagination.

When Claw and Gaillimh left the Irish scene Frankie kept it going for a while but then it died away. We had less and less privacy at training and that kind of behaviour wasn't on when the outside world was looking in. None of this carry-on had anything to do with the real world outside camp.

My birthday always fell during the Six Nations and I suffered my share of public nudity. For the 2005 season, though, I was rooming with Donncha and he had a more subtle way of drawing attention to the birthday boy. When I came down for dinner the table was decorated with balloons, party hats and a nice cake. That was embarrassing in its own way but at least I was fully clothed. The pay-off was that I had to sing. If I didn't give them 'Lady in Red' it would have been the Neil Diamond song 'When It Began'. I only sang songs where people could join in after the first line.

The serious business was our third match of the Six Nations, at home to England. They had lost their first two games and it was a real chance for us to kick on. We did enough to win but it wasn't handy. I slotted a couple of drop-goals in the first half and missed another on my left foot that I should have got. I lost my rhythm a bit in the second half. Drico came up with another match-winning try on a big day and we hung on for dear life, 19–13. Job done.

I got the Man of the Match award, which I didn't think I deserved. I suspect the fact that it was my fiftieth cap came into the equation. They made a presentation to me at the banquet that night and I had to make a speech. I don't remember the words but the tone of what I said was serious and from the heart.

Maggsy always impressed me when he talked about playing for Ireland. He spoke with fierce passion and sincerity and I wanted to get across some of that in my speech because I shared those feelings.

The lads were a bit taken aback. In those days the lads would probably have seen me as cheeky and quick with a smart comment. I turned a lot of things into a laugh and maybe that was a front. Behind that mask rugby was an intensely serious part of my life. Winning fifty caps for Ireland was a huge honour and I didn't think it was appropriate to make light of it in any way.

I think my image among the lads has changed in the last couple of years. I suppose I've changed. It wasn't something I thought long and hard about. I wasn't looking to put on an act. But I remember thinking that time was moving on in my career. I was moving into my late twenties, I was the starting out-half, a key decision-making position. I wanted to be a leader in the group and I had that opportunity. To be a leader, though, I knew I needed to carry myself a little differently.

How I'm perceived by strangers in the street is a different thing. I'd say people find me rude. A couple of people have told me so straight out. They were right. I'm not comfortable being a face that people recognize. On match days I'm brutal. I can't chill out. I hate walking through the lobby of the team hotel and being approached by people who want an autograph or a picture or a quick word. All I'm thinking about is the match. My nerves are in shit, my stomach is turning. I can't just break away from that and make small talk with strangers. I really struggle with match days. Even afterwards. I don't like the back-slapping. I'd love to play the game and go home. Or else go into a quiet room with the lads and have a few cans. I know it's only a game and I should relax a bit more but I don't believe I could think like that and still perform.

Away from match days I'm a bit better but I'm still not comfortable with attention. If I'm at mass or out shopping I hate the feeling of people looking at me. If a group of kids stop me and look for a picture I won't disappoint them. But the chances are I'll tell them to hurry up because all I can think about is the attention that this is drawing on me. After all these years I'm still embarrassed by that. On the pitch is different. Out there I never think about who's looking at me. It doesn't cost me a thought.

Anyway, it doesn't matter what people see, or think they see, because the video misses nothing. On the Monday after the England game Eddie and Mervyn Murphy, our video analyst, gave a great presentation for forty-five minutes about the mistakes we'd made. The conclusion was that we didn't do anything wrong without the ball but when we were in attacking positions we wasted a lot of opportunities with poor decision-making and bad execution.

Eddie liked the idea of criticizing players in front of their peers. That can be tough on new guys but I think all of the experienced players recognized the value of it. If your mistakes are highlighted in the presence of your team-mates you're less likely to repeat them. In his years with Munster, Deccie had a different style. Less confrontational. More gentle.

France were next in Lansdowne Road and they did a number on us. They won the toss and gave us the wind in the first half but they refused to give us the ball. We cocked up a couple of times and they turned our mistakes into tries. Overall we were off the pace and they punished us. Turning to face the wind in the second half we were 9 points down and we had to keep the ball in hand a lot more. That helped to get our intensity up and Drico's try brought us back into the game. We hauled them back to 2 points but when we were pushing they hit us with another try to clinch it.

One of the things people wondered that season was how we would cope with being favourites. It wasn't a problem in the first three matches. Did we cope with it against France? We made so many mistakes in the first half that you'd have to doubt it.

I passed Humphs on the all-time scoring list for Ireland that day. The papers picked up on it. It wasn't something I celebrated.

We still had a chance to save our season in Cardiff a week later. Wales were going for the Grand Slam but if we beat them we'd win the Triple Crown. If we beat them by 13 points we'd win the Six Nations Championship. To be honest, we weren't focused on either of those things. The Triple Crown was hardly mentioned. Our season had been about moving beyond that and the chances of achieving that were slim now.

It was a bad day for me. After seventeen minutes I was charged down by Gethin Jenkins and he controlled the ball brilliantly to score their first try. For an out-half being charged down is an occupational hazard but you never expect it to happen against a loose-head prop. I never saw him coming. The usual set-up is that a forward would screen the kicker when he's making a clearing kick but Jenkins dodged my protection, managed to stay onside and caught me a beaut. He hasn't stopped thanking me since.

Like the France game we didn't have much possession in the first half and we didn't have great control over the ball we managed to get our hands on. Wales targeted our 10–12 channel so myself and Maggsy saw a lot of Tom Shanklin. He hurt us and ultimately that hurt me.

We were 22–6 behind eleven minutes into the second half when Humphs came on. I couldn't believe it. I felt I was playing all right. I knew I was. A big part of my reaction was anger, another part was shock. I hadn't been taken off for tactical reasons since the summer tour to South Africa nine months earlier. We'd been involved in three or four high-pressure, down-to-the-wire matches since then and I had stood up to the demands of those games. We were in trouble now and they doubted my ability to turn it around. That was the message as I understood it. We ended up losing by 12 points in the end, but for the first time in the match we had some go-forward ball in the last twenty minutes and I could have done something with that.

I was told afterwards that our defensive coach Mike Ford influenced the call. I probably shouldn't have blamed him because ultimately Eddie makes the decisions and he can reject advice from any of his coaches. But I was steaming mad and the thought of Mike hauling me off made it worse. I always believed that he favoured Humphs anyway but that wasn't necessarily a problem. Eddie favoured Humphs for long enough too. Mike had worked very hard on my tackling and my effectiveness in our defensive system, I respected his expertise and there was no question that he was good for us as a team. But why was he calling for me to be taken off? I couldn't get my head around that.

Back in the team hotel after the match I confronted him. I didn't even do it privately. I collared him by the lifts in the Hilton Hotel and for all I knew the whole world could have been watching. I was so wound up that I didn't notice and I didn't care. I don't think I raised my voice – I'm pretty sure I didn't – but in that state you're not in total control.

Then Mike denied it, which left me with nowhere to go. We couldn't even thrash it out because, as far as he was concerned, it wasn't true. My source was adamant and I was in the middle. Still fuming. Mike and I put the whole thing to bed later on and it wasn't a problem in our relationship after that. The issue it raised, though, was serious and it wasn't just going to disappear. Eddie hadn't trusted me to turn that game around. He was the guy I needed to confront.

CHAPTER 14

I knew I was in trouble. A second after the impact I could sense it. With the bad ones you always know. It was my first game for Munster after the Six Nations and I was back in Wales for a Celtic League match against the Gwent Dragons at Rodney Parade. The quarter-final of the Heineken Cup against Biarritz was a couple of weeks away. Beyond that, the Lions tour to New Zealand. All of a sudden my season was on the line.

I had cleared a ball to touch and my leg was still up, in the finishing position, when yer man came flying through. He was late, I was in a weak position and he hit me with such force that my leg buckled. The pain was instant. Mad pain. They carted me off and I sat under an ice pack by the entrance to the dressing room. All I could think of was ligament damage. I had hurt my medial ligament five years earlier, just before I won my first cap. But there was no tear and I was back in a couple of weeks. This time?

The first scan showed up nothing but our physio wasn't convinced. The second scan confirmed his hunch. The medial ligament was damaged but that wasn't the problem: my cruciate ligament was partially torn. A grade two tear. Not ruptured but bad enough that surgery was a serious probability. Either way I had no chance of playing for Munster against Biarritz. With surgery I had no chance of making the Lions.

I was in the care of Ray Moran, a brilliant knee specialist in Dublin. He wanted to open up my knee and take a closer look. I signed a consent form which gave him licence to do whatever repair work he deemed necessary once I was on the operating table. At that point there would be no further consultation. My last hope was Ger Hartmann in Limerick.

A physio I know in Dublin called Alan Kelly said that Ger might be able to help. He worked with a lot of international athletes like Sonia O'Sullivan and Paula Radcliffe and anybody he ever treated swore by him. Ger had a relationship with Ray too and my scans were sent to him so that he could evaluate my chances. A day before I was due to go into the operating theatre Ger said he could rehab me without surgery. It was going to be torturous but if I had the stomach for it we could do it.

For me, the decision to work with Ger was straightforward. I needed massively intensive, one-on-one attention and he was the best in the business. He was my only chance of making the Lions tour. The Munster physios, though, didn't see it like that. They were seriously pissed off with me and I could understand their reaction. As far as they were concerned I was going outside the system, which made it seem like I didn't trust the system.

That wasn't the case. The reality, though, was that Nick Green had about twenty Munster players to look after in Cork and Kirsty Peacock was under the same pressure in Limerick. They were busy at Munster training sessions, they were going away to matches. They didn't have the time to give my rehab the attention that Ger could. Kirsty no longer works in the Munster set-up but our relationship was damaged for a while. A lot of craic goes on in the physio's room where fellas are getting rubbed down or strapped, but during my rehab Kirsty and Nick used to blank me when I went near them. I hated that awkwardness between us but for that rehab I had tunnel vision.

Hiring Ger cost me seven or eight grand and the IRFU didn't pick up the tab or help with the cost in any way. But that was the price I was prepared to pay to get myself right. I was in Ger's clinic five days a week, six hours a day and sometimes we'd do a Saturday session as well. I used to stay with Quinny in Limerick for three nights during the week and do the 120-mile round journey from Cork on the other days.

The regime was murder. The hardest thing I ever had to do in my career. After lunch I used to have a kip for an hour and you'd need it before the afternoon session. It was like he took me apart and built me back up again. I went to him with an injured right knee and he identified about five other areas of serious weakness in my physical make-up. My left knee, he said, was weak and unstable. That was my good knee.

There were days in his clinic when I broke down. My body couldn't take it. My mind was making demands that my body couldn't meet. I went through every emotion from hope to despair and back. You spend so much time trying to push through the pain barrier that it wrecks your head and drains your body. One of Ger's partners was a Kerryman called Ger Keane and he was incredibly positive. When things were getting on top of me he kept me going.

Clive Woodward named me in the Lions squad only about three weeks after the injury happened. I got a call from Clive's PA on Saturday morning, 10 April, asking what number I would be at between eight and ten that Sunday evening. A couple of minutes past eight he rang to tell me that I was selected and to say that he was going to give Jonny Wilkinson every chance to prove his fitness. He wanted to know if I was comfortable with that. It was typical of Clive to ask the question and as it happened I didn't have a problem with it. But what if I did? I could hardly raise an objection. Wilkinson's season had been destroyed by injury and he wasn't named in the squad the following morning but I understood Clive's thinking and I knew he was desperate to have him on board.

Clive sent one of the Lions' fitness men, Craig White, to observe me in Ger's clinic one day but they weren't looking for daily updates or anything; they seemed cool enough about my recovery. I trained with Munster in the first week of May but I didn't risk playing against Leinster in the semi-final of the Celtic Cup. The lads won, which set up a final against Llanelli: the last team I had played against seven weeks earlier.

The match went like a dream. We won, I scored 17 points, including an early try, and got the Man of the Match award. I felt fresh and strong and sharper than I had felt in about three years. I had done full-on tackling in training so there were no doubts in my mind that my knee could take the strain. Before I left Ger's clinic I was doing one-legged hops, jumping off small tables and all kinds of other things. I knew it was all right. I felt like a new man.

After all the additional work that Ger had done I had about an extra 5 metres on my pass off either hand. I had practised with an old leather ball filled with sand to give it a medicine ball effect and those drills had paid off. I was pretty euphoric in a television interview afterwards and I didn't hold back in my praise of Ger. I'm sure it wasn't what Kirsty and Nick wanted to hear but my relief was overwhelming and my gratitude to him was huge. Until you've experienced a serious injury you've no idea how lonely and challenging it can be. I was over that now.

The Lions' training camp was at the Vale of Glamorgan Hotel near Cardiff. Man United were preparing for an FA Cup final against Arsenal that weekend and they were in the same hotel. Malcolm loved that. I passed the café one day and he was drinking coffee with half of the Man U team. I bumped into Roy Keane once in the lobby but we were only talking for a minute when others joined us. Lawrence Dallaglio asked him how he thought the series would go. Roy told him straight out: All Blacks, 3–0. Lawrence was a bit stunned.

I didn't find the camp nearly as difficult as I had four years earlier. I wasn't awestruck this time either. My goal was to make the Test team. Jonny proved his fitness and was on the plane but it was clear from early on that they were going to play him as an inside centre. The other out-half on tour was Charlie Hodgson but the way I saw it the number 10 shirt was between me and Stephen Jones. He had a very good Six Nations and I didn't. I had peaked in the autumn internationals but that was nearly nine months earlier. While I was injured I watched videos of Ireland's games in the Six Nations and it was obvious that a spark was missing from my game. The creativity wasn't there. I needed to get that back.

The first match on tour was against Bay of Plenty and Clive told me a week in advance that I was starting. There were six tour matches before the first Test but I knew that if I cocked up I wouldn't get another serious chance to prove myself. Some guys would have had a hard job playing themselves off the team. I didn't have that luxury.

Everything went well at first. We scored three tries in the first thirteen minutes and were 17–0 in front. But by half-time they were level and, effectively, my tour was over. Why? Because I missed three tackles. Every one of them looked desperate: I was fended off for one, I came out of the line for another. Bad. We missed nine tackles in the first half and a third of those were down to me.

We ended up scoring six tries to win by 14 points. I was involved in five of the tries and was heavily involved in three of them. I took the ball hard and flat and my passing was on the money. We changed our strategy in the second half and my tactical kicking couldn't have been better. Eddie O'Sullivan, who was one of Clive's assistants, said that it was a 'masterclass'. Clive said that I was the 'outstanding player' in the second half.

None of that mattered. The two stats that killed me were my missed tackles and my missed shots at goal. I only converted two from six and was wide with an easy drop-goal chance. Eddie and Clive did their best for me at the post-match press conference but they were trying too hard. You know when you're being over-praised that you're in trouble. No matter how good the positives were in my performance the negatives were crushing.

I was savaged in some elements of the New Zealand press. 'Knows how to kick to the corners but Ronan Keating would be a better tackler,' wrote one guy in the *New Zealand Herald*. 'Kiwis know their rugby and they know a lemon when they see one,' wrote another reporter. 'O'Gara should have painted himself yellow and jumped in a gin and tonic. His kicking was duff and he didn't look like he could run a pack of girl guides.'

When I got back to my room and thought about the match I knew that the mud was going to stick. First impressions are the hardest things to reverse. I got on as a blood sub for a few minutes in the third game of the tour against New Zealand Maori and I played for ten minutes at the end of the fifth match against Otago but I was basically out in the cold. I made my next start three days later against Southland when the Test squad had already been separated from the dirt-trackers. Before that I approached Clive to ask him where I stood. Charlie Hodgson had already started twice as many games as I had. Charlie is a good player but I didn't believe he was better than me. Clive assured me that I was next in line behind Jonny and Stephen. Whether that was his thinking or not I'm sure he knew that's what I wanted to hear.

The Southland game was good for me. I was named as vice-captain and I took over the captaincy for the last twenty minutes when Michael Owen went off. I only missed one kick from seven and that was from the half-way line, and I led the tackle count with thirteen – which probably shows how anxious Southland were to target me. Clive looked at the video and said that I was one of about six players who had improved their chances of being involved in the next Test. Maybe that was just his way of keeping our morale up. It worked for me. He said if there was an injury I'd be straight in. Before I came on tour that wasn't the route I had planned to take into the Test squad but in my circumstances I was happy with any crumb of encouragement. You couldn't last on a Lions tour without hope.

We had good craic after the Southland game. The match was played in Invercargill, where John Hayes had played for a couple of years. There was a dinner after the match with a few speeches and a band and we tormented Hayes until he got up to speak. There were a lot of Irish lads in the squad that day: myself, Hayes, Donncha, Geordan Murphy, Denis Hickie, Simon Easterby (who had been called up when Lawrence Dallaglio injured his ankle in the first game of the tour) and Gordon D'Arcy. Eventually he caved in. Hayes took the microphone and said a few words about how much he loved this part of the world. When I say a few words I'd say it was less than thirty. But still, we were all shocked. None of us had heard him speak in public before. His wife Fiona said it was longer than the speech he made on their wedding day.

The first Test was a disaster. The All Blacks destroyed us and Drico's tour was ended by a spear tackle after two minutes. I went up to his room that evening and we had a bite to eat. Brian's a very good friend of mine but there was nothing I could say that was going to ease the trauma for him. We were all in single rooms on that tour but when something like that happens you don't need to be alone. He's a strong guy and he coped with it as well as you could possibly expect.

On balance I didn't like the idea of not sharing rooms on that tour. There are always nights when you wish you were on your own but it didn't help the overall mood. People finished their dinner, went up to their rooms and watched television. The quality of television in New Zealand is desperate and during that tour every time you turned it on somebody seemed to be talking about how brilliant the All Blacks were and how crap we were.

In terms of logistics the tour was massively well-organized. We had chartered planes taking us everywhere with a bus meeting us on the runway. We never went through airport check-ins and the way our itinerary was structured they minimized the amount of hotel hopping we did. But it wasn't great craic. It pissed rain a lot of the time, the Test team were being hammered and the highlight of most days was just going somewhere nice for a cup of coffee and a chat. The lads went to the casinos a few nights and I tagged along a bit, but I'm not a fan of casinos and if it meant changing out of my tracksuit to get past the door man I regarded that as too much effort.

The only good thing was that the mid-week team was winning and the spirit in that group was good. Ian McGeechan was in charge of us and we called ourselves the Midweek Massive. Our target was to go through the tour unbeaten and we achieved that. We put 109 points on Manawatu in our second-last match and I got my first tries for the Lions that night. Two of them. I couldn't remember the last time I scored two tries.

They were useless but Auckland was our last game on tour and we regarded that as our Test match. Charlie started but I was told that I would get forty minutes. As it happened Charlie went off injured after twenty and I was in. It lashed rain but they still tried to play an expansive game. We didn't. The crowd booed me when I sat back in the pocket for a drop-goal attempt shortly after I came on but our game plan was clear. Play it tight. And win.

The final Test was four days later. Paulie was rooming across the corridor from me that week. It had been a tough few weeks for him in the front line. He'd be a fierce man for keeping his spirits up but that tour just got on top of him. He didn't play as well as he would have liked and morale in the Test team was poor. He was still up for a bit of slagging though. There were no shortage of performance-based stats being thrown at us and Paulie had bad numbers for knock-ons. I took my opportunity to put the boot in but with Paulie you never get the last word.

'Yeah,' he says, 'and you're leading the stats for the most tackles on Casper the Ghost.'

Beauty.

Jess arrived in New Zealand for the last week. We had planned to go on holiday in Fiji on the way home straight after the tour but I couldn't face it. Because it was their winter the weather wasn't great and it got dark at six o'clock. I'd had enough of that. I needed some heat in my bones. After the Auckland match I told reporters that I was sick of the place and I needed to go home. The press knew before Jess that Fiji wasn't happening. She was cool about it. Once we got back to Ireland we were on a plane to Portugal within twenty-four hours.

Typical of Jess, though, she made the most of her time in New Zealand. After the Auckland match she was at a reception with other wives and girlfriends and they were chatting to Brian O'Driscoll's dad Frank. Then Prince William walked into the room. The girls were dying to meet him. Frank had met him earlier in the tour so he brought them into his company and Jess introduced herself as my girlfriend.

'Oh yes,' said Prince William, 'I met Ronan after one of the matches. I couldn't understand a word he was saying.'

Stephen Jones started the last Test but Jonny and Charlie were both ruled out with injuries so I was on the bench. I got on for the last fifteen minutes. The All Blacks were well ahead and getting my first Test cap for the Lions didn't feel like the realization of a dream.

Plenty of people said that Charlie and myself were the form out-halves on that tour and that we should have been involved in the Test 22, but I think Clive had his mind made up long before we got to New Zealand and my defensive performance against the Bay of Plenty made it easy for him to leave me on the outside. The Lions used forty-eight players on that tour and twenty-two of them got more game time than I did. That probably sums up my place in the scheme of things.

I went there with big ambitions. None of them were met.

CHAPTER 15

Thirteen minutes into the second half he took me off. We were 7 points down against Australia in Lansdowne Road and we had just suffered our worst period in the game. Two bad turnovers had gifted them 10 points. Neither turnover involved me but I was dragged. I wasn't playing well but I wasn't alone. As a team we were shocking. Still, the finger was pointed at me. Australia beat us by 16 points and the only tactical change Eddie made was to replace the number 10.

I stewed on it for two days. I kept my mouth shut after the match but I was furious. I knew I couldn't let this pass. I had to stand up for myself. The days of being taken off and just accepting it were long gone. In the last Six Nations game against Wales in Cardiff he took me off at the same stage of the match in similar circumstances. We were in trouble and Eddie's solution was to take me off. Where was the trust? Where was the belief that I could turn it around? All I saw was doubt. I didn't need that. I didn't deserve it.

I spoke to my dad and he said be calm. Ask him for reasons and don't lose your head. I worked out what I wanted to say and all of it was clear in my mind. At the beginning of our next training session on Monday morning I asked Eddie for a word. The rest of the lads were doing warm-up laps and we went over to the side of the pitch.

Why had he taken me off? He felt Humphs could make an impact. Nobody admired Humphs more than I did but he was thirty-four now and I don't believe he was the player he used to be. Chris Latham went straight through him for the try that clinched the match and he threw an intercept pass for their last try. An intercept can happen to anybody but the tackle was a poor effort. Defence was always my greatest weakness but that tackle was unacceptable.

Eddie didn't buy my line about Humphs. 'Hindsight is a wonderful thing,' he said. He was adamant that sending him on had been the right call. Anyway, this wasn't about Humphs – it was about me and where I stood with Eddie.

'I'm here,' I said, 'trying hard, obeying your tactics, doing what's right for the team. I'm trying to take on extra responsibility because Paulie and Brian aren't here. I'm trying to organize the backs and the second things start going wrong you whip me off. I don't intend hanging around for that. I'll gladly go home and play for Munster and be happy for the rest of my career. I think I'm respected down there.'

At that point he flipped. 'What's your fucking problem? You're over-reacting here. Don't be throwing the toys out of the pram.'

'I tell ya, I'll go and play for Munster. There's no enjoyment in this, being fucking whipped off and ridiculed. I'm meant to be a senior player and when things don't go well the out-half gets turfed out first. I've had enough of it. I'm not enjoying it. I'm happy to go.'

The argument must have lasted twenty minutes. Mickey McGurn, our fitness guy, relocated the warm-up to a different part of the ground but the lads didn't need to hear a word to know that the conversation had turned heavy. Donncha told me later that I was jabbing my finger, like I'd done with Duncan McRae on the Lions tour in 2001. That was a sure sign I was wound up.

I don't think I was raging with him. At least, I don't think I let my rage get out. I don't know, maybe I did. I had stuff to get off my chest, I had worked out how I wanted to express myself and I said my piece. He was thick with me for doing it at the side of the pitch. He said I should have come to his room in the hotel and he was probably right. Humphs was watching this scene too, looking at me putting pressure on the coach. But at that moment I wasn't thinking about anybody else.

There was a bigger picture here. Drico and Paulie were both injured and missing for the autumn internationals. A week before the Australia match we played New Zealand and I thought I had a chance of being captain. At that stage of my career that's how I saw myself in the group. A leader. He gave the armband to Simon Easterby and I respected that decision. Simon is a guy I have huge time for – incredibly brave with a good head on him. But I knew that if Humphs had started that match he'd have had a really good chance of being captain. Why did Eddie see me differently?

New Zealand destroyed us and we were hammered in the media for our strategy. The plan was to keep the ball in hand as much as possible and kick it as little as possible. I agreed with the plan and carried it out to the letter. But in the media I got it in the neck for not kicking. I was big enough to take that. I went public in defence of our strategy which, by extension, was also a defence of Eddie. He was getting fierce heat. The 2005 Six Nations had ended badly, the autumn internationals were going badly. A couple of newspapers were calling for his head. I was happy to stand by him. I believed in him. He had shown great loyalty to me over the years and I felt real loyalty to him.

That's why the Australia match fried my brain. I'm not the kind of fella that jumps ship. Did he not know that? The match was going against us but we were still in there. I wasn't panicking and I wasn't going to shrink from the challenge. My head was in the right place. I was carrying out the agreed game plan and I needed him to trust me.

That match, though, changed my attitude in one critical respect. I needed to realize that you can't follow the game plan over a cliff if the game plan isn't working. If I was going to be taken off and fingered for a malfunctioning game plan I needed to react on the hoof and make changes. After the Australia game George Hook hit the nail on the head in the *Sunday Independent*: 'There are now real questions about O'Gara's decision making. He is becoming an automaton of the back room directions rather than directing play as he does for Munster.'

That made sense. I wasn't talking about mutiny here but I needed to start backing myself. I had over fifty caps, I'd played a world of games for Munster in the Heineken Cup, I was used to high-pressure situations and I had to start using that experience. For the benefit of the team and for my benefit. Both.

Once my row with Eddie was finished there was no more said about it. Neither of us raised it again. I saw him quoted in an interview a few months later where he said that he preferred to be confronted about an issue rather than have people bitching behind his back. That's exactly my thinking too. In the Irish set-up, though, nobody confronted Eddie. I think the lads were shocked to see me take him on because none of them had ever done it. Eddie's demeanour didn't really invite dialogue. Some fellas didn't say two words to him from one end of the season to the next. He wasn't good at small talk or easy conversations. He didn't hang around the team room very much, although he made a conscious effort to change that in later years. Not many fellas behaved in a relaxed way in his company. Drico did, Shane Horgan. Paulie, Simon, Denis Hickie, Quinny. After that? It seemed to me that fellas didn't feel they could just be themselves when they were around him.

Over the years I got beyond that with Eddie. At the beginning

I would have been like the others when he walked into the room. You were quieter, you were conscious of his presence, you didn't want to say the wrong thing. Quinny was able to slag him but he was the most fearless slagger of all time and he has a special gift for relating with people. Apart from that the overall attitude was that nobody took on the boss and nobody joked with him. Eddie didn't drink much so that avenue for breaking down barriers didn't exist. I'd say Eddie would have liked fellas to feel more comfortable in his company but at the same time he wouldn't have wanted to be everyone's buddy either.

I suppose I got over that fear of him. That was basically the key to it. We had a good relationship then. It wasn't a personal relationship I suppose. You couldn't call it a friendship. But it was a strong, close working relationship and that survived everything.

Was the row a watershed in our relationship? Did he start looking at me in a different way? Maybe. He never said.

I didn't go around avoiding him for the rest of the week. We tried to carry on as normal even though we both knew there was some awkwardness between us. Romania was the last fixture of the autumn internationals and Humphs was always going to start in that match. Eddie told me not to read anything into the selection. I didn't. Humphs was made captain.

The slagging started at the first available opportunity after the row. 'Eddie, pick me! Eddie, pick me!'

I was wide open. They couldn't resist.

The test of whether anything had changed in Eddie's attitude towards me came in Paris three months later. We had beaten Italy by 10 points in the first game of the Six Nations at Lansdowne Road but we had played poorly again and the criticism continued to rain down on us. A week later we played France in Paris and we trailed by 40 points early in the second half. We went there to play ambitiously but our execution was pathetic for an hour and they murdered us for every mistake. This was meltdown. Eddie's neck was on the block. Our credibility as a team was on the line.

Fourteen of their points came directly from my mistakes. One was a charge-down, another was a risky chip ahead outside our 22. The ref had awarded us a penalty but he was playing advantage and the moment I kicked he called 'advantage over'. The ball landed softly in French hands and they were in again.

Did it cross my mind that he would take me off? No. That probably sounds crazy because for an hour I played worse than I had against Australia. Much worse. But the match against Australia had been in November. After that I was back with Munster and we did well to get out of our pool in the Heineken Cup. There had been big games and big performances. My confidence was up. It had been up for weeks. When I pulled on the green jersey again I didn't revert to being the angry, undermined player I was in November. I was pumped up with Munster confidence and that dictated my state of mind. Bullish.

But if I hadn't stood up for myself in November would Eddie have whipped me off again? I'm only guessing but I'd say, probably, yeah.

Paulie and Drico were back in the team but I still saw myself as a leader and the time for leaders to stand up is in a crisis. Three players spoke at half-time: Drico, Paulie and me. I had been part of the problem but I needed to be part of the solution. In my mind shrinking into a corner of the dressing room and saying nothing wasn't an option.

For the last twenty minutes of that game I played as well as I ever did for Ireland. We were six tries down and then we got the next four. I got the first one – took a short line off Strings at a ruck and got in without a hand being laid on me. Suddenly we had momentum and all the passes that went wrong for an hour were sticking now.

For a while it was like a sevens match. Loose and wild. If you

Above: Winning the AIL with Cork Con in 1999. Philip Soden lifts the cup, with Frankie Sheahan on my right.

Below: Quinny and I met the Pope with Ireland in 2001.

Right: Heineken Cup Final 2000: The Kick. That experience probably made a man out of me.

Left: Gaillimh with some words of advice after we won at Castres in October 2000.

Below: More happy days in 2000 and another famous win in France, against Toulouse in Bordeaux.

Above: My try against Leicester at Welford Road in the quarter-finals of the Heineken Cup in April 2003. It was sweet revenge for defeat in the final the previous year.

Above: 18 January 2003: The Miracle Match and a perfect day at Thomond Park.

Right: Frankie and I celebrate the Celtic League Final victory against Neath in Cardiff in February 2003.

Above and below: The Heineken Cup semi-final against Leinster at Lansdowne Road in 2006. I can't describe the buzz I got from scoring that try, but we'll probably never play such a big match again where we'll have personal feelings for the losers.

Left: Wasps and Lawrence Dallaglio have always been fierce opponents, but I was a proud captain when we beat them in January 2008.

Below: 24 May 2008, Millennium Stadium, Cardiff. The kick that made it 16-13.

Above: There could be no better way to end Deccie's reign at Munster.

Below: Munster: 2008 Heineken Cup winners – with a few Heineken drinkers!

Left: I threw back my head and roared.

Below: Paulie keeps a hold of the cup after the game.

Left: Happy times with Tomas.

Below: Three contented men: me, Jim Williams and Deccie.

Below: The homecoming: I'm on the other side lifting the cup now.

looked at the stats afterwards we had the kind of numbers that you would expect from France in Paris. Line breaks, territory, passes completed: you couldn't look at those stats and believe we had lost. At one stage they were heading for a record score against us and at the end they were out on their feet. We brought them back to 12 points and we had chances to close them down further. The French manager Jo Maso said afterwards that we would have won if the game had lasted another ten minutes and out on the field that's how it felt too.

In those last twenty minutes our season turned.

A couple of days later there was a story in the papers that Humphs was retiring at the end of the Six Nations. From his point of view I could understand it. He wasn't getting much game time any more but being in the squad was keeping him away from his wife and three kids for weeks at a time. I didn't think it was the end of him though. I always thought he'd come back for the World Cup eighteen months later. I'd say that's what Eddie would have wanted too – although neither of them said that to me. I used to slag Humphs about taking early retirement before returning as a hero to rescue us the following summer. That didn't happen in the end.

I was sorry to see him go. It's hard to believe that we were rivals for so long without ever falling out. There was never any tension or bad feeling between us. I liked him and admired him and I think those feelings were mutual.

The other long-term half-back in my life was Strings. Against Scotland later that season we made our fortieth international start as a pair and the papers picked up on it. By then we had made more than twice as many appearances together as the next half-back partnership on the list, John O'Meara and Jack Kyle in the 1950s.

Over the years people made a lot of assumptions about our

relationship. Because we'd played together as kids and played together with Munster and because we were both from Cork and started off with Cork Con people thought that we were bosom buddies. The reality was different. As people we're not alike. We have different interests, different friends, different personalities. Take a simple example of dealing with the public; he's comfortable signing autographs, standing for pictures, talking to strangers about the upcoming match. I'm not. We get on well but outside of training and Irish camps we don't seek out each other's company. There are about thirty players in the Munster squad and fifteen or twenty guys from outside Munster in the Irish squad and on a certain level you would have a relationship with all of them. But friendship is a stronger and more permanent thing. How many of those relationships will continue after our playing careers are over? I hope six or seven of them will. That would be a lot. Think back to your school days or college days or old jobs you've had. How many of those friendships have lasted? Only the special ones.

I've always had a good working relationship with Strings. If you asked him he'd probably say I was a pain in the ass at times on the field. Part of my job is to be demanding of those around me. If he wasn't giving me the ball the way I wanted it I'd bark at him or eat the head off him, depending on my mood, I suppose, or how much pressure we were under. Most of the time he'd be composed and patient and just take it. Other times he'd turn around and tell me where to go. The same exchange could happen at training but there was never a time when I didn't apologize afterwards.

His passing has always been incredible and for his size he's a great tackler, especially in one-on-one situations when the stakes are high. Because he's small teams often target him but he never backs off. On the field he has presence too. It's very hard to define that or describe it but you will always recognize it in someone.

He's good at making decisions and organizing the forwards. You could see it when we played Llanelli in a rain storm at the end of 2007. That was a day for forwards and Strings was directing the traffic, establishing a zig-zag pattern, getting the pods going, staying on their case, telling them when to pick and go. You couldn't do that without a good understanding of the game.

For years he didn't kick the ball enough and that was a problem. It meant that every team we played against could focus on closing me down when we were trying to clear our lines, knowing the ball was going straight from him to me. He worked on that element of his game, though, and it's better now. He'll probably say it's one less thing for me to bitch about.

We got our season on track against Wales and Scotland at home. Nothing special but we beat them, which meant that we travelled to Twickenham on the last day of the Six Nations with a chance to win the Triple Crown again.

With the clock running down it didn't look like it was going to happen. They were 3 points ahead and we had the put-in to a scrum 10 metres from our own line. Drico asked the referee what was left. Two minutes. We spoke about what we'd do and we decided to gamble. The call was an ID chip. In that move the centres switch, which makes the defence think we're going to pass. Then, at the last second, I put foot to ball and dink it into space behind the opposition for one of the lads to run on to. My kick was a little over-cooked but we got a great bounce and Drico did brilliantly to gather possession and make a break.

We kept it going and I thought Shane Horgan was going to score until Lewis Moody nailed him. A ruck developed and you could see they were trying to kill the ball. I was the fourth Irish player at the ruck and Shaggy said I hit it like a back-rower. Nobody had ever said that about me before. Thanks, Shaggy. Drico took it up again but Shaggy was screaming for it on the blindside. Strings spotted him and played a great pass but Shaggy still had a lot to do. It was an amazing piece of power and agility to stretch out and ground the ball for a try.

The referee went upstairs to the Television Match Official but I was convinced he'd got there. I jumped on Shaggy's back and our fitness coach Mickey McGurn joined me a second later. Try given.

That put us 2 points in front with the conversion to come. Mickey told me to take the full minute permitted for the kick. He'd already kicked the ball away after tangling with a ball boy, not realizing that the clock was stopped. Getting the kick, though, was more important than killing a few seconds. They were going to have time for one more attack and we had coughed up 11 points from restarts earlier in the match.

My kicking had been patchy. Missed three. Needed this one. Got it.

Going back to the All Blacks match in November it had been a desperately hard season. The criticism never really ceased. Everyone kept saying that we weren't fulfilling our potential as a team. We knew that. England were there for the taking that day in Twickenham and we nearly didn't do that either. But we came through it. We pulled it off. We had enough confidence, enough bottle, enough faith in each other, enough class to execute a big play exactly when we needed to. In the very last minute of the Six Nations we looked like the team we believed we could be.

CHAPTER 16

On New Year's Eve 2005 Leinster stuffed us in the RDS, 35–23. We had a chance to rob the game from an attacking scrum near the end but we fluffed it; then they broke up field and took away our bonus point. In the big picture, it didn't matter. They were miles better. We looked like plodders. We were top of the Celtic League but we were struggling to qualify from our pool in the Heineken Cup and nobody thought we were going anywhere.

I wasn't good and I was cranky. One of the reporters wrote that I looked 'tetchy and careworn' on the field. Somebody else said that my body language was all wrong. Felipe Contepomi scored 25 points for Leinster, including two tries. My influence on the game didn't compare to that. I was frustrated and before the match finished I was angry. My blood was boiling. I hated everything about that match.

As a team, we had problems. We'd known for years that we weren't going to win the Heineken Cup without scoring tries in the biggest matches but there was still no sign of improvement. In the dressing room after the match I let fly. We were content to keep the scoreboard ticking over with penalties: 3–6–9 . . . But that wasn't going to take us where we wanted to go. We'd done that for years and it hadn't been good enough. Tries change the mood and the momentum of a game in a way that penalties never can. We needed to play with ambition. We needed to cut teams open.

I was the first person to speak in the dressing room. Back then I wasn't a voice that people expected to hear every week. I was wound up. I blew my top. Not irrational. Emotional. Sometimes the lads call me Keano because of my outbursts. That day I was Keano.

Jim Williams had finished playing and was part of the backroom staff now. He backed me up and then a few other guys spoke. It was a good meeting. The only good thing that came out of the match.

My brother Colin got married a day before the game so I didn't travel with the rest of the squad. I drove up on my own and I drove home with Denis Leamy for company. By the time I dropped him in Cashel, more than 100 miles south of Dublin, we hadn't spoken two words.

That was the day we won the European Cup.

Two weeks later we played Castres away in our second-last pool match. They couldn't qualify and if we didn't win we couldn't either. Deccie had returned as our coach at the start of the season and that night he took a punt. He threw in Barry Murphy at centre and Ian Dowling on the wing to make their first starts in Europe. Both of them gave us something different. It was a risk but that's exactly what we needed to do: take risks.

Castres weren't up for it and we murdered them, 46–9. Seven tries was the most we'd ever scored away from home in Europe. This was the performance we'd needed to ignite our season. I should have got a try too. I was yards clear going into their 22 and was nabbed. Murder. I off-loaded to Tomas O'Leary and he touched down instead. Chris White was the referee and he said that he'd seen tired horses go up the hill at Cheltenham faster than me. Great line.

Eight days later we had Sale in Thomond Park. They were top of the pool and to overtake them we had to win with a bonus point. They had beaten us by 14 points three months earlier and since then they had dominated the Premiership in England. Their profile was similar to the Gloucester team we had turned over a couple of years earlier in the Miracle Match – except that Sale were better. On the day of the match the bookies were offering Munster at 20/1 to win the Heineken Cup. Factored into the price was their belief that we weren't going to get out the pool alive.

The atmosphere in Thomond Park was different to anything I'd experienced before. Even for the warm-up the ground was nearly full. You could feel the tension. There was anger or something in the crowd. They were psyched. We were up for it and they were up for it. The kick-off was late, 5.30. The grass was a bit dewy and it was a still evening. No wind. It was like playing in a frozen arena. The best atmosphere I played in. Anywhere. Ever.

I don't think the bonus point was mentioned. They hammered the fundamental stuff into us. Work rate, get up off the ground, go round the corner, get up, go again: at them, at them, at them.

They scored first, a penalty. Then we got first blood.

For the restart Axel Foley shouted over at me, 'Put it into them.' He wanted a target for the pack to make a big hit, a statement of aggression, something to make the crowd go wild. I hung it up to give our forwards a chance. I didn't aim for Sébastien Chabal but he was the natural receiver and he stood in the landing area. A giant of a man and the heart of their team. Paulie lined him up. He charged up so quickly that he had to check his stride for a second in case he arrived too soon. Then he nailed him. Axel, Donncha and Leamy joined in and drove him back 20 metres. Chabal should have gone to ground but he's such a proud bastard that he fought the tackle and stayed on his feet as long as he could. It was a massive moment. Their strongest man, flattened.

By half-time we had three tries on the board, one of them a

beauty from Barry Murphy. My clearance was deflected and he picked it up on the bounce just inside their half. Against Leinster in the RDS Barry made a break but he passed when he should have trusted his pace and gone for it. The coaches told him he needed to back himself. Against Sale he did. He had options to pass and he kept looking to pass. And he kept going for the line.

One more try and we were there. It didn't come quickly and then we tried to force it. We couldn't get good field position and they were defending for their lives. Without a fourth try we would have been playing a quarter-final in the south of France. We didn't panic but we went away from the things we said we'd do.

They survived until stoppage time and then Wally killed them with a piece of brilliance and power. From 5 metres out nobody was going to stop him. Got there.

The first that most of the Munster players knew of Conrad O'Sullivan's tragic death was when we arrived for training in Thomond Park, less than two weeks before our Heineken Cup quarter-final against Perpignan. In the room under the stand where we have a snack after games there were candles lit. Deccie had arranged for a priest to be there as well as a grief counsellor and our sports psychologist Declan Aherne. Some of the lads, like Denis Leamy, Stephen Keogh and Frank Murphy, knew him very well. He made his debut for Munster with Leams. Mick and John O'Driscoll were his cousins. Those lads, especially, were in bits.

Conrad was four years younger than me so my brother Fergal knew him better than I did. They went to school together, played on the same teams in Cork Con, went on holiday. But Conrad was on a Munster contract and that made him part of the Munster family. In different ways his death affected all of us. We started the session with prayers and carried on with training. Nobody's heart was in it.

I was asked to do a reading at the funeral mass. Conrad was an out-half too. I felt like I was representing the jerseys we both wore: the white of Con and the red of Munster. I was honoured to do it. He was a talented rugby player, a lovely man and great fun to be with. Before the Perpignan match there was a minute's silence. For thirty or forty seconds I lost it. Donncha was standing next to me and I could hear him whispering, 'Hold it together, hold it together.' Donncha was closer to Conrad's age and knew him very well. I knew he was feeling it too. All of us were.

Apart from Conrad the other thing on my mind that day was my hamstring. On the Wednesday at training I heard it pop. Thought it was gone. I walked straight off the pitch. Training wasn't going well that day and Deccie thought I was pissed off over something. The week of a big match can be like that. Everyone on edge. It wasn't as bad as I feared and I minded it for the rest of the week but I've had hamstring trouble before and in the back of my mind was the thought that this could go at any second.

We did a light warm-up in the Radisson Hotel on the morning of the game: kicking, sprinting. Fine. Then we were hitting tackle bags in our warm-up at Lansdowne Road and I felt a twinge. I was on my way over to tell Deccie when I stopped myself. Where was the sense in telling him? He knew I'd hurt it on Wednesday. I felt strong enough to start. If it went, it went.

I got away with it. No more than that. There were a couple of times when I saw a gap and wanted to have a cut but there was no spurt in my leg. If I had tried to sprint flat-out I risked tearing it to pieces.

The match was a grinding battle and we did enough. Paulie got a try in the first half and I kicked five from five. A few days earlier we had played a ruthless, no-holds-barred, full-scale war of a match in training. Not everybody was happy about it but it worked. We were prepared for everything they threw at us.

Almost everything. I got bladed. I slid in for a 50/50 ball and yer man caught me just below the knee with his studs. The pain was wicked. Agony. Suddenly I couldn't feel my hamstring. I played on until the last minute, when Jeremy Manning came on, but then I spent most of the next week in hospital. The cut was deep, right through to the bone, but the problem was that it got infected.

I was on a trolley bed in Cork University Hospital for five days hooked up to an intravenous drip. They blasted me with four or five different antibiotics but the infection was desperate. I was on fire. I was walking the corridors in the middle of the night because I couldn't sleep and when I was in bed I was using towels to mop up the sweat.

Then Jess came to visit me. I showed her the wound and she fainted. In fairness, she had just come from her power yoga class and she was dehydrated, but she had a history of fainting in certain situations. Deccie was visiting at the same time and he caught her as she fell. I was shifted onto the chair and Jess was given my bed. They wouldn't let her go home for a few hours so they put her in a different room, which meant that I ended up visiting my visitor.

A side-effect of sweating so much in bed was that I got a terrible rash on my backside and my private parts. I asked the doctor for a cream and he said he'd send down a dermatologist. I thought it would be a fella. A stranger. I thought we could get through this quickly with the minimum of embarrassment.

No.

'Hi, Ronan, I'm the dermatologist. I'm here to have a look at you.'

It was a girl I knew from our road. A woman now, of course, and a medical professional, but I couldn't see beyond the girl I grew up with. She used be on the bus to school every morning. Now she was treating the most delicate condition I had ever suffered. I got down on my hands and knees and she went to work.

Me? Mortified.

I was on a crutch for about a week when I came out of hospital but there was never any danger that I was going to miss the semi-final against Leinster. The build-up to that match was incredible. It was the biggest rugby match ever played in Ireland by a mile and you couldn't escape it. I remember being in the car that week having to switch channels on the radio because they couldn't stop talking about it and I didn't need to hear any more about it.

They had played brilliantly to beat Toulouse away in the quarter-final and I was worried about them. I knew the lads were bullish. Fellas like Paulie and Leams were very confident that we would win and I took comfort from that. I kept my doubts to myself. I had huge respect for their back line and I didn't make any secret about it over the years. That was an invitation to be slagged. I was very pally with Drico, Shane Horgan and Denis Hickie and the lads reckoned my dream was to wear blue and play with them. I suppose I had more buddies on the Leinster team than most of the Munster lads. Malcolm O'Kelly had been my room mate with Ireland for a long time and I really liked him too.

Drico texted me on the morning of the match: 'Let's go hard.'

'Not too hard,' I replied, trying to turn it into a joke when my stomach was turning inside out. Texting him that morning would never have crossed my mind but Drico isn't like anybody else on the day of a big match. He can laugh and joke and be chilled out. Then he crosses the white line and he's a completely different animal. I can't do that. I was suffering like mad. I hardly slept. I hardly ate. The last twenty-four hours before the match were horrific. You wonder why you put yourself through it. These are the games we live for, you want to enjoy everything about it but you can't. It's hell.

When we got to the ground I relaxed a little. I went out for the warm-up and the South Terrace was completely red. I put my kicking tee on top of the padding beside the left-hand post and jogged around the goal-line. The crowd gave me a massive cheer and I was taken aback because you never get that playing for Ireland at Lansdowne Road. The sun was shining, there wasn't much wind. I felt good.

Everyone knew that this wasn't an ordinary big match. Under the surface there were all kinds of things going on. When I was in hospital people came up to me to talk about the match and they were asking had we 'any chance at all against Leinster?' I gave a polite answer but inside I was fuming.

Our defeat at the RDS was in the back of everyone's mind. Felipe Contepomi had controlled that game for them. He was playing out of his skin and, in the build-up, there was a lot of attention on him. That laid down a challenge to me. Wally says he could see that I was feeling the pressure that week. I didn't discuss it with him or anybody else. He just knew.

We had to go after Contepomi. Get into his space, get into his head. No out-half likes to make tackles all day. It's draining and it's distracting. You want to be on the front foot, directing traffic. He got cranky after a while. Giving out. His kicking fell apart quickly and he didn't really get it back. We knew we had him.

Deccie, Jim and Dumper – Tony McGahan – came up with a really smart game plan. One element was to crowd the midfield. For their lineouts between the 22s we competed with one forward less. Because John Hayes is incredible at one-man lifts we could still put a man in the air to try and steal their ball. We put Jerry Flannery at the tail of the lineout and that released Wally to come into the centre and close down the space against Drico and D'Arcy.

Once the game kicked off I knew we were in business. I think our mindset was different to theirs. That probably sounds strange when the prize was the same for both teams but it had to mean more to us. We had suffered so much more hurt than them in this competition and we carried that onto the field. Bitterness, as Axel calls it.

We got an early penalty and turned down another shot at goal to kick for the corner. Axel and myself talked about it beforehand, what we would do in certain situations. You can't plan for a decision like that – you just get a feel for it out on the pitch. We knew that a try would be huge, we had started well and we backed ourselves. We got it. In a match like that 10–0 was a massive lead.

I was in the game from the beginning, my kicking was going well and my defence was strong. I knew that Drico and D'Arcy would try to run over me and I couldn't let that happen. I put in a good hit on Drico before half-time and they basically didn't get any change out of me.

We were 16–3 ahead going in at the break and we were in control. But it wasn't over. They had a good spell in the second half, brought it back to 10 points with eleven minutes left and missed chances to get closer. Freddie Pucciarello was in the sin-bin and if they scored next it would have been tricky. Instead, we killed the game.

I handed off Malcolm inside their 22 and there was no cover behind him. Clear run. All I could see was a mass of red in front of me behind the goal. It was an amazing feeling. Total euphoria. I grounded the ball and jumped the advertising hoarding. I don't remember making a conscious decision but from the way I put the ball down you could see I was angling to do it. I was so wrecked I barely cleared it. Hendo said I was like a nag at Beecher's Brook, hitting the top of the fence and nearly falling over. I wasn't expecting to be engulfed by the crowd but I guess I wasn't thinking about the consequences.

I said afterwards that I did it in the heat of the moment and if I had my time again I wouldn't do it but that's not true. I wasn't being disrespectful to the Leinster players but I can't describe the buzz I got from scoring that try. All the pressure of the week, of the match, of the comparisons with Contepomi – all of it came out in that moment. I got carried away. That was it. For every Munster person in Lansdowne Road and everywhere else around the world it was a day for being carried away.

I was interviewed on television shortly after the final whistle. In those situations you hardly ever speak from the heart. You're trying to be composed and diplomatic. But there is a difference between Munster and Leinster and it was part of the reason why we won that match. 'I'm a proud Cork man,' I said, 'and Paulie here is a proud Limerick man and we have to walk the streets amongst our people tomorrow.' That was basically a home match for Leinster but most of Lansdowne Road was covered in red. That gives us something that you can't quantify.

There was about a month before the final so we didn't hold back that night. We needed a good blow-out and we got it. The Munster branch hired the bottom floor of a big restaurant near Heuston Station and that's where the party started. The drinking continued on the train and for the rest of the night.

On the journey home texts started coming through from Leinster players. Drico, Shaggy, Reggie Corrigan, Denis Hickie, Malcolm. They must have been hurting like mad but they had the decency to get in touch and say well done. When the Limerick-based lads got off the train at Limerick Junction I rang Malcolm. I didn't know whether he'd want to hear from me or not but I took a chance. Handing him off for my try didn't look good and he was bound to get stick for it. I'd say he just took it for granted that he was going to nail me. He was out having a few drinks too and we only chatted for a couple of minutes. I'd say he was surprised to get the call and I don't even remember what I said to him but I just thought it was the right thing to do.

We'll probably never play such a big match again where we'll have personal feelings for the losers. In every way that game was a one-off.

Two days before the final Quinny was told he was in the match-day 22. It was seven months since he did his cruciate ligament in the first pool match against Sale. He stayed in my house that night when the Heineken Cup final seemed a million miles away. Quinny was in the bedroom, suicidal, I was freaked out of my head because we'd lost the match and Jess was strumming on the guitar in the sitting room, singing to herself – the only person in the house who felt like singing. I brought Quinny to the hospital the following morning. All he had to look forward to was a long, lonely winter in the gym.

Getting a place on the bench for the final was a massive reward for Quinny's work and typical of his unbelievable survival instincts. Frankie got injured in the same match as Quinny and worked just as hard but he didn't make it back in time for Cardiff. One of Quinny's nicknames is Bertie, after Bertie Ahern. The amount of times Quinny has looked dead and buried during a campaign because of an injury or suspension or whatever and all of a sudden he's back, running the show. Even at the 2007 World Cup he came home a hero because he didn't get a game and everyone said he should have been playing.

The flip side was that Stephen Keogh was left out. It was tough on him and he was fierce disappointed. He was leaving for Leinster that summer but he was a hugely popular player in the Munster squad. When the craic was good on the team bus he was one of the guys on the microphone up the front, keeping it going. Really witty. Losing out on the final was tough for him but the week of the final is like that: everybody is dealing with something.

Paulie and Marcus were struggling with injuries. I got food

poisoning. Deccie was cranky. There were nervous people all over the place. On the morning of the match Wally lost the plot with me at a lineout session after breakfast. I wanted him to move immediately he saw the ball leaving their number 10's hands. I feel that to get the best out of Wally I've got to control him. Sometimes he doesn't like that and he snapped at me. I could see his point of view. I knew he was trying to get himself right for three o'clock. I was trying to get myself right too and that's what happens. I was wound up and he was suffering with nerves. It only lasted twenty seconds. We could have one of those a month. The bottom line is that I can't do without him. He knows that.

We went to the stadium on the day before the game. I picked out my targets around the stadium for line-kicking: loudspeakers, advertising hoardings, just something to focus on. The Millennium Stadium is good for that. I only got to practise my kicking at one end of the field. We weren't given enough time and I was hunted off the pitch. That might have upset me before but not now.

The roof was going to be closed for the match. I don't like that. It creates a condensation effect which puts some moisture on the ball. That was a negative thought in my mind on the night before the game. No matter how positive you are negative thoughts will still get in. Because of the food poisoning I felt a little weak but I promised myself that I wouldn't use that as an excuse. No excuses.

I sat in my usual place on the bus – two from the back on the left-hand side. Shaun Payne and Paulie in front of me. Hendo and Wally behind me. A lot of fellas have iPods. I don't. Everybody finds their own way to cope. I was coping. A lot better than the Leinster game. I don't know why. I said to myself in the build-up, 'It's one thing Munster winning but you've got to do yourself justice too.' I hadn't done that in the other two finals. I knew there was pressure. I was living with it but it wasn't crowding me.

I walked down the tunnel and onto the pitch feeling happy with myself. It was a strange feeling for me before a big match. I felt settled. Confident. I felt we were going to do it. I guess that was it. I felt our day had come.

Biarritz scored a try after three minutes. I was outside John Kelly and he told me to wedge – shove out. I expected Bidabe to pass it to Brusque but he got a fend on John, pushed him off, went through the gap and fed Bobo. He brushed against the touchline and went over in the corner. Rags put his hand up in the huddle afterwards. Missed tackle. He was big enough to get over it. Carry on.

My first kick at goal wasn't handy but I expected to get it. About 35 metres from the posts, out on the left. For that minute I step out of the match and into my routine. The routine is a constant. Wherever I find myself in the world the routine is a familiar place. If I trust it the pressure doesn't matter. That trust is never in doubt.

I look for the valve because that's the heaviest part of the ball and I face that directly over the black spot on the crossbar. I take a line from the middle of my chest, through the middle of the ball, through the middle of the posts and walk three steps back. I make an angle, depending on the position of the kick in relation to the posts. Then I take a step to the left. My mind is cleared of everything except my swing thoughts: stay tall, follow through.

In the quarter-final and the semi-final I had missed only one kick from twelve attempts. Over it went.

Our next penalty was in a similar position. I looked over at Axel.

'Corner?'

'Yeah – let's go for it.'

That was the attitude we brought onto the field. No fear. Controlled. Bullish. We had to make a statement. We had to establish ourselves in the match and earn their respect. We had to tell them that giving away penalties wasn't going to make us take 3 points and go away. We felt we had them on the rack and we gambled. For the next penalty we did the same thing. The breakthrough didn't come from either of those attacks but we knew we couldn't back off. To win we needed tries.

A couple of minutes later we made it happen. I started the move with a dinky chip down the short side and we ended up with a four on two overlap in the far corner. At that point I nearly messed up. I expected Trevor Halstead to be a little deeper because I couldn't hear him so I didn't put the ball exactly where he would have wanted. He did well to catch it. There were two players outside him but Trevor saw a gap and with his power he wasn't going to be stopped so close to the line.

Trevor was huge for us that season. Great team player. His physique was incredible. Sculpted. Mr Body Perfect. He needed a kick in the ass for Celtic League matches where he probably wasn't too bothered but he could turn it on for the big games. During those weeks we'd have a chat. I'd make sure his head was in the right place.

'You're going to smash a few fellas over this weekend I hope, Trevor.'

'Oh yeah, Roger, I'll be there.'

I stood over the conversion near the touchline and felt I wasn't going to miss. I was in the groove. I felt bullet-proof.

The next try was priceless. Strings on the shortside. A brilliant piece of thinking and homework. I was expecting the pass: 999 times out of 1,000 I'd have received that ball from Strings. The move didn't have a name because nobody knew it was coming. 'Braveheart' we called it later in honour of its creator. We've always been poor at getting tries out of nothing and on the biggest day of them all Strings did it for us. The lift it gave everyone was huge. He gave me the ball for the conversion and I gave him a massive hug.

We went in 17–10 ahead at the break. The dressing room was calm. My face was red. My heart rate was through the roof. I was blowing hard. They were getting iced towels for me. The pace was crazy, much faster than the Leinster game.

A couple of minutes after the restart we got another penalty. It was my easiest kick of the match but for the only time that day I thought about the significance of it and I lost concentration for about ten seconds. I snapped out of it but I didn't catch the kick as sweetly as I wanted to. I had to look at it a second time to make sure it was over.

We were 10 points in front but then we had twenty bad minutes. They got three penalties in a row and we were hanging in there. I put a couple of balls out on the full. The way their back three were set up there wasn't much room kicking for the corners. I was trying to put it over the wingers but the margin for error was very small and without perfect execution it wasn't going to work.

We knew that Yachvili wasn't going to miss anything but I don't remember any panic. There wasn't much arguing. We didn't lose our confidence. I remember thinking that if they go 2 points in front it won't be a disaster. We just needed some territory.

Then we got a penalty. Their prop Johnson was penalized for coming in from the side. The clock next to the giant screen said seventy-three minutes. I didn't know whether there was seven minutes' actual time left or seven minutes, plus stoppage time. Didn't matter. We hadn't scored for half an hour and we were only a point in front. All of our first-half momentum was gone. Had to get it. I knew it was an important penalty but I had to kill that thought before it killed the kick.

Jim Williams was running on with the kicking tee that day. It was a handy way of getting him onto the pitch with messages. He had a word with me and whatever he said he made me feel completely relaxed. I don't think it was even what he said but the way he said it. All of a sudden it was like I was playing in a minor B final. I drew breath for a few seconds but I was running on empty. Because of the food poisoning I hadn't eaten enough before the match and I was depending on adrenalin now.

Put it down. Lined it up. Struck it beautifully. Over.

I turned to run back and John Hayes gave me the outstretched hand. I'd say it was the first time he'd ever done it in his career because he doesn't do any fancy shit. It threw me for a second. It would have looked to the rest of the world like a small thing but that was a massive thing for Hayes to do. I was emotionless until then but that gave me shivers down my spine.

For seven minutes they came at us and we held on for dear life. The final whistle went. Joy. Relief. Incredible joy.

Quinny was on the field before the finish and he lifted me up on his shoulder like a bag of spuds. Munster players were dancing and hugging all over the place. When Quinny put me down, though, I went in search of Biarritz players. Seven, eight, nine of them. Yachvili was nearly at the tunnel when I caught up with him. Brusque, the full-back, was sitting on the grass in their half of the field. I grabbed him by the hand and didn't let go until I'd levered him to his feet.

I knew what they were feeling. I'd been in that desperate state. You wish that you could play the final again the following Saturday. Do it differently and win. Both teams bring the same dream to the final and theirs was shattered in the same way that ours had been twice before. We had been good losers and it was important for us to be good winners.

The celebrations would go on for days but the dressing room straight afterwards was a special place. In there it was just us and old friends. Claw, Gaillimh. Dominic Crotty had come home from the States and it was brilliant to see him. He'd been there at the start of this journey and for many of the hard yards.

Jess and my parents and my brothers were at the reception

afterwards. You'd be dying to see them too. The people close to you live it in a different way and suffer just as much. Maybe more. Jess sat next to Morgan and my parents in the stand and she said they could hardly talk at half-time even though we were 7 points in front. In the last few minutes Jess was squeezing Morgan – freaking. I gave Jess my medal and she wore it for the rest of the evening. I didn't trust myself not to lose it. With her, it was safe.

When I turned on my phone there were about 200 messages from all sorts of people. One that stands out came from the Cork hurler Sean Og O hAilpin. I got to know Sean Og through Ger Hartmann and he's an amazing guy. This is what he wrote.

'Words can't describe how delighted I am for you. I even cried after the final whistle myself. No better guy deserves it more than yourself, especially after years of perseverance. I remember a coach once said, "Tough times don't last and tough guys do." Enjoy a well-deserved celebration. I always admire your guts and determination.'

Coming from him those words meant the world to me.

CHAPTER 17

> *'No, it's too far, it's TOO FAR! . . . Everything is against him here. This will be the kick of the northern-hemisphere season so far if he gets it . . . Oh my God!'*
>
> Stuart Barnes, Sky Sports, Leicester v. Munster, 22 October 2006

I opened my mouth and landed myself in it. I wasn't misquoted or taken out of context. I stand over everything I said to Donald McRae in the *Guardian* and looking back I wouldn't change a word of it. But my sincerity was no defence that week. Our first pool match as European champions was away to Leicester and as far as they were concerned I had rubbished English rugby and the Premiership they played in. As far as my team-mates were concerned I had armed Leicester with bullets to fire at us. Going to Welford Road is one of the biggest challenges you can face in the Heineken Cup and, single-handedly, I had raised the stakes.

I don't know how many people read the interview in full – the circulation of the *Guardian* in Ireland is very small. But everyone knew about it. All the other newspapers and all the radio stations picked bits out of the interview and in the media it dominated the build-up to the game. I was portrayed as a loud-mouth and, by implication, a fool for giving Leicester an edge. The interview had taken place a couple of months earlier, which probably accounts for how open and relaxed I was in the piece, but McRae didn't mislead me about when it would appear. I knew it was tied into our defence of the Heineken Cup.

Over the years I've been quite frank in a lot of interviews, depending on the reporter and the circumstances. Press conferences are different – in general nobody says anything interesting at a press conference. But this was a one-on-one interview and, in those situations, when I have something to say, I let it out. Would I have spoken so freely in the week of the match? Probably not. Definitely not if I'd thought about the fuss it was going to cause. At the same time, I didn't disown any of the opinions I expressed. I apologized for an unintentional offence but I didn't retract anything.

The lines that caused all the hassle were contained in three long quotes in the middle of the article.

'We no longer suffer from being beaten before we even travel to England or France any more. That's the level we're at in Munster. We expect to win when we go over there. It's the same with Ireland. I've played against England six times and won four of those matches. That's not surprising to me because, between the walls of our dressing room, we always expect to beat England. But the English public and their team have a hard time believing that. They still assume they should come out on top every time because, apparently, the natural order in rugby is that England are the greatest. It's probably down to the way they've been brought up . . .

'All the old clichés about us being gallant losers or the plucky Irish is absolute nonsense. I honestly think that, both for Munster and Ireland, we've got more talented players than the English in many positions. Maybe that will surprise a few people in England – but our Celtic League is looked down upon because it isn't covered by Sky Sports. I watch some Premiership rugby and I have to switch off the sound because I wonder if I'm seeing the same game. Their commentators are enthusing about the quality and excitement and I'm just like, "Oh my God!" . . .

'Sky do an incredible job in dramatising the whole of English rugby, but the way they hype these English guys is unbelievable. I've toured with some of the players they're now saying are the best in England – and it just doesn't make sense. We all talk about the English players so this is the general opinion in Irish dressing-rooms. Some of the people they are trying to put on a pedestal just don't deserve to be there.'

It wasn't the first time I had expressed those views about the Premiership but in the past I had done it in an Irish newspaper and it wouldn't have been in the week of a big Heineken Cup match against an English team. My saying it in the *Guardian* meant the English boys couldn't miss it. At the Munster press conference that week Graham Simmons of Sky Sports asked me nicely to do an interview and I politely declined. It was still the lead item for discussion in the *Rugby Club* programme on Sky Sports that Thursday night. Needless to say Stuart Barnes and Dewi Morris didn't agree with a word of my criticism.

In the Munster dressing room I was on the back foot. The slag was that I had given everyone an escape clause – if Leicester beat us now it was my fault. Underneath the slagging, though, I'd say a few of them were pissed off. Nobody said it but I could tell. Deccie didn't say anything to me until after the match, which was decent. He reckoned I had enough on my plate and he was right. He didn't give out to me then either but I'd say he was quietly fuming. Everybody knows the way Deccie is in the media, especially before a big match. My interview had been the opposite of that.

I really felt the pressure that morning. I had brought this on myself and now I had to carry it. Before we went out on the field in Welford Road I said a few words. I apologized for the difficult position I had put us in and I said I'd do the rest of my talking on the pitch. I promised to play well for the team – something that I had never said in a dressing room before. Thankfully, I delivered on the promise. That day of all days.

We led from the start but the match still went down to the wire. They got a penalty try with ten minutes left and I botched the restart, sending it straight into touch. Leicester got a shove on us in the next scrum; we conceded a penalty and Andy Goode converted to put them ahead for the first time.

A few minutes later I saw a gap outside our 22 and I went for it. I nearly made it to the 10-metre line before Shane Jennings whacked me. I lost control of the ball in the collision and it fell from my chest to the top of my leg. I thought I was going to be pinged for a knock-on but the referee let the play continue and instead they were penalized for coming in from the side. Shane complained about not getting the knock-on decision and the referee moved it forward 10 metres.

That left it a metre inside our half. From there the kick was on.

Welford Road is not a big pitch. In the quarter-final against Leicester a couple of years earlier I had kicked a penalty from a similar distance – the kind of kick I wouldn't attempt at Lansdowne Road unless I had a big wind behind me. The only issue was the conditions. The rain got worse as the game wore on and it was lashing by the end. That made it tough. You're trying to kick through the ball with your body while trying to stay tall but your standing foot could slip any second and that would destroy the kick. I had missed a long-range penalty earlier in the half when I didn't catch it right, but I felt good about this one.

Paulie was the new Munster captain and he asked me what I thought. I told him straight out I'd kick it. At that moment there wasn't a doubt in my head. I put it down and nailed it.

If I had crashed out in that match I'd have been accused of talking the talk but not walking the walk. I didn't think about missing but what if I had missed? What would the papers have said about me on Monday morning? I'd have been hammered.

Walking the walk was a massive buzz.

As champions there was a lot of focus on us. The ERC hosted a big launch to the new season in Paris and they used me for a laugh. Straight after the final in Cardiff I had been interviewed by French television. I studied French in school and for a year at university so I felt confident enough to handle the conversation in French. Naturally, I kept it simple.

'C'est notre troisième final.' (This is our third final.)

'C'était très dur.' (It was very hard.)

'Mais nous avons gagné et nous sommes très jolis.' (But we have won and we are very pretty.)

Class.

We weren't bothered by the attention. As soon as we beat Biarritz we talked about winning it again. If we were satisfied by winning it once we were dead as a team and there were too many people in that dressing room who wouldn't allow that to happen. Every chance we got we repeated that sentiment in public. When we won the Team of the Year at the RTE Sports Awards I said it on stage at the ceremony: 2006 was in the past, something we could reflect on when our careers were over. For now, our only thought was defending the title.

At our strategy-and-goals meeting at the beginning of that season we agreed we would have to alter our style of play. Not move away from our strengths but apply them differently. The hardest thing in rugby is to stay one step ahead of the video analysts. Every team is picked apart in the video room now and the smart teams had been making it increasingly difficult for us to play the game we had always played. We needed to play with more variety and less boot.

We didn't get it going in the Celtic League at the beginning of the year and Leinster beat us badly in Musgrave Park. We didn't play with enough intensity and they exposed us. But after the Leicester game we dominated our pool in the Heineken Cup until the last two rounds of matches in January.

We played Bourgoin away knowing that a victory guaranteed our place in the quarter-final. They were doing well enough in the French championship but they were bottom of the pool and we were expected to win. The match was played in Geneva on a hard pitch in beautiful weather. It was a perfect opportunity for us to throw the ball around and road-test the 15-man rugby we'd been talking about. The problem, though, was that we didn't know when to stop. We were like fellas who drank pints all our lives and went out one night and drank shorts: we got drunk quickly and kept drinking. Gerry Thornley in the *Irish Times* described us as a rugby version of the Harlem Globetrotters. For us that was much more than a shift of emphasis – it was a personality transplant.

We scored three tries but they scored four and with one exception all of them were gifts. I was at fault for one of them. They got a late try to leave only 3 points between the teams and for a few minutes it was hairy. We were hard on ourselves in the dressing room afterwards. There had been too much sloppiness, too many errors, too many suicidal passes. Leicester were coming to Thomond Park six days later and we knew that performance wouldn't be good enough against them.

Our failure to get a bonus point put us just 3 points ahead of Leicester, which meant that a win of any description would be enough for them to top the pool. Everybody knew that it was a huge game, everybody agreed that they were a serious team and yet everybody expected that we would find a way to win. Why? Because that's what we always did at Thomond Park.

That was the last game in the old Thomond Park before the redevelopment started and there was a lot of hype and history in the media that week. As a team we've always played with emotion, but emotion and sentiment are not the same thing. In the build-up to the game our home record was mentioned in the dressing room and nobody wanted to surrender it in such a significant match, but we weren't hanging our performance on that.

In the end we didn't hang our performance on anything. Big Heineken Cup matches at Thomond Park in January had been the making of us as a team but that night we didn't produce anything. They killed us. It was only 7 points on the scoreboard but they beat us by more than that. The pack has driven us for as long as Munster have been a force in the Heineken Cup and that night we lost the forward battle. Leicester didn't take a backward step. We thought we were mentally right for the match and Leicester showed us that we weren't.

We played with the wind in the first half and went in trailing at the break. They walked off the pitch as if they owned the place. We were better in the second half and there was a pivotal spell in the game when we had them on the rack. We had a handy penalty to take the lead for the first time, 9–8, but instead we elected to take the scrum and go for the try.

The decision was between Paulie, Axel and myself and there was no argument. In those situations you're talking and listening nearly at the same time. It happens in seconds. We were agreed. Go for it. We were criticized for the decision later because it didn't come off: they forced a turnover in the scrum and a few minutes later they got their second try. But in those situations you go on feel and intuition and that time we got it wrong. A try for us in those circumstances would have been huge; not getting a try was massive.

In the two biggest games we'd played the previous season – against Leinster and Biarritz – that strategy had produced crucial scores. It became a signature play for us. Backing ourselves, going for the jugular, taking a risk. It was a big part of what made us champions. But we weren't playing like champions now and all of us knew it.

Ireland were on a different track. A year out from the World Cup we felt we were going places. In the summer of 2006 we toured New Zealand and blew a chance to win in both Tests. Getting close against them, over there, supported our belief that we were players on the world stage.

Indiscipline cost us in the first match. We were 8 points in front ten minutes after half-time and were still in front with ten minutes to go, but we cracked and they made us pay. A week later it came down to the last ten minutes again. From 0–17 behind in the first half we dragged it back to 17–20 after fifty minutes. They were rattled, something I'd never experienced against New Zealand before. They were missing passes and getting cranky with each other. Then the game blew up in our faces.

My face.

They leaned on us with a couple of scrums inside our 22 and when Byron Kelleher gave it to Luke McAlister he came straight for me. I went too low in the tackle, slipped off it and he blew me away. The power in his quads is unbelievable. I couldn't live with his leg drive. From 5 metres out he steamrollered me and that was it. I was lying there like road kill.

I didn't hide away afterwards. I came out, faced the media and confessed to my weakness. 'I have to put my hand up for a bad missed tackle,' I said. 'It's as simple as that. I am a leader in this team. I have to put my hand up. I missed a tackle that effectively ended the game.' It was a big topic at the press conference later and in fairness to Eddie O'Sullivan he stood up for me as much as he could. 'He isn't the biggest back in the world,' he said, 'but he is an incredibly skilful player and is fantastic at running a game. What happens in the modern game is that teams try to create mismatches. They get a guy who is ten kilos heavier and he runs at you. It's car wreck stuff . . . McAlister got a one-on-one with him five metres out. It was a bit like a dump truck hitting a bike.'

I was shattered afterwards but it wasn't like the last time we had toured New Zealand, when my kicking fell apart and I had serious issues to address. This time I had played well and they had exploited my biggest weakness in one explosive moment. My tackling and my body mass were probably as good as they were ever going to be and once in a while I was going to suffer for not being bigger or for not being a better tackler. I cocked up. I'll try harder. If you dwelt on every mistake you made in your career you'd be a basket case. Move on.

Australia beat us well a week later but by then we were flattened and after coming so close against the All Blacks we couldn't get it up again. I scored a try after half-time to put us 15–11 in front but we didn't score again and they beat us by 22 points in the end.

Five months later it was a different story in Lansdowne Road. Australia came to town a week after South Africa for the autumn internationals and we hammered both of them. South Africa put out an experimental team and we had four tries on the board before they got a couple of cheap scores at the end. The Australia match was different. They fielded a serious team and it was a real test of where we stood. The weather was appalling but our control in the conditions was superb. Our confidence was high, our execution was excellent. We expected to win and we delivered on those expectations.

Twelve months earlier the autumn internationals had been a disaster. Drico and Paulie were out injured, Eddie was under enormous pressure, the media was on our case and we seemed to be going backwards. The lessons we learned from that period, though, were valuable. We realized we couldn't be programmed.

We needed to have game plans within a game plan. A kicking game only works if you have a running game and a running game works better with the threat of ball in behind them. On the summer tour we worked on playing expansive rugby and some of the tries we got were as good as we ever scored. If we were going to be a force at the World Cup we needed to play with that kind of variety.

My own game was flying and I was playing with massive confidence. Throughout my career I had always set goals to challenge myself. A lot of the time I wouldn't have talked about those goals in public but in the first half of that season I was very open in the press. In the famous *Guardian* interview I spoke about my desire to be the dominant number 10 in Europe, but with all the other stuff swirling around that week nobody paid any attention to that. A few times in the following months I repeated my ambition to be the second-best out-half in the world behind Dan Carter.

Some people would have read that and said I was cocky, other people would have said I was putting unnecessary pressure on myself. That's an Irish thing. False modesty is valued more than straightforward honesty. I didn't see it in those terms. For me the greatest pressure to perform always came from inside. Nobody was imposing these goals on me: I was setting them for myself. Without challenges you can't improve.

Humphs had retired from international rugby and anyway I felt I had won the argument with Humphs a few years earlier. I didn't see a serious threat for the Irish jersey so my goals needed to be much broader than that. I had reached a stage in my career where I wanted to be regarded as one of the best out-halves in the world. I felt it was a realistic target but I also knew it involved another leap forward. I needed to perform close to my very best, more often. On demand.

Naturally, I was slagged in the squad for saying this stuff in public. Paulie's reaction, though, was different to everybody else's. He was amused at the thought of somebody striving to be the second best in the world. Paulie's only desire, his greatest need, is to be the best. He wants it for himself, he wants it for us. If he heard that Canterbury had devised a new fitness regime that was giving them an edge he'd want to know every detail about it and he'd demand to know why we weren't using it. If you asked me to name the three most influential people in my rugby career Paulie would be one of them. I knew he'd see it differently.

For us the 2007 Six Nations was dominated by two things: playing in Croke Park and chasing a Grand Slam. It was built up as our date with glorious destiny.

Lansdowne Road was closed for a massive redevelopment and the Gaelic Athletic Association had agreed to open Croke Park for rugby and soccer internationals. For all kinds of historical reasons it was a massive decision for the GAA and the debate had rumbled on for a couple of years before the motion was finally passed. France and England were coming to Dublin and the hype was like nothing we'd witnessed before. After our performances in the autumn we were hailed as the best Irish team for generations. That kind of talk was neither here nor there: we needed a Grand Slam. That was our stated goal. That was the standard by which we would judge ourselves and be judged by others. Nothing less.

Wales in Cardiff was our first match. Ropey. We beat them 19–9 – and by three tries to nil – but we didn't play well and it was close for a long time in the second half. I was brutal for the first twenty minutes but I got through it and came up with our third try near the end. Touched the ball three times in the move and showed good strength to resist the tackle and get over the line. Earlier in my career I wouldn't have been capable of that finish. It's probably the only one of my Irish tries that I brought straight from the gym.

Drico did his hamstring, though, and he didn't recover in time for the France game in Croke Park seven days later. With the form he was in that was a massive setback. Did it cost us the match? No. We threw it away. Blew it.

It was a strange occasion. The build-up was incredible: the nerves, the roar when we came out of the tunnel, the pressure of expectation, the weight of history. Everything was different to any other international we'd ever played. You felt it. The feeling was unavoidable. It was everywhere. In the dressing room Paulie had told us to play with 'manic aggression' and that was everybody's honest intention. But it didn't happen. Did we bottle it? No. Were we affected by the occasion? A little bit, yeah. Our biggest problem, though, was France. For the first twenty minutes they were brilliant.

The capacity of Croke Park is 30,000 greater than Lansdowne Road but the atmosphere was muted for most of the first half. You knew that the crowd were dying to get into the match but we had to get into the match first. We couldn't get our hands on the ball and then they scored the first try. It was a nothing move. It had no pace, it was going sideways, we had every man covered. But Geordan Murphy missed a tackle on Raphaël Ibañez and he was in. Soft. Too soft. Before we did anything in the match we were 13–3 down.

We got a try before the break and I was on the end of it. When the ball came to me first a drop-goal was on my mind but I went left instead, Denis Hickie did brilliantly to make space and Wally played a lovely flip pass to me on the loop. Decent score. First try by an Irishman in Croke Park. Delighted.

Inch by inch, we found a way into the match. Fifteen minutes into the second half we took the lead for the first time and four minutes from the end we got a penalty 30 metres out. Nailed it.

They hadn't scored for 65 minutes and we were four in front. Then we blew it. We thought we had it won. I thought we had it won. Some of the lads switched off. Suicidal.

We didn't deal with their restart and they got lucky with the bounce. But after that it had nothing to do with luck. They needed a try and we should have been able to stop it. At one stage in the move I had a chance to go in from an offside position, clean out Pierre Mignoni and concede a penalty. I would have been sin-binned but it would have been worth it. The thought only came to me in the video room days later. It would have been cynical but it might have been the difference between winning and losing. In rugby, all of the best teams cheat. That day it was all about getting over the line in front. We were second. Nowhere.

They did us with a try in the last minute but they beat us for lots of reasons. Our intensity wasn't good enough, especially in the first half. For our first game in Croke Park it was a crazy thing to get wrong. Against England that was never going to happen.

So much of the build-up to that match concerned stuff other than rugby. It was about history and politics and possible protests and whether 'God Save the Queen' would be respected. You can't cut yourself off completely from all that but it wasn't a distraction. We had too many other things on our minds.

I didn't think we'd win by 30 points but I knew we'd win. We were better than them. The mistakes we made against France wouldn't be repeated. We were confident. Bullish. Jonny Wilkinson was playing at 10 for England and for the first time in my career I felt I had the measure of him. Ever since the 2001 Lions tour his standards were the ones I aspired to reach and to a certain extent his example was the one I followed. But until that day I never went into an Ireland–England game feeling that I was better than him. That sense of superiority was repeated all over the field and we blew them away. I have been blessed with so many good and happy days in my career but that will always be one of the best and the happiest. That evening, when we really needed it, we were nearly as good as we could be.

The banquet was held in the Shelbourne Hotel and it was a crazy night. Jonny and his girlfriend were at our table along with Mike Tindall and his girlfriend, Zara Phillips. A round of shots was ordered early in the evening and trays of shots kept coming to our table. The madness took off from there. A gang of us went to a nightclub later and Mike and Zara came along. As a member of the royal family she attracted a lot of attention during the evening and outside the hotel a posse of photographers were waiting to grab a picture as she left. So her minder and our security people organized a taxi around the back and we made our exit through the kitchens of the hotel. It must have been 5 a.m. when we finished in the club. Twisted and exhausted.

In Edinburgh two weeks later I was in a much different state. We had struggled to beat Scotland but the struggle was nearly over. We were 19–18 in front and time was nearly up when I made a half-break in traffic. Like a fool I charged into Nathan Hines as hard as I could. Hines is a massive second-row forward and in that collision there could only be one winner.

I hit the ground but I wasn't thrown to the ground. I went down on my terms and a ruck formed. All of a sudden I was trapped in a bad position. Bodies on top of me. No air. I could feel myself suffocating. I roared at them to get off but after about five seconds I had no breath left. Nobody budged. I could feel myself drifting off. Lights out. Unconscious.

John Hayes spotted that I was in trouble and he responded quicker than anybody. He thought I'd swallowed my tongue so he checked for that straightaway and rolled me onto my side, which is what any first aid person would have done. Typical Hayes. You could depend on him for your life. I tried to thank him afterwards but he just brushed it off. Credit never sits easily with him – for anything. An incredibly humble man.

I didn't really know what had happened but a couple of the lads thought I'd been choked and Leamy said it to Eddie. This was straight after the match in the dressing room and I was in no fit condition to contradict anybody. Eddie was bulling. He brought that story to the press conference and the media ran with it. I still hadn't changed out of my gear when Eddie came back and told me what he'd said. I couldn't give him any confirmation for that story and over the next couple of days I became uneasy about it. I had no memory of anybody's hand around my neck before I passed out. The video evidence was inconclusive but I didn't believe I'd been choked. For a couple of days the papers were full of the story, kicking it over and back.

Nobody had named Hines as the aggressor but the weight of suspicion rested on him and after a couple of days he came forward to face the media. The citing commissioner found that there was no case for any Scottish player to answer and the IRFU accepted that decision, but, in a way, that didn't put Hines in the clear, at least not over here. The Irish media and the public in general still seemed to believe that something had happened. Eddie wasn't backing off what he had said in the post-match press conference and I wasn't in a position to contradict him in public.

After a few days it fizzled out but in the back of my mind there was unfinished business. I didn't meet Hines again until the Scotland match in Croke Park a year later. As we were leaving the pitch I approached him, we shook hands and I made it clear that I had never accused him of choking me. He accepted that. As far as I was concerned that was the end of the matter.

By beating Scotland we had won the Triple Crown again but you wouldn't have thought so from our dressing room. We had played badly and got away with it. It was our third Triple Crown in four years and nobody was getting excited. It didn't mean much to me. Our goals had moved on.

Because England had beaten France we had an outside chance of winning the Six Nations going into the last match against Italy in Rome. Our game was on first and then France played Scotland in Paris, which meant that all we could do was set France a target and hope that was enough.

On the night before the game Denis Hickie made a great speech. The gist of it was that we should play without fear. Challenge ourselves. We could beat Italy by 5 or 10 points and that wouldn't be a bad result in Rome, but where would that leave us? Everything he said struck a chord. The following day we played the way Denis said we should: with daring and ambition.

With time nearly up we had eight tries and 51 points in the bag but nobody knew if that would be enough. We were awarded a penalty just inside their half, Strings picked up the ball and threw it to Leams. Gordon D'Arcy and Wally were shouting, 'Points', but I shouted, 'Go, go, go.' So he tapped and went. That was the way we had played throughout the second half and that was where our tries had come from. By that stage Drico had left the field injured, Paulie wasn't on the field to begin with and the way Leams saw it the captaincy was being shared between me and Simon Easterby. I made the call.

Nobody could have predicted what would happen next. We lost the ball, they counter-attacked from miles out and they scored a try in the corner. When the final totting up was done a couple of hours later that try had swung the championship in France's favour. Leams took some criticism for taking the ball on but that wasn't fair. It wasn't a solo run and in my opinion he did the right thing. Nobody in our dressing room criticized him for it.

When we got back to the team hotel there were eight minutes left in Paris. A crowd had gathered in the lobby watching a television in the corner and we stood there with them. Scotland were hanging tough. They scored a late try and if France didn't reply we were champions. It was too good to be true. The Television

Match Official had to adjudicate on France's last try but he gave it and we'd been done on the line.

In our hearts, though, we knew we hadn't lost the championship in Rome. We lost it in Croke Park against France. That was the day when we needed to stand up and dominate the championship.

Didn't do it.

A couple of weeks later Munster had a Heineken Cup quarter-final, away to Llanelli. Paulie was out, which meant that I was captain. For the previous season I had been joint vice-captain with Paulie but when Axel stepped down there was only one man for the job. Now, in Paulie's absence, it was down to me. I thought I was ready for it. I was wrong.

I didn't think there was any great mystery to it. Decision-making had always been part of my job on the field and as a senior player with Munster and Ireland I had been consulted about strategy for years. I believed that the most important thing I could do for the team was to get my performance right and the captaincy would look after itself. I spent half of the next season as captain and only then did I realize how far off the pace I'd been on the week of the Llanelli match. Most of all, I neglected the needs of other people. I should have done more to make sure that other players were in the right frame of mind for that game and I failed to do that.

On the field my decision-making was poor. They got an early try, I missed a couple of penalties in the first half and we didn't chase the game with enough patience. I turned down three shots at goal before the break and another couple later on. I wouldn't have got all of those kicks but I should probably have attempted three or four of them. The upshot was that we didn't score for over an hour and by the time we did we were 17–0 behind. People said that being captain had affected my performance and they were probably right.

There were bigger issues in our performance that night though. There was no heart in it. They wanted it more than us, which should never happen to a Munster team in the Heineken Cup. We played like lame ducks. Not enough desire, intensity, aggression – all the things that make us so hard to beat. We got a late try but they were worth more than a 9-point win.

As a group we had to confront this. Something wasn't right and there was no sense waiting until the beginning of the following season to address it. We had issues that could only be sorted out with honest, hard, straight talking. A day-long meeting was organized for the Radisson Hotel near Limerick. Our old team-mate Killian Keane was brought in to facilitate the meeting with the management coming in and out of the process at different stages. Management were part of the problem too.

Video analysis needed to be better, fitness needed to be better. One of the conditioning coaches, Damien Mednis, seemed to want full control over our physical preparation and that wasn't possible: in our system we had a speed coach, a strength coach, we had people based in Cork and Limerick and Damien wanted to run all of it. This led to rows and to the players it looked like there was a bad atmosphere in the management. Damien left at the end of that season.

Deccie's role was another issue. He had taken charge of attack but that wasn't playing to his strengths. He excels at man-management, at getting a team of coaches working around him, at making everybody feel included; he excels at team selection, at creating the environment in which we can succeed. But being an attack coach is a highly technical and specialist job. That wasn't his strength. At the end of that meeting Deccie knew the players' feelings on that issue and he accepted it in the right spirit.

I don't know how other teams operate but in the Munster set-up there is a huge emphasis on honesty. If something needs to be said nobody is too big or too important to hear it. Without that ethos we couldn't be who we are. That day in the Radisson we needed to find ourselves again.

We had no chance of winning the Magners League and in a World Cup year the international players could have coasted until the end of the season. We decided, though, that Munster needed a positive end to the season and we won our last four games.

For those few weeks Munster probably needed us. The next time we put on the jersey six months later we needed Munster.

CHAPTER 18

Autumn 2007

We flew home from the World Cup on Monday, 1 October. As we walked through the airport in Paris Irish supporters stood aside and clapped. It was a weird feeling. For the previous month they were cursing us. You couldn't blame them. Huge Irish crowds had travelled to our matches and all we gave them was crap. They could have taken the chance to hurl abuse. Instead they clapped. It was an act of decency and we were grateful.

We lost as a team but you can't share the suffering. The pain is there last thing at night and first thing in the morning rattling around in your head. There's nothing that anybody can say or do to change that. You must live with it. Suffer it. Deal with it. I kept thinking, 'There must be a better life than this somewhere.' Totally irrational stuff. I knew what disappointment was: bad defeats, bad performances, Heineken Cup finals. Northampton. But rugby had never made me feel this desperate before. The World Cup only lasts a few weeks but we'd been living with it for months. A piece of every day was dedicated to it until a time came when it dominated most of every day. We had given it everything and got back nothing in return. Less than nothing.

I didn't want to know about the outside world that week. I

went for a drink one night with Denis Leamy and John O'Driscoll just to get out of the house. We sat at the bar watching a soccer match. We didn't talk about rugby and nobody bothered us. It wasn't an escape because there was no escape.

Garrett Fitzgerald, the Munster chief executive, called to the house one night and I appreciated that. After the World Cup I knew that Munster was the only way out of this for me. Axel Foley sent round a welcome home text to all of the returning heroes: 'Ye're not the first Irish team to bring disgrace on the nation and ye won't be the last.' That's exactly the reception I expected. There wasn't going to be any sympathy in that dressing room, which was fine. I didn't want to be treated any differently. Munster represented normality, something I wasn't ready for yet.

We had two weeks off but I went back to the gym on the Monday after we came home. I had injured my knee in the first couple of minutes of the France match and I needed to get that looked at by Ray Moran in Dublin. He told me not to play for another couple of weeks so that was October written off.

For those few weeks I laid low. My manager, Brendan Lenihan, fielded interview requests from various talk shows and Jess and I thought hard about them. I agreed to meet a researcher from *The Late Late Show*. She travelled to Cork and we had a long chat. It was a good opportunity. They had the biggest audience of any Irish television programme, which made it a great platform for me to tell my side of the story, to address all the rumours and put them to bed. But I took advice and we decided to let it go. The story had gone quiet since the World Cup and whatever we said on television was bound to resurrect it in the newspapers. Why should we let vicious, worthless rumours dictate an agenda to us? Our happiness was a private thing that we didn't need to prove to the nation.

Trevor Halstead was getting married in South Africa at the end of the month and he had invited myself and Jess. I'd have loved to have gone but how could I have avoided talking about the World Cup? Impossible. Instead we went to New York for a few days. Over there nobody knew the tournament even existed. Perfect.

We got back from New York on a Thursday and I played a Magners League match against Edinburgh two days later in Musgrave Park. It was over a month since the Argentina match and I was ready to play again. I'll never forget the warmth of the crowd. When my name was called out before the game the cheer was bigger than usual and anything good I did in the match received more applause than it was due. We won by 3 points and I kicked two penalties in the last few minutes. I was named Man of the Match but I don't think I deserved it. That was the final bit of exaggerated applause.

Everything about that match, though, was a relief. I could start to put the World Cup behind me. Begin again.

A week later we played Wasps away in our opening match in the Heineken Cup. Paul O'Connell was injured at the World Cup and he wouldn't be back until the end of January so I took over as captain. We led by 10 points thirteen minutes into the second half and ended up losing by one.

I was furious. We conceded bad tries and lazy penalties. We took soft options. The attitude we live by is 'Refuse to Lose'. That was missing. Fellas were talking in the dressing room afterwards but I didn't listen to a word. I was fit to explode. I didn't sense the anger or hurt that should have been there. I didn't think fellas were suffering. It seemed to be a case of 'bonus point in the bag, not a bad performance, long way to go'. That wasn't good enough.

A few days later there was a meeting between Deccie and the Cork-based senior players at the Munster branch offices. I vented my frustration. I said we needed to spend more time on attack and we needed to be harder on each other. Denis Leamy spoke up too and he was very strong. There was no need for panic but the stuff that went on in the Wasps game had the capacity to kill our season if we didn't address it immediately. Our pool in the Heineken Cup was cut-throat and after one match we had very little room for error.

I wondered if we would have won if Paulie had been on the field. I know the same thought crossed other players' minds. As captain he would have been barking at us, making sure fellas didn't take the soft option. I couldn't be the kind of captain Paulie is but I needed to demand everything from everyone around me and I was prepared to do that.

Clermont Auvergne came to Thomond Park on the following Sunday. They made fourteen changes from the team that had beaten Llanelli comprehensively in their first pool match and their coach, Vern Cotter, came in for stick about that afterwards. We couldn't worry about them. It was all about us. We beat them well and nailed a bonus point with four minutes left.

The ground was a building site and the crowd is never as fired up for a Sunday lunchtime kick-off as a Saturday evening game but the atmosphere was still brilliant. Leading Munster out in Thomond Park for a Heineken Cup match was a massive day in my rugby life. I had only played two games for Munster since the World Cup and already I was unrecognizable from the player who had stumbled from one mistake to another in France. I could feel my confidence flooding back.

It's hard to explain because I probably feel more pressure in a red jersey than a green one. I guess it comes back to attachment. It's a tribal thing. You're playing for your neighbours, the people you meet on the street. That brings demands and expectations too but we embrace that and take energy from it. Among sports followers – not just rugby supporters – there's a huge credibility about Munster that the Irish team doesn't really have. People know what to expect from Munster and nine times out of ten that's what they'll get. Expectations of Ireland keep changing and those expectations are not always met. I've played internationals in Lansdowne Road and Croke Park where the crowd didn't really get involved. I've never played a meaningful match for Munster where that was the case.

Our next European match against Llanelli in Stradey Park was exactly the kind of performance that feeds our reputation. We were going back to the ground where we had been dumped out of the Heineken Cup nine months earlier and we needed to front up. The rain and wind were incredible, one of the three worst conditions I had ever encountered for a match. The pack was fantastic. We played with huge aggression and control and beat them well.

They came to Thomond eight days later and those back-to-back fixtures are tricky if you've won the away game first. We tell ourselves all week that it's going to be tough but deep down we can't see how we can lose. In those situations we always struggle. Stephen Jones was back for them and that made a big difference. He scored an early try. A bad try from our point of view. Breakdown in communication. They played against the wind, contained us, went in at the break just 7 points down and sprinted off the field at half-time as if there was a million pounds waiting for them in the dressing room, bumping into fellas as they went.

With less than fifteen minutes left we were only 4 points in front and Marcus was sin-binned. Then we produced our best move of the match and Brian Carney scored in the corner. No fear we'd do it before the heat came on. Typical.

After the match our manager, Jerry Holland, walked up to me at the reception and put his arm around me. 'The captaincy is really suiting you,' he said. 'It doesn't suit everybody but it's going really well.' After the mess I'd made of it for the quarter-final the previous season it was a relief to be told that. It doesn't matter how long you've played or what success you've had in your career, everybody needs to be told they're doing all right every now and again. I was enjoying it. I knew when Paulie was fit he would resume as captain and I was cool about that. He was the best man for the job but for now the job was good for me.

Two days after Christmas John Kelly played his last game for Munster. It was a bracing thing for a lot of us. During my season with University College Cork I had played alongside John in the centre and we had both been contracted by Munster around the same time. In our dressing room he had been a massively positive influence. A hard trainer, a good talker, a smart player, honest, a great fella to have by your side walking into battle. He represented everything you would want in the ideal Munster player.

And then it was over. His contract was up at the end of December. They offered him an extension for a month but he declined. I don't blame him; I wouldn't have taken it either. I tried to use whatever influence I had to sort out an extension until the end of the season but there was no changing their position. This was the ruthlessness of the professional game. John's time was up, he had struggled with injury and he was surplus to requirements. Dougie Howlett was arriving from New Zealand in January and the train was moving on. John played against Connacht on a miserable night in Musgrave Park and later that evening we had a few drinks in Douglas. That was it. Game over.

Howlett arrived before our next European match against Clermont Auvergne. Straightaway he made a good impression. We all knew from the beginning of the week that he would be starting in France and he really got into it. When we discussed attack he wasn't afraid to make suggestions. Not in a pushy or overpowering way because by nature he's a polite and quietly spoken guy. We were all ears. The guy talking was the All Blacks' all-time top try-scorer – of course we were listening.

His work ethic was clear from the start. On the day before the match we went to the ground for an hour. Normally that session is optional and a lot of fellas don't go. For that match Deccie made it compulsory. Dead right. I did some kicking at the end of training and Dougie asked if he could join me. He wanted to familiarize himself with his area of the pitch for catching and clearing. Get his bearings. He was looking after the little things that make a difference.

The Clermont game was huge. The pool was fierce tight and if we came away empty-handed we were basically eliminated. The atmosphere was cranked up from early in the week. During training on Wednesday at the University of Limerick, Axel called the squad into a circle and fucked us out of it. He said that mentally we were miles off the pace. That set the tone for the next few days.

As captain I was glad he did it. The Munster dressing room has never been short of leaders and Axel had been an outstanding captain. He wasn't sure of his place on the team any more but that didn't diminish his status in the group. Respect for him never changed. His words carried the same weight as ever. I always regarded him as a reassuring presence. Over the years he was somebody that I bounced things off and in all that time I'd say we only had about three arguments. I couldn't tell you who won them because we'd be a pair of stubborn bastards.

Tony McGahan made a big call that week to change the shape of our defence. Since he'd arrived at the beginning of the previous season Tony's contribution and influence had been huge. He has a brilliant rugby mind and he saw something in the Clermont tapes that we needed to address. They play with a lot of width and he wanted to set us up in a way that half of our defence wouldn't be taken out with one pass. Rua Tipoki wasn't happy with the change but Tony stood his ground and he was proved right.

At the squad meeting on the day before the game Deccie questioned our ambition. It was the first time he'd done that for years. The timing was perfect. He said we'd won a Heineken Cup, a Celtic League and a Celtic Cup and we seemed satisfied. As a group we know we have problems getting motivated for every Magners League match but for the European games it's never an issue. That's what Deccie was questioning now: our desire. What he said was perfect material for my captain's speech on the morning of the match. Our season was on the line.

For the first thirty-five minutes it looked like it was over. We couldn't get our hands on the ball, I was missing touch and they were 17 points in front, 20–3. In the middle of it all Audebert stood on the side of my head. Cut my ear with his studs. I was bandaged up and they put in a few stitches at half-time. By then our performance needed more urgent treatment. Jim Williams was pretty fired up. Our ball retention had been shocking. On the couple of occasions that we kept the ball we looked dangerous. We needed to get that sorted.

We were still 17 points down with twenty minutes left but at least we were in the game, and when Lifeimi Mafi got over for a try you could feel the momentum changing. They seemed to have loads of energy when they had the ball but when we had it they were out on their feet. We got the next two scores and with only 4 points in it we went for the jugular. Maybe we were a bit reckless because as things stood we had a bonus point. But we could feel they were there for the taking. If we had tried to play for penalties they might have done us. We had to be bold and go for them.

In the end they got another penalty and failed with a drop-goal attempt in stoppage time. We got out of jail. Our season was still alive. Paulie sent me a text after the match. 'Know you are disappointed with the loss but that took bottle.' We made a lot of mistakes but the ambition was there for everyone to see and the outcome was reasonable. Not acceptable but reasonable. We fought for each other and we dug in.

They did a proper job on my ear afterwards: twenty-three stitches. Audebert got an eight-week suspension. He wrote me a letter saying he was sorry. I respected that. While I was waiting to be stitched the Clermont hooker Mario Ledesma came into the room and pulled up a chair. In Ireland–Argentina matches over the years we had some fiery exchanges. I thought he was going to take the head off me at a post-match banquet in Dublin one night. Anyway, he obviously wanted to make peace.

I congratulated him on Argentina's performance at the World Cup and apologized for all the bad stuff between us over the years. He couldn't have been nicer. 'You are a good man,' he said. 'Good player.' His English seemed to have improved a lot too. Maybe he just preferred giving out to me in Spanish. I didn't ask him.

The pool came down to our final home match against Wasps a week later. They were 3 points ahead of us in the table. To go through we needed to win by more than a point. If they got a bonus point in defeat we would still go through as long as they didn't score more tries than us. With Munster the permutations are never straightforward. First things first: win the match.

We had a good review of the Clermont game two days later. Ten turnovers in the first thirty minutes. Criminal. I thought a lot about what I wanted to say to the players that week. Over the years when we've played an English team in the final pool game at Thomond Park the atmosphere has been unbelievable and we've always drawn strength from that. It wasn't enough against Leicester a year earlier but that wasn't the crowd's fault.

I thought we needed to strip our build-up of emotion. It was no secret that Axel was in his last season and that he was going to officially announce his retirement sooner rather than later. There was a debate that week about timing. One argument was that we could use his announcement as a motivational tool in the days before the game. In the end, though, we decided against it. We didn't want to use any emotion that we would need at teatime on Saturday. Axel made his intention public two days after the game. By then we were through.

The conditions were desperate. Not as bad as they had been in Stradey Park but not far off it. It was a night for the pack and the boot, aggression and control. The Wasps' number 10, Danny Cipriani, came to Thomond Park as the new whiz-kid of English rugby. In the circumstances he did as well as you could expect behind a beaten pack. Jason Holland, who had joined our backroom staff as a video analyst, did some great video work on him before the first Wasps match in Coventry. Cipriani is a talented guy but he didn't hurt us in either game. When Denis Leamy touched down for a try with seven minutes left we were safe. Mick O'Driscoll was immense that night. He became a real leader on the field.

The relief was massive. As captain I felt a personal responsibility for the team and our results. If we had failed to reach the quarter-finals I would have taken that as a reflection on my captaincy. Not having to deal with that outcome was a huge load off my mind. The challenge of being captain had been a positive thing since the World Cup. My form was back to where it was in the Six Nations nine months earlier. Munster had put me on my feet again.

CHAPTER 19

Winter 2007/08

On the Thursday before Christmas every member of the World Cup squad was asked to attend an all-day meeting in the Berkeley Court Hotel in Dublin. It was nearly three months since we came home from France, humiliated. Since then the IRFU had commissioned an independent report into our failure by a Scottish company called Genesis; the professional players' union of Ireland had circulated all of us with a questionnaire; the dopey rumours were still flying around.

None of that mattered to us. Eddie O'Sullivan was staying on as coach and we were less than seven weeks away from the first match of the Six Nations against Italy. We needed to move on. Without confronting the World Cup that was impossible. The pain doesn't just leave you one morning. You learn to manage it. That day we had to face it, head on.

Eddie spoke first and set the tone. He said he had cocked up. Our preparation was wrong and it was his fault. We had spent too much time on hard physical conditioning and not enough time on rugby. None of us had ever heard him admit to a serious error of judgement before. That wasn't his way. In team meetings he was strong, impressive, direct. He always had his stuff together and there was an air of certainty about him. As his power grew over the years his authority grew with it. His demeanour didn't invite challenges from the floor. I don't know if he was challenged by other members of the coaching staff. It didn't happen in front of us very often. When it did Eddie won the argument.

Over the years there may have been half a dozen of us who took him on over various issues, but not necessarily in front of the group. Eddie tried to be a facilitator but there was an atmosphere in the room where fellas felt intimidated to speak. That wasn't entirely Eddie's fault. He had a certain kind of personality but I don't think his mind was closed to other opinions. Players needed to get over whatever inhibitions they had and speak up if they had something to say. I guess the handy option was to keep your mouth shut and do what you're told. For a long time that had worked for us too.

After Eddie's speech we were split into small groups of four or five and it was clear to everybody that nothing was off the agenda. It was a blank page. All kinds of stuff came back. There had been too many training sessions at the World Cup and they had been too long. Because of that two things suffered: the intensity of the sessions and the freshness of players on match day. Overall fellas were tired, they had lost weight, there was no buzz in their legs. Eoin Reddan made the point that at Wasps the conditioning coach would get tired players off the training pitch. Mickey McGurn didn't have that power in the Ireland set-up and players were keen for that level of input from him. Players felt that they weren't trusted enough by the coaches to take stuff on board and retain it. That contributed to longer sessions too.

There was a strong feeling that training should be more enjoyable. It should have a fun element. Play soccer for ten minutes or Gaelic football or throw a Frisbee. Something. From a strategic point of view a number of points came up: we needed to be less predictable; we needed to address our consistently poor starts with a specific game plan for the first quarter; we needed to play what was in front of us more often and play off the cuff; there needed to be a better balance between forwards and backs in attack with forwards carrying more ball.

The feedback was gathered and presented to the players under various headings. Under the heading 'Attitudinal Discussion Points' the focus came back on the players. These were not management's observations; it was us challenging each other.

1. We go into ourselves and go quiet when things go wrong in the game. Trust the game plan and stick to it.
2. Take more ownership of performances and coach ourselves more.
3. Players work regularly after training on their weaknesses.
4. Take individual responsibility to adapt and improve as individuals in the future.
5. Win games even if we have to 'win ugly'.
6. Have the confidence to voice individual opinions to senior players and management.
7. Leave the World Cup behind and bring no baggage into the Six Nations.

The final point posed the biggest test.

Eddie was late. The Italy match was at two o'clock. His pre-match talk at the hotel was due to start at 12.20. It was 12.23. Eddie is never late. We were sitting around in a circle. Waiting. Nobody talking. Tense. I went out to see what the hell was going on. Some issue with the bus.

'What's your problem?' he said to me, sharp as you like. 'Relax, relax – go in and sit down.'

Everyone's a bit edgy. We're starting again but not in credit. The World Cup emptied our account. The crowd didn't want to know. The atmosphere was dead. Jess was sitting near a crowd of Ulster supporters who were freaking. They wanted Humphreys brought back. I was doing all right. We played some really good stuff in the first half an hour. Cut them open three or four times but the problem was that we had only one try to show for it. Poor execution, nothing else. If we'd gone 15 points ahead they'd have given up. We kept them in it and they made us sweat. The second half dragged. They never looked like winning but we needed a late penalty to win by five.

It was a shocking performance. I've no problem with players and management coming out and holding their hands up after a display like that. There's no point trying to swear to the public that black is white. They could see with their own eyes how bad we were. In fairness to Eddie, though, none of the players could come out and say it that day. He was under enough pressure already.

A week later we were in Paris. People assumed that would be emotionally difficult for us and for me. I didn't feel that way. I didn't feel in any way threatened about going back there or under any extra pressure to perform. I was playing well. Confident. For me it was like the World Cup had happened in a different season. Munster had put that distance between then and now. In my pen picture in the match programme the French seemed to recognize that things had moved on. '*Fantomatique durant la dernière Coupe du Monde Ronan O'Gara semble être de retour sur la voie de la rédemption.*' (Ghostly during the last World Cup Ronan O'Gara seems to be on course for redemption.) I wouldn't have put it like that but I felt good.

With the media I kept my head down. No interviews. As Munster captain I had to attend press conferences during the pool stages of the Heineken Cup and that was fine, but I was keeping my contact with the media to a minimum. I saved my talking for the captain's meeting on Friday night.

A lot of the time Drico would ask me quietly if I had something to say. Most of the time the answer to that question would be no. This time I had something prepared. I questioned what the jersey meant to us. Are we taking it for granted? Do we care enough? Where was the emotion? The desire? I picked out Bernard Jackman and Rob Kearney, who were starting a Test match in Paris for the first time. I told them to think of the pride they were bringing to the people close to them back home. I wanted us to put feeling back into the jersey.

I also thought we were giving in to the negativity that was surrounding the team. Our attitude needed to be more powerful than anything other people could throw at us. I spoke about the class players we had in the room. Twelve months earlier nobody would have had to spell that out. We were in a different place in our careers but our abilities hadn't changed. I wanted us to be positive and stand up for ourselves.

Ten minutes after half-time we were 20 points behind. Then we stood up.

They already had four tries in the bag. A couple of their tries were good, a couple were down to us and our sloppiness. In attack some of our old spark was back. I can't ever remember an Irish team playing that well and being 20 points down. If the French put on another 20 points though, the good stuff in that first half would have been buried with us.

The last half-hour was the best thing we'd done did as a team in nearly a year. Two quick tries and they were rattled. We had all the momentum. They were dead on their feet. We had the scent of blood. We were only 5 points down with five minutes left and our pack was killing them. Only one team was going forward. We were pounding them near their try-line and all we needed was a little more patience. Their forwards had cracked. But we threw it out. Went wide. Geordan Murphy had hardly any room to work with. If you needed somebody to come up with a genius solution in that situation Geordan is the man but his little grubber kick went dead. We should never have let the ball out.

I played all right. Kicking from the hand was poor at times. Defence not great. No breaks. Average. We had given a reasonable performance but we needed a win. Scotland were next in Croke Park. That was our chance.

At the captain's meeting Drico wrote our 15 on a flipchart and their 15 alongside. He said Scotland think they're as good as us but not one of their players would get into our team. He was right. We had to go out and show that. After a while we did. Five tries. We weren't getting carried away but we needed to suck up the positives too. The backs played really well. The crowd got behind us. We had taken the second half in Paris and turned it into something. The games that would define our season were coming next though. We all knew that.

For the Wales match the media were obsessed with the tense relationship between Warren Gatland and Eddie O'Sullivan. It goes back to the time when Warren was the Irish coach and Eddie was his assistant. Warren was sacked, Eddie was promoted and Warren felt shafted by the whole process. I was a young player on the scene when all that was going on. Warren had given me my international debut but we didn't have a close relationship. I met him by chance in a bar in Wellington during our tour of New Zealand in 2006, but in the seven years since he left the Irish job I can't remember any other contact.

Warren criticized Drico before the game in Croke Park and, privately, our captain made no bones about his intended response on the pitch. As players we were conscious of Eddie too. It wasn't the rallying call for the week and we didn't talk much about it. In the professional game I don't know if it's possible to have a relationship with your coach that involves something as strong as friendship. I respected Eddie, I liked him, and I know there were others who shared those feelings. In his approach to matches he didn't appeal to our emotions. Not his style. We wanted to beat Wales for a whole load of reasons. The pleasure it would give Eddie was one of those reasons.

We kept it tight for the first twenty minutes, half an hour. Nothing fancy. Possession, territory. When we lost, Eddie was criticized for that. The line was that we had been fearful and too conservative. I don't buy it. The senior players had been consulted fully and we all agreed this was the way to go. Poor starts had been an issue for us for a long time. Against France and Scotland it had happened again. We needed to get into the game first, then go and win it.

It nearly worked. We were 6–0 in front when Shane Horgan was inches from getting a try near the posts. At 13–0 we could have controlled the game. Instead they got into it and in the second half they did a number on us. There were only 4 points between the teams at the finish but it wasn't really close. In the last few minutes they killed the clock like Munster do on our good days away from home. Being on the other side of the ball in that scenario was incredibly frustrating.

I was sipping sparkling water in the lobby of the Shelbourne Hotel when the Welsh team arrived for the post-match banquet. Warren and his wife Trudy walked over to me and Jess. Warren said he was surprised how little rugby we had played in the match. I was taken aback. As far as I was concerned we were the only team trying to play rugby. I argued the point and then he hit me with a stat that finished the discussion. I don't remember the stat but I know it was conclusive. Basically, he was right.

When it came to the speeches Paulie got up to speak for the Irish team. Drico had pulled his hamstring so he was in his room, icing it. Paulie was back in the team and he was asked to step in for the captain. Normally that wouldn't cost me a second thought but the captaincy had crossed my mind. Drico wasn't going to be fit for the England game a week later, Paulie was feeling his way back from a four-month lay-off and the captaincy had gone well for me with Munster. If I was ever going to get it I thought this was my chance. Then Paulie got up to speak and I thought, 'Well, that's that.'

On Monday night I got a text from Eddie asking me to come to his room. It was nearly eleven o'clock. He doesn't sleep much. I was in bed. I guessed it was about the captaincy but I couldn't be sure if it was good news or bad news. Since the banquet there hadn't been any signals either way. I'll never forget his words: 'I'm happy to offer you the captaincy of the team,' he said, 'subject to two issues.'

The first was controlling my temper with the referee. I have a reputation for losing it with refs. I think it's overstated. I get cranky with them at times but I don't abuse them. Not in my view. He also wanted me to assure him that I'd take the 3 points when we had penalty opportunities – within reason and especially at the start of the game. I had no problem with either of those conditions. I was probably there for about fifteen minutes – longer than I expected. With Gordon D'Arcy and Drico both injured he was piecing together a new centre partnership and he wanted to bounce his thoughts off me. He wasn't looking for nominations for the positions just wondering if I had anything to add.

Before breakfast the following morning Paulie came over and shook my hand. Eddie must have told him. Paulie is a great friend and my respect for him is huge. Knowing him he would have wanted to get the nod just as much as I did but he didn't show any disappointment. He was very generous and supportive. Exactly what you'd expect from him.

The following day the texts and calls kept coming. My old Munster team-mate Christian Cullen rang from New Zealand; Denis Hickie was travelling the world in his rugby retirement and he called from Argentina. My old school Pres sent flowers to Jess.

Ollie Campbell got in touch. When I got home a few days later there was a stack of cards and letters. I was hugely conscious of the honour and the responsibility but I didn't feel it was a burden. I don't know how I would have felt without the experience of captaining Munster through our pool in the Heineken Cup. Without that experience I mightn't have been offered the chance.

For the first time in the Six Nations I noticed a change in Eddie that week. The story going around was that he was told his fate on the night of the Wales game and even a win against England couldn't save his job. I don't know whether that's true or not. I've learned to pay no attention to rumours. His demeanour got worse though as the days passed and by the weekend he looked like a man under siege.

The players weren't buzzing either. The Wales game was a kick in the teeth. The impetus we had generated from the second half in Paris and the Scotland game in Croke Park seemed to be gone. Training was very flat on Thursday. Dead. Fellas were quiet during the drills when they should have been talking and shouting. Confidence was low. You could sense it. See it.

I prepared my speech for the captain's meeting. Simon Easterby wasn't starting but everyone suspected that it would be his last day in an Ireland jersey. I had a quiet word and he confirmed that he was retiring but he didn't want any big deal about it. At the meeting I couldn't let it pass. Simon made his international debut on the same day as me and he had been a hugely positive influence in our dressing room. I told the players that I wanted this game to be a fitting end for Simon. With the affection and respect he commanded in our group I knew that would strike a chord with everyone.

I tried to be positive. I told the lads that I wanted them to express themselves. I wanted us to be bold and take the game to them. At the start that's exactly what we did. Rob Kearney's try was brilliant. Everything I'd hoped for. After ten minutes we were 10 points up. After that? The wheels came off. Danny Cipriani had a blinder for them and once they built up a head of steam they rolled us over. Blew us away.

In the second half I was brutal. I had carried my Munster form into a green jersey for all the other games but in the second half I made more mistakes than I had in the rest of the Six Nations put together. All over the field we were in meltdown. Eoin Reddan said to me later on that a confident team runs itself and he's right: everybody concentrates on their own job and trusts the next man to do his. That trust had been damaged because our confidence was so low. Without saying it we doubted each other.

Some of our fellas never stopped trying. Other fellas? I'm not so sure. I was sick about the whole thing. As captain that performance had happened on my watch. I felt responsible. It was no reflection of the talent we had in the team or the passion I felt for the jersey. It wasn't the real Ireland out on the field but it was what we had become. I was glad the Six Nations was over. We'd hit rock bottom. We needed a break from each other. In my speech at the banquet that night I expressed some of those thoughts. I said we needed to take a long hard look at ourselves. My mood was the mood of the speech too.

Eddie said a few words in the dressing room after the match. He didn't say it was his last game but he didn't need to spell it out. To us it sounded like farewell. On the following Wednesday he sent a text to everyone in the squad.

'I'd like to let you know, before it becomes official, that I'm stepping down as coach. Thank you for your professionalism and commitment during my time with the team. It has been an honour to work with you. I wish you every success in the future. I would ask you to keep this confidential until it becomes official. Good Luck. Eddie.'

I didn't ring him for a few weeks. Let the dust settle. He was in good form when we spoke. He wouldn't have wanted it to end the way it did but a huge load had been lifted off him too. You could hear it in his voice. I was grateful for everything he'd done for me. He had been good for my game and he'd been good for Ireland.

He can hold his head up high. He should be proud of what he achieved.

CHAPTER 20

Spring 2008

You can make all the plans in the world but stuff still happens. On the day before we played Gloucester in the quarter-final of the Heineken Cup, Paul O'Connell called round for Alan Quinlan to bring him to the airport. The front door was open but there was no sign of Quinny. Paul beeped the horn. Still no sign. He walked in to see what the story was and found Quinny lying on his kitchen floor. Out cold.

He had taken a carbohydrate drink but gulped it too quickly and did something to his windpipe that knocked him out. He hit the deck fairly hard and there was a fine big lump on his head. There was no question of him pulling out of the match but he was groggy for a good while on Friday.

As he was getting better I was getting worse. I had felt rotten for a couple of days. During Friday night I got a dose of the runs and I felt like I was getting sick. The Doc sorted me out with something on Saturday but at lunchtime I wasn't sure whether I'd be able to play or not. I was dying. All I wanted was my bed. Deccie asked the Doc if he thought I might be suffering from nerves. Christ. At this stage of my life I know the difference between nerves and being sick.

Then Marcus Horan did his back during a tackling drill in the pre-match warm-up. He was out and Tony Buckley was in. That meant Freddie Pucciarello was promoted to the bench. When they located Freddie he was behind the stand at Kingsholm, eating his second burger. His gear was on the team bus which was now parked in some other part of Gloucester. They had to send a motorcycle cop to get Freddie's stuff.

After less than half an hour Freddie was on. They were screwing us in the scrum and we were lucky to be level. Chris Patterson had missed three penalties and they were camped in our half. We had suffered at Kingsholm a couple of times in pool matches over the years but this didn't feel like one of those games. We had to dig in but we were all right. Once we got our hands on the ball and built a few phases we went through them pretty easily. The move for Ian Dowling's try before half-time lasted about three minutes, from inside our 22 right up to the top corner when Ian touched down. It was a brilliant score and it changed the game. From the outside it looked close and tense for an hour but out on the field we knew we had them and they knew too. Mike Tindall said to me afterwards that once it went to 8–0 they knew they were in trouble. They didn't believe they could beat us coming from behind. On the field you can sense that attitude. We won the match pulling up.

We really went for their out-half, Ryan Lamb. Jason Holland had done some great video work on him. He has a habit of planting his foot and throwing out these long, windy passes. The second he planted his foot our defence could ignore him. Rua Tipoki got into his head as well. Lamb tackled him once and he just laughed at him. 'Is that your best shot?'

Deccie made a couple of big calls that night, picking Tomas O'Leary and Denis Hurley ahead of Strings and Shaun Payne. It was tough on Strings after what happened at the World Cup. I sympathized with him but there's not much you can say in that situation. With Munster, most of us have been in that position. With me it was early in my career but I haven't forgotten what it was like.

Tomas had been waiting a long time for his chance too. The last time we were in the Heineken Cup quarter-final two years earlier he filled in at centre because of injuries. He made plenty of appearances on the wing too. Scrum-half is his spot though and I knew he'd have the head for a big game. He's a good player: he can break, he can kick, he can tackle and his pass has improved a lot over the years. He did really well against Gloucester and so did Denis Hurley at full-back.

Denis had very little experience compared to Tomas but he's a serious athlete and we probably needed his pace against their back three. His kick ahead for Dougie Howlett's try was sheer class. Shaun, though, had been brilliant for us in the pool matches when we needed his cool head and his intelligence. At the beginning of the year we didn't know whether he was going to play or not because he had done a deal to take over as manager. For a while he was juggling both. Myself and Paulie were freaking at Deccie about that. As far as we were concerned he was too good to be sitting at a computer. We needed him on the training field.

There was no big fanfare when Alan Gaffney brought him in but Shaun was one of the best signings Munster ever made.

About ten days before the semi-final Axel rang me. He'd been talking to Gaillimh about Saracens and he made a good point. They reminded him of the Northampton team that beat us in the 2000 final: they couldn't do it week in, week out in the Premiership but they had big-game players. That struck a chord with me. If they lost, it was going to be Richard Hill's last game for them so there was going to be a lot of emotion in their performance. Saracens were dangerous. We knew we were better than them but we had to get our heads right.

Training was good that week. Heated. Cranky. Paulie and Leamy got stuck into each other. If you were a complete stranger listening to them having a go you'd wonder how they could play together at the end of the week. That thought never crosses our minds. Within reason that tension is a good thing in our group. Nobody gets away with anything. Everyone is pushing.

Nicknames are part and parcel of the slagging that goes on and sometimes they change – always to make a point. Donncha started calling me Victor Meldrew during the Six Nations; it was his way of saying that I was a cranky old bastard who was always giving out. Paulie's new nickname with Munster this season was Psycho. I don't think he liked it but nobody has a veto on their nickname. When it comes to deadly slagging Paulie is well able to dish it out. There are times when we think he should relax a little bit more. For his own good. Would that be good for us as a group? Probably not. Paulie being the way he is contributes a lot to Munster being the way we are.

He made a great speech before the Saracens match. He said that all the bickering and chopping at each other on the training pitch had to lead to something. We're always knocking ourselves and finding fault – now we had to put all that into practice. Into a performance. Everyone was conscious of what had gone on between himself and Leamy during the week and Paulie turned it into something positive: going into battle the one fella he wanted behind him, he said, was Leamy. Paulie pushed all the right buttons. We'd done our homework. We had trained well. We wanted to play well. We didn't.

They scored a try after a couple of minutes but we got over that and by half-time we were 15–7 in front. Quinny scored a great try and I got in from close range. A mismatch for pace between me and one of their props. The conversion should have been routine but I cocked it up. Got my angles wrong. The referee went to the Television Match Official for a ruling. I thought it was

50/50, at best. The uprights were low and it looked like it had gone over one of them. They didn't give it and it was such a bad kick it didn't deserve to be given. When I was running back out I thought of our pool match against Saracens at Vicarage Road in 1999. I landed a match-winning conversion with a kick that looked like it had gone over a post. The referee didn't have the option of going upstairs and the points were given. What goes around . . .

We were buzzing at half-time. We weren't playing great but we believed we were in control of the match. We thought if we got the next try we could put 30 points on them. Then they came out and kicked two penalties and our performance went to pot. The conditions had something to do with it. The rain was incredible and in the second half the turf was squelching under our feet. But our difficulty was much bigger than that. We dropped passes, we made poor decisions, my kicking was bad. They got a sniff of it and tore into us.

The penalty at the end could have gone either way. The referee penalized Hill for not releasing but he could just as easily have done Wally for hands in the ruck. We had put ourselves in the only position where we felt they could beat us: with a last-minute score in a one-score game. We got away with it.

Nobody was celebrating in our dressing room. Nobody was talking. It was like we'd lost. Eventually Deccie tried to break the ice. 'Give the fella next to you a pat on the back, we're going to the final.' None of us were in the mood to have our spirits lifted. We were disgusted with the performance. Disgusted with ourselves. The fear of losing hadn't been there. That was our biggest problem. In our hearts we didn't believe they could beat us. Without that fear of losing we're not the same team. You can talk about it until you're blue in the face before the match. You can be aware of it. Guard against it. But if you don't feel it you're missing an edge. We need that edge.

A few of the lads had swapped jerseys and that caused trouble too. After all these years we're still not allowed swap jerseys after matches. Can you believe that? Deccie had a go at Quinny about it and Quinny didn't back down. It was something and nothing. Deccie and Quinny get on fierce well but the whole atmosphere in the dressing room was just cranky.

We had a month to get it right. Against Toulouse in Cardiff fear of losing wasn't going to be an issue.

Speculation had been going on for weeks that Deccie was going to get the Irish job. He was the obvious candidate. His achievements with Munster spoke for themselves. He had served his apprenticeship and he was ready to step up to another level. He bounced it off me one day in the car park in Musgrave Park. I told him he should take it.

Deccie knows his strengths and he's aware of his limitations. That's why he's been successful. With Munster he had a strong team around him: guys like Tony McGahan, Jim Williams, Paul Darbyshire, Jason Holland, Jerry Holland. None of those guys were short of expertise or strong opinions but Deccie didn't feel threatened by that. He welcomed it. We needed top-class technical input from other people to keep us moving forward and Deccie recognized that too. By the end of his time with Ireland, Eddie had taken too much on himself, was too powerful. He needed people to challenge him. Deccie won't make that mistake.

I was in Spain when Deccie's appointment was formally announced. Jess was on mid-term break and Deccie told me to head away for a few days. Munster played Llanelli in the Magners League on the first Saturday of May and we were on the plane to Marbella the following morning. My brother Fergie and his wife and my parents came with us. I needed a break. We'd scraped past Llanelli but we had played badly and I was poor again. Paul

Warwick came on for me and got us out of a hole. My form had held up from the start of November to the start of April but it was in a dip now. I wasn't worried about it and I wasn't happy about it.

Other fellas were struggling a bit too. A week later we played Glasgow at home in the Magners League. The team was a mixture of first choice and squad players. Leamy and Donncha were left out but it was made clear to them that they were dropped, not rested. It was the last game before the final. I guess Deccie was trying to wind them up.

I did my ankle after a couple of minutes. Quinny was tackling a fella, I couldn't get out of the way in time and he fell on me. I didn't think it was too bad at first but after an hour I had to come off. I went for a scan the following morning. It was mad sore. They came back and said they were happy with the ligaments but there was a lot of fluid around the ankle and they suspected that the bone might be chipped. A day later they told me it wasn't but the twenty-four hours in between were hell.

Training was good. We really stepped it up. Including the Saracens game we had put in a string of four bad performances. Were we concerned? Deep down? No. We regard ourselves as a big-day team. The big day was coming.

I didn't attempt kicking until late in the week but I worked hard in the gym. For the first time in my life I lifted 100 kg on the clean weights. The forwards would tell you they'd lift that with one hand. For me it was a personal best. In the gym I call myself 'The Machine'. You're better off mocking yourself.

We were starting to crank it up. On Friday Deccie told us to refuse all outside requests on our time. He said if people really wanted us they'd still want us on the Monday after the final. I brought home one of the laptops from the team room and watched footage of Toulouse over the weekend. The coaching staff had already come up with a strategy and discussed it with the senior players. The plan was good.

I promised myself that I wouldn't worry about the game too far out. A week of worry was too much. But I couldn't help myself. I kept thinking the match was going to come down to kicking. Elissalde is a great kicker. How many will he miss? I started thinking that I couldn't afford to miss anything. Then I tried to tell myself, 'So what if you miss?' I could kick six out of eight and still kick brilliantly. Did I convince myself? I didn't stop worrying.

There are days that I think my life would be so much easier without kicking. I know it's only a game. I know it's only sport. I know we're putting too much importance on it. But it's what makes me tick. When I retire I wonder what I'll do without it. The pressure of the big games seems to be getting worse and I wonder how many more times I can cope with it. But I love it. I need the pressure. Kicking is a burden but I want it. Need it. It's what I do. If a fella thought he was a better kicker than me I'd take him on until I destroyed him.

On Wednesday I kicked for two hours with Mark Tainton in the wind and rain at Musgrave Park. You can cod yourself and say 'You don't need to do this. The roof is going to be closed. There won't be any wind and rain.' But it stood to me. It was a tough session and mentally I got through it. Two days later I kicked beautifully at the Millennium Stadium. Missed one practice kick from forty. I was delighted and then I thought, 'I'm going to have to do this all over again tomorrow.' That annoyed me. Why? It wasn't rational. I wasn't in a rational state of mind.

The nerves were crazy. Later that evening I went for a walk. Just to get out. There's a golf course at the hotel and I ambled around for twenty minutes. I didn't know where I was going. What was going through my mind? The thought of losing three finals out of four. How could we live with that?

The team meeting was good that night. Calmer than any of the meetings before the other three finals. That was a help. I didn't need to be revved up any more. I was rooming with Quinny. He was suffering too. We agreed it was the worst ever. On Saturday morning I thought I was going to get a nervous breakdown. I told Quinny. I knew he'd understand.

Getting on to the field was like being released from prison.

My first kick in open play went straight to their number 8, Shaun Sowerby. Breakdown in communication with Rua. The kicking calls are K, I, C: K for down the left, I for up the middle, C for down the right. Rua saw space up the middle but I thought he said K. When you don't have time to look you trust the call. Great start. I was chilled though. The worry was gone. Whatever happens out here I can deal with it.

For twenty minutes we couldn't get our hands on the ball. Our plan was to dictate the tempo from the start with our kicking game and target their winger, Yves Donguy. Put the ball in behind him, make him turn. All we were doing, though, was tackling. I missed touch a couple of times and even when I found touch they were hitting us with quick throws. They were taking the game to us.

Denis was a bag of nerves at full-back. I could see it during the week. He had just finished exams and then he was straight into the biggest game of his life. His mistakes were being highlighted too much in training. I said it to a couple of lads on Tuesday. He needed to be picked up. Praised. Over-praised. But then the day comes and nobody can hold your hand. I was about the same age as Denis in my first final. I haven't forgotten how hard that was and how many mistakes I made. You go through it and come out the other side. He's going to be a star for us.

They missed a couple of chances. Twenty-five minutes of pressure for 3 points. Nothing. We got down the field and made them pay. I thought Leamy had scored the first time he got over the line. He was convinced too. All the lads ran to half-way while the Television Match Official was having a look. Fabien

Pelous was holding the ball and he wouldn't give it to me for the conversion. No try. Go again.

It was their put-in to a 5-metre scrum but we got a shove on and Tomas did brilliantly to nail Byron Kelleher. I was having my own battle with him. A couple of shoulder charges, a bit of cursing and swearing. The usual lip. Quinny was in his ear the whole time. He didn't like it. The next put-in was ours and we battered them. Leamy got over again. Try.

A few minutes later I had my first penalty. For every kick I have my swing thoughts and a couple of key phrases to trigger them. That day I added another. In the hotel that morning I watched the semi-final of the Super 14. Dan Carter was playing. He was brilliant. As a rule he doesn't miss and I said to myself, 'Why should I miss? I do everything he does. I put in the hours of practice, I have the technique, why should I miss?'

Dutchy was bringing on the kicking tee during the match and I confided my swing thoughts to him. If things weren't going well I wanted him to repeat them to me when he gave me the tee. Dutchy wasn't taking any chances: he gave me the swing thoughts every time.

Every kick is my first kick. Stay tall. Follow through. Carter doesn't miss.

Four points up at half-time. After the pressure we'd absorbed that was huge. Everything was calm in the dressing room. Anybody who wanted to speak had his say. I wanted us to move the ball more. I felt our backs were dangerous all day. I knew we could hurt them out wide if we could get the ball going through the hands. Dougie's disallowed try proved it. The pass from Rua was only a fraction forward but it showed what we had behind the scrum. It must have made them think.

I was struggling to get my own game going. There was a time, years ago, when that would have bothered me. Affected me. Not now. My confidence doesn't just desert me at the first sign of trouble. What use is confidence like that? The mentality I have now I have spent a lifetime building, consciously and unconsciously. Early in the second half I was charged down twice, a couple of minutes apart. It's always a shock. I didn't see the guy coming. I thought I was in the clear. I was annoyed but I wasn't rattled. Dump it.

Next ball.

They had a lineout around half-way and I anticipated an overthrow. Got a hunch and gambled. I jumped high for the ball and got milled. Took a hammering in the ribs but secured the turnover. After the charge-downs that was the next ball.

A few minutes later they were down to fourteen men. The sin-binning of Pelous was classic Quinny. I don't know what Quinny said but it doesn't matter. Pelous is the most capped French international of all time. Discipline is his big thing and Quinny cracked him. The chat was between Quinny and Kelleher, there was no need for Pelous to get involved. Once he kicked Quinny in the backside he was bound to go to the sin-bin. Some people argued it was a harsh yellow card. How can it be harsh? The guy raised his foot.

When Pelous was penalized I landed the kick to put us 7 points in front. Cedric Heymans made a brilliant break down the line and kicked ahead. Once. Twice. I was the last man back and I thought I had it. I didn't get my body down quickly enough. I was concentrating too much on getting my hands on it and bouncing up again. If I'd dipped to the ground a little bit quicker I would have got a boot in the back but I would have stopped the try. Jauzion got a great toe-poke to the ball and Donguy got the touch down. 13-all. Game on.

They should have scored again before we did. Elissalde put in a cross-kick when they had men over. I was the second-last man in our defensive line and Marcus was 40 yards from me. I was thinking what the hell was I going to do? The risky play was to come out of the line and try to take man and ball. If you time it wrong the show is over and you're the villain for leaving the line. Elissalde kicked. Panic over.

The next score was huge. We got it. The penalty was moved forward for dissent. Either way, distance wasn't an issue. I felt totally relaxed. The mistakes I had made in the match didn't matter. This could be the winning kick. Didn't matter. This was just about me and my kicking. My technique, my practice, my ability to cope with the pressure. This is what I'm here to do. Dutchy gave me the kicking tee and my trigger phrases. It crossed my mind that he was getting a laugh out of this and inside I was nearly laughing too. I couldn't believe it. The last fifteen minutes of a European final with the sides level and I nearly got a fit of the giggles. Totally relaxed.

Put the ball down. Lined it up. Bang. 16–13.

Then the forwards took over. They thought they could keep the ball for eight minutes. Incredible. In my own mind I was thinking three minutes. Tomas was keeping them going and they were all volunteering for carries. Every one of them was getting smashed and nobody was hiding. To watch your pack doing that was awesome.

Then Rua started roaring at me to get the ball out and I was roaring at Tomas. He was preoccupied with keeping the forwards going and with the volume of noise in the stadium he couldn't hear me. I went in to him but he's well able to stand his ground too. 'I'm trying,' he said, 'I'm trying.' They kept it going for seventeen phases before they were penalized. I was demanding the ball after eight phases.

Toulouse kicked it downfield from the penalty but they lost it at the lineout and we were attacking again. They were pinged just over half-way and there was only half a minute on the clock. I went to the referee straightaway to see what the story was. He said there's another play after this.

I went over to Paulie. What are our options here? He said kick it. I said, 'What if I hit the post?' And even if I scored, 6 points was no better than 3 points against them. The ref was going to allow them take the restart. France only needed a restart to do us in Croke Park.

Hayes and Leamy were shouting at us, 'Take the points,' but they didn't know there was another play coming. We kept talking. Will I kick it to touch? He said we could lose the lineout. So he said, 'Right, kill the clock. Tap it to me.'

I gave it to him too quickly. They weren't back 10 metres but I should have pointed that out to the ref. I should have given Paulie twenty seconds to get ready. The clock wasn't going to resume until I touched the ball anyway. Instead I popped it to Paulie and they gang-tackled him. They could have turned him over. They didn't.

The ref blew.

Thanks be to God.

Rua, Mafi and Jerry Flannery were next to me. The buzz was unreal. The noise, the elation, the relief. I went round to a few of the Toulouse players. Elissalde wouldn't shake my hand. I caught him on the calf in the first half with my studs and he thought I had tried to hurt him. It was a complete accident. Twenty minutes later he apologized. I was glad about that. There was no reason for any bad blood between us.

Then Paulie wanted a word.

'I'm not taking no for an answer here,' he said, 'I want you to lift the cup with me.'

My first instinct was 'no'. He was the captain, a giant in our dressing room, he deserved the honour. He wouldn't take no for an answer.

This season had started with the World Cup. A miserable failure. The toughest time in my life. Out of that nightmare had come this dream. For all the Munster players who failed at the World

Cup this campaign was a chance to redeem ourselves. More than a chance it was a challenge. For our credibility as men and rugby players we had to stand up and do it. We'd done it. In the hardest campaign you could imagine, we'd done it.

Paulie and I walked up last onto the podium. The stadium went dark. I could feel the cup in my right hand. I thought of Jess and Mum and imagined the joy on their faces. And I thought of Dad. This moment. Lifting the cup. This was for him and all he had done for me. My thanks for everything.

Paulie and I lifted the cup together. I threw my head back and roared.

CAREER RECORD

APPENDIX ONE – RONAN O'GARA – RECORD FOR IRELAND AT SENIOR INTERNATIONAL LEVEL

CAP	DATE	OPPONENTS	VENUE	COMPETITION	RESULT	ROG POINTS
1	19/02/2000	SCOTLAND	LANSDOWNE ROAD	6 N	W 44–22	10 (2 con, 2 pg)
2	04/03/2000	ITALY	LANSDOWNE ROAD	6 N	W 60–13	30 (6 con, 6 pg)
3	19/03/2000	FRANCE	STADE de FRANCE	6 N	W 27–25	4 (2 con)
4	01/04/2000	WALES	LANSDOWNE ROAD	6 N	L 19–23	14 (con, 4 pg)
5	03/06/2000	ARGENTINA*	BUENOS AIRES	SHORT TOUR	L 23–24	Did not score
6	10/06/2000	USA	NEW HAMPSHIRE	SHORT TOUR	W 83–3	16 (8 con)
7	17/06/2000	CANADA*	TORONTO	SHORT TOUR	D 27–27	9 (3 pg)
8	11/11/2000	JAPAN	LANSDOWNE ROAD	AUTUMN TEST	W 78–9	23 (10 con, pg)
9	19/11/2000	SOUTH AFRICA	LANSDOWNE ROAD	AUTUMN TEST	L 18–28	8 (con, 2 pg)
10	03/02/2001	ITALY	STADIO FLAMINIO	6 N	W 41–21	21 (try, 2 con, 4 pg)
11	17/02/2001	FRANCE	LANSDOWNE ROAD	6 N	W 22–15	17 (con, 5 pg)
12	22/09/2001	SCOTLAND	MURRAYFIELD	6 N	L 10–32	3 (pg)
13	13/10/2001	WALES*	MILLENNIUM STAD.	6 N	W 36–6	2 (con)
14	20/10/2001	ENGLAND *	LANSDOWNE ROAD	6 N	W 20–14	6 (2 pg)
15	11/11/2001	SAMOA	LANSDOWNE ROAD	AUTUMN TEST	W 35–8	15 (3 con, 3 pg)
16	03/02/2002	WALES*	LANSDOWNE ROAD	6 N	W 54–10	7 (try, con)
17	16/02/2002	ENGLAND*	TWICKENHAM	6 N	L 11–45	5 (try)
18	02/03/2002	SCOTLAND*	LANSDOWNE ROAD	6 N	W 43–22	2 (con)
19	23/03/2002	ITALY*	LANSDOWNE ROAD	6 N	W 32–17	5 (con, pg)
20	06/04/2002	FRANCE*	STADE de FRANCE	6 N	L 5–44	Did not score
21	15/06/2002	NEW ZEALAND	CARISBROOK DUNEDIN	SHORT TOUR	L 6–15	3 (pg)
22	22/06/2002	NEW ZEALAND	EDEN PK AUCKLAND	SHORT TOUR	L 8–40	Did not score
23	07/09/2002	ROMANIA	THOMOND PARK	CHALLENGE GAME	W 39–8	12 (3 con, 2 pg)
24	21/09/2002	RUSSIA	EAST SIBERIA	RWC QUALIFIER	W 35–3	15 (3 con, 3 pg)
25	28/09/2002	GEORGIA	LANSDOWNE ROAD	RWC QUALIFIER	W 63–14	19 (5 con, 3 pg)
26	09/11/2002	AUSTRALIA	LANSDOWNE ROAD	AUTUMN TEST	W 18–9	18 (6 pg)
27	22/11/2002	ARGENTINA	LANSDOWNE ROAD	AUTUMN TEST	W 16–7	11 (con, 3 pg)
28	22/03/2003	WALES*	MILLENNIUM STAD	6 N	W 25–24	3 (dg)
29	30/03/2003	ENGLAND*	LANSDOWNE ROAD	6 N	L 6–42	Did not score
30	07/06/2003	AUSTRALIA*	SUBIACO OVAL PERTH	SHORT TOUR	L 16–45	3 (pg)
31	14/06/2003	TONGA	STAD NUKU A'LOFA	SHORT TOUR	W 40–19	10 (2 con, 2 pg)
32	20/06/2003	SAMOA	APIA PARK	SHORT TOUR	W 40–14	32 (2 try, 2 con, 5pg, d)
33	06/09/2003	SCOTLAND	MURRAYFIELD	RWC WARM UP	W 29–10	9 (3 con, pg)
34	11/10/2003	ROMANIA*	CENTRAL COAST STAD	RWC – 5 POOL	W 45–17	2 (con)
35	19/01/2003	NAMIBIA	AUSSIE STAD SYDNEY	RWC – 5 POOL	W 64–7	14 (7 con)
36	26/10/2003	ARGENTINA*	ADELAIDE OVAL	RWC – 5 POOL	W 16–15	6 (2 pg)
37	01/11/2003	AUSTRALIA	TELSTRA DOME	RWC – 5 POOL	L 16–17	8 (con, 2 pg)
38	09/11/2003	FRANCE	TELSTRA DOME	RWC – 5 Q-FINAL	L 21–43	Did not score
39	14/02/2004	FRANCE	STADE de FRANCE	6 N	L 17–35	7 (2 con, pg)
40	22/02/2004	WALES	LANSDOWNE ROAD	6 N	W 36–15	11 (try, 3 con)
41	06/03/2004	ENGLAND	TWICKENHAM	6 N	W 19–13	14 (con, 4 pg)
42	20/03/2004	ITALY	LANSDOWNE ROAD	6 N	W 19–3	4 (2 con)
43	27/03/2004	SCOTLAND	LANSDOWNE ROAD	6 N	[illegible]	[illegible]

45	19/06/2004	SOUTH AFRICA	NEWLANDS, CAPE TOWN	SHORT TOUR	L 17–26	5 (con, d)
46	13/11/2004	SOUTH AFRICA	LANSDOWNE ROAD	AUTUMN TEST	W 17–12	17 (try, 3 pg, d)
47	27/11/2004	ARGENTINA	LANSDOWNE ROAD	AUTUMN TEST	W 21–19	21 (5 pg, 2dg)
48	06/02/2005	ITALY	STADIO FLAMINIO	6 N	W 28–17	13 (2 con, 3 pg)
49	12/02/2005	SCOTLAND	MURRAYFIELD	6 N	W 40–13	13 (2 con, 3 pg)
50	27/02/2005	ENGLAND	LANSDOWNE ROAD	6 N	W 19–13	14 (con, 2 pg, 2 d)
51	12/03/2005	FRANCE	LANSDOWNE ROAD	6 N	L 19–26	14 (con, 4 pg)
52	19/03/2005	WALES	MILLENNIUM STAD	6 N	L 20–32	6 (2 pg)
53	12/11/2005	NEW ZEALAND	LANSDOWNE ROAD	AUTUMN TEST	L 7–45	Did not score
54	19/11/2005	AUSTRALIA	LANSDOWNE ROAD	AUTUMN TEST	L 14–30	6 (2 pg)
55	26/11/2005	ROMANIA*	LANSDOWNE ROAD	AUTUMN TEST	W 43–12	Did not score
56	04/02/2006	ITALY	LANSDOWNE ROAD	6 N	W 43–12	16 (2 con, 4 pg)
57	11/02/2006	FRANCE	STADE de FRANCE	6 N	L 31–43	16 (try, 4 con, pg)
58	26/02/2006	WALES	LANSDOWNE ROAD	6 N	W 31–5	16 (2 con, 4 pg)
59	11/03/2006	SCOTLAND	LANSDOWNE ROAD	6 N	W 15–9	15 (5 pg)
60	18/03/2006	ENGLAND	TWICKENHAM	6 N	W 28–24	13 (2 con, 3 pg)
61	10/06/2006	NEW ZEALAND	WAIKATO STADIUM	SHORT TOUR	L 23–24	13 (2 con, 3 pg)
62	17/06/2006	NEW ZEALAND	EDEN PK AUCKLAND	SHORT TOUR	L 17–27	7 (2 con, pg)
63	24/06/2006	AUSTRALIA	SUBIACO OVAL	SHORT TOUR	L 15–37	10 (try, con, pg)
64	11/11/2006	SOUTH AFRICA	LANSDOWNE ROAD	AUTUMN TEST	W 32–15	12 (3 con, 2 pg)
65	19/11/2006	AUSTRALIA	LANSDOWNE ROAD	AUTUMN TEST	W 21–6	11 (con, 3 pg)
66	26/11/2006	PACIFIC ISLES*	LANSDOWNE ROAD	AUTUMN TEST	W 61–15	Did not score
67	04/02/2007	WALES	MILLENNIUM STADIUM	6 N	W 19–9	9 (try, 2 con)
68	11/02/2007	FRANCE	CROKE PARK	6 N	L 17–20	17 (try, 4 pg)
69	24/02/2007	ENGLAND	CROKE PARK	6 N	W 43–13	21 (3 con, 5 pg)
70	10/03/2007	SCOTLAND	MURRAYFIELD	6 N	W 19–18	19 (try, con, 4 pg)
71	17/03/2007	ITALY	STADIO FLAMINIO	6 N	W 51–24	16 (try, 4 con, pg)
72	11/08/2007	SCOTLAND*	MURRAYFIELD	RWC WARM UP	L 21–31	Did not scor
73	24/08/2007	ITALY	RAVENHILL BELFAST	RWC WARM UP	W 23–20	18 (try, 2con, 2pg, d)
74	09/09/2007	NAMIBIA	BORDEAUX	RWC – 6 POOL	W 32–17	7 (2 con, pg)
75	15/09/2007	GEORGIA	BORDEAUX	RWC – 6 POOL	W 14–10	4 (2 con)
76	21/09/2007	FRANCE	STADE de FRANCE	RWC – 6 POOL	L 3–25	3 (dg)
77	30/09/2007	ARGENTINA	PARC des PRINCES	RWC – 6 POOL	L 15–30	5 (con, pg)
78	02/02/2008	ITALY	CROKE PARK	6 N	W 16–11	11 (con, 3 pg)
79	09/02/2008	FRANCE	STADE de FRANCE	6 N	L 21–26	3 (con, 3 pg)
80	23/02/2008	SCOTLAND	CROKE PARK	6 N	W 34–13	9 (3 con, pg)
81	08/03/2008	WALES	CROKE PARK	6 N	L 12–16	12 (4 pg)
82	15/03/2008	ENGLAND (c)	TWICKENHAM	6 N	L 10–33	5 (con, pg)
83	07/06/2008	NEW ZEALAND	WELLINGTON	SHORT TOUR	L 11–21	6 (2 pg)
84	14/06/2008	AUSTRALIA	TELSTRA DOME	SHORT TOUR	L 12–18	2 (con)

* caps (17) as a replacement

IRELAND RECORD

P – 84, W – 51, D – 1, L – 32
Points: 835 (14 t, 129 c, 158 p, 11 d)

APPENDIX TWO – RONAN O'GARA/MUNSTER'S EUROPEAN/HEINEKEN CUP RECORD

GAME No.	ROG APP	DATE	MUNSTER'S OPPONENTS	VENUE	ROUND	RESULT	ROG POINTS
1		01/11/1995	SWANSEA	THOMOND PARK	POOL D	W 17–13	Did not play
2		08/11/1995	CASTRES O	MAZAMET	POOL D	L 12–19	Did not play
3		12/10/1996	MILAN	MUSGRAVE PARK	POOL D	W 23–5	Did not play
4		16/10/1996	CARDIFF	ARMS PARK	POOL D	L 18–48	Did not play
5		19/10/1996	WASPS	THOMOND PARK	POOL D	W 49–22	Did not play
6		02/11/1996	TOULOUSE	STADE les SEPT DENIERS	POOL D	L 19–60	Did not play
7	1	07/09/1997	HARLEQUINS	THE STOOP	POOL D	L 40–48	15 (3 con, 3 pg)
8	2	13/09/1997	CARDIFF	ARMS PARK	POOL D	L 23–43	8 (con, 2 pg)
9		20/09/1997	BOURGOIN	THOMOND PARK	POOL D	W 17–15	Did not play
10		27/09/1997	CARDIFF	MUSGRAVE PARK	POOL D	L 32–37	Did not play
11	3	04/10/1997	BOURGOIN	STADE PIERRE RAJON	POOL D	L 6–21	Did not score
12		12/10/1997	HARLEQUINS	THOMOND PARK	POOL D	W 23–16	Did not play
13	4	19/09/1998	PADOVA	MUSGRAVE PARK	POOL A	W 20–13	7 (2con, pg)
14		26/09/1998	NEATH	MUSGRAVE PARK	POOL A	W 34–10	Did not play
15		10/10/1998	PERPIGNAN	STADE GILBERT BRUTUS	POOL A	L 24–41	Did not play
16		17/10/1998	NEATH	THE GNOLL	POOL A	D 18–18	Did not play
17		31/10/1998	PERPIGNAN	MUSGRAVE PARK	POOL A	W 13–5	Did not play
18		08/11/1998	PADOVA	STADE PLEBISCITO	POOL A	W 35–21	Did not play
19		13/12/1998	COLOMIERS	STADE SELERY	Q-FINAL	L 9–23	Did not play
20	5	20/11/1999	PONTYPRIDD	THOMOND PARK	POOL 4	W 32–10	22 (2 con, 5pg, d)
21	6	28/11/1999	SARACENS	VICARAGE ROAD	POOL 4	W 35–34	15 (3 con, 3pg)
22	7	11/12/1999	COLOMIERS	STADE les SEPT DENIERS	POOL 4	W 31–15	11 (con, 3 pg)
23	8	18/12/1999	COLOMIERS	MUSGRAVE PARK	POOL 4	W 23–5	8 (con, 2pg)
24	9	08/01/2000	SARACENS	THOMOND PARK	POOL 4	W 31–30	16 (2 con, 4 pg)
25	10	15/01/2000	PONTYPRIDD	SARDIS ROAD	POOL 4	W 36–38	21 (3 con, 4pg, d)
26	11	15/04/2000	STADE FRANCAIS	THOMOND PARK	Q-FINAL	W 27–10	17 (con, 5 pg)
27	12	06/05/2000	TOULOUSE	BORDEAUX	S-FINAL	W 31–25	21 (try, 2con, 4pg)
28	13	27/05/2000	NORTHAMPTON	TWICKENHAM	FINAL	L 8–9	Did not score
29	14	07/10/2000	NEWPORT	THOMOND PARK	POOL 4	W 26–18	11 (con, 3 pg)
30	15	14/10/2000	CASTRES O	STADE J-P ANTOINE	POOL 4	W 32–29	22 (try, con, 5pg)
31	16	21/10/2000	BATH	THOMOND PARK	POOL 4	W 31–9	16 (2con, 3pg, d)
32	17	28/10/2000	BATH	RECREATION GROUND	POOL 4	L 5–18	Did not score
33	18	13/01/2001	NEWPORT	RODNEY PARADE	POOL 4	W 39–24	29 (try, 3con, 4pg, 2d)
34	19	20/01/2001	CASTRES O	MUSGRAVE PARK	POOL 4	W 21–11	11 (con, 3 pg)
35	20	28/01/2001	BIARRITZ	THOMOND PARK	Q-FINAL	W 38–29	23 (con, 7 pg)
36	21	21/04/2001	STADE FRANCAIS	LILLE	S-FINAL	L 15–16	15 (5 pg)
37	22	29/09/2001	CASTRES O	THOMOND PARK	POOL 4	W 28–23	23 (con, 6pg, d)
38	23	06/10/2001	HARLEQUINS	THE STOOP	POOL 4	W 24–816	(try, con, 2pg, d)
39	24	26/10/2001	BRIDGEND	THE BREWERY FIELD	POOL 4	W 16–12	6 (2 pg)
40	25	03/11/2001	BRIDGEND	MUSGRAVE PARK	POOL 4	W 40–6	15 (3 con, 3 pg)
41	26	05/01/2002	HARLEQUINS	THOMOND PARK	POOL 4	W 51–17	21 (3 con, 5 pg)
42	27	12/01/2002	CASTRES O	STADE J-P ANTOINE	POOL 4	L 13–21	8 (con, 2 pg)
43	28	26/01/2002	STADE FRANCAIS	STADE JEAN BOUIN	Q-FINAL	W 16–14	11 (con, 2 pg, d)
44	29	27/04/2002	CASTRES O	BEZIERS	S-FINAL	W 25–17	20 (con, 6 pg)
45	30	25/05/2002	LEICESTER TIGERS	MILLENNIUM STADIUM	FINAL	L 9–15	9 (3 pg)

47	32	19/10/2002	PERPIGNAN	THOMOND PARK	POOL 2	W 30–21	13 (3 con, 3 pg)
48	33	06/12/2002	VIADANA	MUSGRAVE PARK	POOL 2	W 64–0	24 (try, 8 con, pg)
49	34	14/12/2002	VIADANA	PARMA	POOL 2	W 55–22	10 (5 con)
50	35	11/01/2003	PERPIGNAN	STADE AIME GIRAL	POOL 2	L 8–23	3 (pg)
51	36	18/01/2003	GLOUCESTER	THOMOND PARK	POOL 2	W 33–6	13 (2 con, 3 pg)
52	37	15/04/2003	LEICESTER TIGERS	WELFORD ROAD	Q-FINAL	W 20–7	15 (try, 2con, 2pg)
53	38	28/04/2003	TOULOUSE	Le STADIUM de TOULOUSE	S-FINAL	L 12–13	12 (2 pg, 2 d)
54	39	06/12/2003	BOURGOIN	STADE PIERRE RAJON	POOL 5	W 18–17	18 (6 pg)
55	40	13/12/2003	BENETTON-TREVISO	THOMOND PARK	POOL 5	W 51–0	11 (4 con, pg)
56	41	10/01/2004	GLOUCESTER	KINGSHOLM	POOL 5	L 11–22	6 (2 pg)
57	42	17/01/2004	GLOUCESTER	THOMOND PARK	POOL 5	W 35–14	15 (3 con, 3 pg)
58	43	24/01/2004	BENETTON-TREVISO	TREVISO	POOL 5	W 31–20	6 (3 con)
59	44	31/01/2004	BOURGOIN	THOMOND PARK	POOL 5	W 26–3	6 (3 con)
60	45	10/04/2004	STADE FRANCAIS	THOMOND PARK	Q-FINAL	W 37–32	17 (4 con, 3 pg)
61	46	25/04/2004	LONDON WASPS	LANSDOWNE ROAD	S-FINAL	L 32–37	9 (3 pg)
62	47	23/10/2004	HARLEQUINS	THOMOND PARK	POOL 4	W 15–9	5 (con, pg)
63	48	31/10/2004	N/ S OSPREYS	THE KNOLL	POOL 4	W 20–18	15 (5 pg)
64	49	03/12/2004	CASTRES O	STADE PIERRE RAJON	POOL 4	L 12–19	12 (4 pg)
65	50	11/12/2004	CASTRES O	THOMOND PARK	POOL 4	W 36–8	9 (3 con, pg)
66		08/01/2005	N/S OSPREYS	THOMOND PARK	POOL 4	W 20–10	Did not play
67		15/01/2005	HARLEQUINS	TWICKENHAM	POOL 4	W 18–10	Did not play
68		03/04/2005	BIARRITZ O	SAN SEBASTIAN	Q-FINAL	L 10–19	Did not play
69	51	21/10/2005	SALE SHARKS	EDGELEY PARK	POOL 1	L 13–27	8 (con, 2 pg)
70	52	29/10/2005	CASTRES O	THOMOND PARK	POOL 1	W 42–16	14 (4 con, 2 pg)
71	53	10/12/2005	N/G DRAGONS	RODNEY PARADE	POOL 1	W 24–8	11 (con, 2pg, d)
72	54	17/12/2005	N/G DRAGONS	THOMOND PARK	POOL 1	W 30–18	15 (3 con, 3 pg)
73	55	13/01/2006	CASTRES O	STADE PIERRE-ANTOINE	POOL 1	W 46–9	9 (3 con, pg)
74	56	21/01/2006	SALE SHARKS	THOMOND PARK	POOL 1	W 31–9	11 (4 con, pg)
75	57	01/04/2006	PERPIGNAN	LANSDOWNE ROAD	Q-FINAL	W 19–10	14 (con, 4 pg)
76	58	23/04/2006	LEINSTER	LANSDOWNE ROAD	S-FINAL	W 30–6	20 (try, 3con, 3pg)
77	59	20/05/2006	BIARRITZ O	MILLENNIUM STADIUM	FINAL	W 23–19	13 (2 con, 3 pg)
78	60	22/10/2006	LEICESTER TIGERS	WELFORD ROAD	POOL 4	W 21–19	11 (con, 2pg, d)
79	61	28/10/2006	BOURGOIN	THOMOND PARK	POOL 4	W 41–23	11 (4 con, pg)
80	62	10/12/2006	CARDIFF B.	ARMS PARK	POOL 4	W 22–12	17 (con, 5 pg)
81	63	16/12/2006	CARDIFF B.	THOMOND PARK	POOL 4	W 32–18	12 (3 con, 2 pg)
82	64	14/01/2007	BOURGOIN	STADE de GENEVE	POOL 4	W 30–27	15 (3 con, 3 pg)
83	65	20/01/2007	LEICESTER TIGERS	THOMOND PARK	POOL 4	L 6–13	6 (2 pg)
84	66	30/03/2007	LLANELLI S. (c)	STRADEY PARK	Q-FINAL	L 15–24	5 (con, pg)
85	67	10/11/2007	LONDON WASPS (c)	RICOH ARENA	POOL 5	L 23–24	13 (2 con, 3 pg)
86	68	18/11/2007	CLERMONT AUVERGNE (c)	THOMOND PARK	POOL 5	W 36–13	11 (4 con, pg)
87	69	08/12/2007	LLANELLI S. (c)	STRADEY PARK	POOL 5	W 29–16	19 (2 con, 5 pg)
88	70	16/12/2007	LLANELLI S. (c)	THOMOND PARK	POOL 5	W 22–13	12 (4 pg)
89	71	13/01/2008	CLERMONT AUVERGNE (c)	STADE MARCEL MICHELIN	POOL 5	L 19–26	14 (con, 4 pg)
90	72	19/01/2008	LONDON WASPS (c)	THOMOND PARK	POOL 5	W 19–3	14 (con, 4 pg)
91	73	05/04/2008	GLOUCESTER	KINGSHOLM	Q-FINAL	W 16–3	6 (2 pg)
92	74	27/04/2008	SARACENS	RICOH ARENA	S-FINAL	W 18–16	13 (try, con, 2pg)
93	75	24/05/2008	TOULOUSE	MILLENNIUM STADIUM	FINAL	W 16–13	11 (con, 3 pg)

HEINEKEN CUP RECORDS

MUNSTER	P – 93, W – 65, D – 1, L – 27; Points: 2348 (240 t, 157 c, 263 p, 15 d)
O' GARA	P – 75, W – 55, D – 0, L – 20; Points: 954 (8 t, 130 c, 206 p, 12 d)

APPENDIX THREE – RONAN O'GARA – TROPHIES AND MILESTONES

1990/91	Captains Cork Constitution U-12 to win a 16-nation tournament in St. Etienne, France.
1991/92	Captains Presentation Brothers College Cork to victory in the Munster Schools JCT Final.
1994/95	Plays for Munster Schools and captains Pres to win the Munster Schools SCT Final.
1995/96	Wins Munster U-20 League and Cup, inaugural all-Ireland U-20 Cup, Irish Universities Dudley Cup and promotion into Division Two of the All-Ireland League with UC-Cork.
1996/97	Wins the inter-provincial Grand Slam with Munster U-20; collects first Ireland U-21 cap.
1997/98	Wins Triple Crown with Ireland U-21; makes senior Munster debut and Heineken Cup debut; wins Munster Senior League with Cork Con.
1998/99	Wins the Irish inter-provincial title with Munster; plays for Ireland A; wins all-Ireland League with Cork Con.
1999/2000	Wins an inter-provincial Grand Slam with Munster and contributes a record 79 points during the competition, makes senior Ireland debut; losing finalist in the Heineken Cup.
2000/01	Wins the IPC with Munster for the third time in a row.
2001/02	Losing finalist in the Celtic League and the Heineken Cup.
2002/03	Wins the Celtic League with Munster, beating Neath (37–17) in the final.
2003/04	Wins Triple Crown with Ireland.
2004/05	Wins the Celtic League with Munster, beating Llanelli Scarlets (27–16) in the final; becomes new all-time top points scorer in Heineken Cup; is top points scorer in the Six Nations; wins first Lions Test cap.
2005/06	Wins Heineken Cup for first time. Wins Triple Crown with Ireland, setting a new Irish points record; regains title of top Ireland points scorer of all time and becomes the nation's most-capped player in the out-half position.
2006/07	Wins Triple Crown with Ireland, becoming one of only six Irish players to do that three times; tops the Six Nations points scorers table for the third consecutive season, with another new Irish points record.
2007/08	Wins 148th Munster cap when the province celebrates a second Heineken Cup success.

INDIVIDUAL SCORING IN THE SIX NATIONS

2000–08

1.	**RONAN O'GARA**	**(IRE)**	**443 (9t-61c-89p-3d)**
2.	JONNY WILKINSON	(ENG)	419 (4-75-74-9)
3.	STEPHEN JONES	(WAL)	338 (4-57-66-2)
4.	CHRIS PATERSON	(SCO)	316 (7-28-74-1)
5.	DAVID HUMPHREYS	(IRE)	195 (3-21-45-1)

APPENDIX FOUR – SUMMARY OF GAMES PLAYED AND POINTS SCORED ACROSS HIS CAREER

	95 /96	96/97	97/98	98/99	99/00	00/01	01/02	02/03	03/04	04/05	05/06	06/07	07/08	TOTALS
UC-CORK														
ALL GAMES	5													5
ALL POINTS	54													54
CORK CON														
AIL GAMES		13	12	13	9	11	5	2						64
AIL POINTS		126	114	153	109	124	58	30						714
MUNSTER														
HC GAMES			3	1	9	8	9	8	8	4	9	7	9	**75**
HC POINTS			23	7	131	127	129	103	88	41	115	77	113	**954**
CL/ML GAMES							7	6	2	8	10	11	6	50
CL/ML POINTS							73	81	9	55	81	90	52	441
I PC GAMES			3	1	5	4	2							15
I PC POINTS			37	0	79	60	17							193
OTHER GAMES			1	2	2	2				1				8
OTHER POINTS			19	19	32	26				17				113
ALL GAMES			7	4	16	14	18	14	10	13	19	18	15	**148**
ALL POINTS			79	26	242	213	219	184	97	113	196	167	165	**1701**
IRELAND U-21														
ALL GAMES		1	2											3
ALL POINTS		6	27											33
IRELAND A														
ALL GAMES				1										1
ALL POINTS				0										0
IRELAND														
6 N GAMES					4	5	5	2	5	5	5	5	5	41
6 N POINTS					58	49	19	3	48	60	76	82	48	**443**
RWC GAMES									5				4	9
RWC POINTS									30				19	49
OTHER GAMES					3	2	3	8	3	2	6	3	4	34
OTHER POINTS					25	31	18	120	26	38	36	23	26	343
ALL GAMES					7	7	8	10	13	7	11	8	13	**84**
ALL POINTS					83	80	37	123	104	98	112	105	93	**835**
LIONS														
TEST GAMES						0				1				**1**
TEST POINTS						0				0				0
OTHER GAMES						4				6				10
OTHER POINTS						26				49				75
ALL GAMES						4				7				11
ALL POINTS						26				49				**75**

All statistics supplied by Des Daly, Irish Rugby Statistician.

INDEX